Yale Southeast Asia Studies, 7

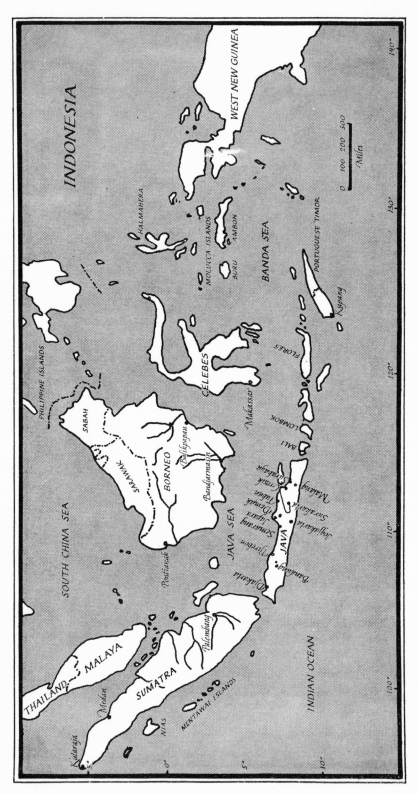

The Republic of Indonesia

ETHNICITY, PARTY, AND NATIONAL INTEGRATION

An Indonesian Case Study

R. William Liddle

New Haven and London, Yale University Press, 1970

Library of Congress catalog card number: 70–99830
ISBN: 300–01206–3
Designed by Marvin Howard Simmons,
set in Garamond type,
and printed in the United States of America by
the Murray Printing Co., Forge Village, Mass.
Distributed in Great Britain, Europe, and
Africa by Yale University Press, Ltd., London; in
Canada by McGill-Queen's University Press, Montreal;
in Mexico by Centro Interamericano de Libros
Académicos, Mexico City; in Australasia by Australia and
New Zealand Book Co., Pty., Ltd., Artarmon,
New South Wales; in India by UBS Publishers'
Distributors Pvt., Ltd., Delhi; in Japan by John Weatherhill,
Inc., Tokyo.

Untuk memperingati saudaraku
Robinson Simanungkalit, 1919–1969
Kepala Dinas Pengawasan Peraturan
Kotamadya Pematangsiantar

In memory of a friend more nearly a brother
Robinson Simanungkalit, 1919–1969
Pematangsiantar Municipal Controller

CONTENTS

LIST OF TABLES, FIGURES, AND MAPS

Tables

Figures

Maps

PREFACE

If it is possible to discern a central focus or underlying unity in the diversity of contemporary comparative political analysis, that focus is surely the concern for theoretical control. Systems analysts, structural functionalists, psychoculturalists, aggregate data collectors, promoters of various kinds of middle-range theorizing, and many others less easy to categorize seem to be in basic agreement on the desirability of enhancing our explanatory and predictive capacities through a symbiotic, mutually supportive process of theoretical and conceptual development joined with hypothesis testing and data analysis in the world of real political events.

At best, studies of Indonesian politics over the past two decades have fit only tangentially into this common orientation. While several contributions of high quality and lasting value have been made, explicit theoretical interest has been eschewed in favor of elaborately detailed elite studies, rather formalistic analyses of political parties, a "contemporary history" approach, ad hoc searches for factors in the country's ancient past that can explain its present, and so on. Books such as David Apter's *The Gold Coast in Transition* (Princeton, Princeton University Press, 1955), Lloyd Fallers' *Bantu Bureaucracy* (Cambridge, University Press, 1956), Myron Weiner's *Politics of Scarcity* (Chicago, Chicago University Press, 1962), Lucian Pye's *Politics, Personality, and Nation-Building* (New Haven, Yale University Press, 1962), Gabriel Almond and Sidney Verba's *The Civic Culture* (Princeton, Princeton University Press, 1963), to mention only a few, represent a frame of reference all but missing from the Indonesian scene.

The present work makes no claim to meet the standards of quality represented by the books listed above. I am, however, committed to the fundamental assumption that the development of comparative politics as a discipline requires a willingness to be guided in one's research by theoretical questions and a desire to contribute through research findings to the further growth of theory.

A concern for theoretical development, conceived in this very broad sense, does not of course provide sufficient criteria for embarking on a specific piece of research. One must further specify the kind of theory that one conceives to be useful and the kind of problem to which the theory is addressed. There are a great many hazards in theory building, not the least of which is the practical irrelevance that may result either from too great abstraction (or too little connection between the most abstract and the most concrete levels of the theory) or from choice of an inutile central concept. One way of minimizing these hazards is to adopt the middle-range position, focusing on an analytical problem, a set of structures, or some aspect of political behavior that is generally conceded to be significant both in its own right and as one element in a constellation of problems, structures, or behavior, but that lacks well-established links with the larger constellation. It is this rather modest theoretical perspective that I have adopted in the selection of a problem—national integration—and in the choice of an analytic approach and research method—the study of national political structures in a local setting through intensive interviewing and prolonged observation. This strategy, because it has been applied here only to a single case, cannot and was not designed to produce definitive conclusions, even for Indonesia. Instead, the purpose (and hopefully the result) has been to generate a few conceptual and methodological ideas and to produce some substantive findings and tentative conclusions of relevance to the specific integrative problems of Indonesia and other new states and to general understanding of the problem of national integration.

A first book, perhaps more than those that follow, is a product of many minds and hearts. Institutionally I am indebted to Yale University, which provided me with seven years of superb undergraduate and graduate education, to the Ford Foundation's Foreign Area Training Fellowship Program, which supported the field research, and to the University of Chicago's Committee for the Comparative Study of New States, under whose auspices writing of an earlier version of the book was begun. Among the many individuals who have commented on the manuscript, I am most grateful to Clifford Geertz, whose influence is evident throughout the analysis, and to Harry Benda, who was the most conscientious, thoughtful, and constructively critical adviser a student could hope for. A. R. Zolberg, Robert O. Tilman, C. E. Lindblom, Joseph LaPalombara, David Kettler, John Champlin, David S. Gibbons, and Joseph Crymes also made many useful comments, too few of which have been adopted. Mrs. Beth Kodama of Yale University Press wielded scissors and paste with a tactful but firm hand and is largely responsible for whatever readability the final product possesses.

In a study of this kind, based on fieldwork and extending over several years, personal debts loom as large as intellectual ones. A successful field experience would not have been possible without the kindness of the people of Simalungun/Siantar who received me in their homes and offices and graciously tolerated a barrage of questions. I am especially grateful to the members of *marga* (clan) Purba Pakpak, whose hospitality included my official induction into the clan, and to the members of *marga* Sitolubatu, whose friendship has given me my warmest memories of life in East Sumatra. Mr. and Mrs. Abdul Kohar bin Abdul Rony not only taught me the Indonesian language but also prepared me for both the joys and the frustrations which a foreigner experiences in contemporary Indonesia. My parents, through what must have seemed to them endless years of schooling, offered unstinting moral and financial support and the assurance that ultimately there is a relationship between effort expended and results achieved. It is to my wife, however, that I owe the greatest debt, for it was she who had to endure the physical and mental rigors of accompanying a single-minded husband to a small Sumatran town. And in the field and during the writing, it was she who encouraged and cajoled, contributed ideas, corrected prose, and did the thousand tasks that make life—even a fledgling author's life—a joy.

However widely one may share the praise, there is no sharing the blame. Final responsibility, at least for the deficiencies, rests with the author.

A Note on Research Procedure

Fieldwork for this study was carried out in the regency of Simalungun and the municipality of Siantar, province of North Sumatra, over a period of seventeen months, from January 1963 to June 1964. During this period I was continually resident in Siantar, the center of administrative and political activity for both the municipality and the regency, for a time in a house generously provided by Nommensen University (where my wife, and later I for a brief period, taught English), then in a private house on the outskirts of town, and finally in the home of a Siantar civil servant.

With the exception of Chapter 1 and parts of Chapter 2, for which published material of varying quantity and quality was available, most of the data analyzed in this book were generated through interviews and observation of local political life. Interviews were conducted, in the Indonesian language, in Siantar with all of the members of the regency and municipality legislatures, most of the regency/municipality leaders of the political parties and their subsidiary organizations, and many civil servants. Frequent trips (eventually including fourteen of the seventeen subdistricts of Simalungun) were made to subdistrict towns and villages, where local political figures and officials were interviewed. Occasional trips were also made to the provincial capital, Medan, to interview individuals who had previously played important roles in Simalungun political life.

The initial interview was conducted in a semistructured fashion, beginning with a series of life history questions dealing with such matters as year and place of birth, father's occupation, respondent's education and occupational experience, prerevolutionary political activities, revolutionary experience, and postindependence political activity. This approach was useful in providing information about the course of events during the past half-century as well as a sense of individual, group, and organizational roles in those events. If the respondent was cooperative (and most were, particularly after my status as neutral observer and chronicler was established), the life history questions were followed by a deeper probing into the individual's political attitudes, the reasons for his particular partisan affiliation, and so on. In many cases repeated interviews were conducted, and about twenty individuals, including leaders of all of the active parties and organizations (except the Communists) and a few government officials, became continuing sources of information about developments within the parties, the legislatures, and the regency/municipality administrations. In this way I was able to follow the twists and turns of political developments during the research period from many perspectives.

In addition to the interviews concerned primarily with the development of party politics, I was also a daily observer of the regional legislatures when in session, attended meetings of subdistrict officers and village heads, traveled with party leaders to the villages to observe organizational activities and meetings of party/organization members, attended ceremonial functions, interviewed plantation administrators about union activities and traditional leaders and others knowledgeable about colonial and precolonial politics, and so on. Finally, three or more Medan newspapers (none are published in Simalungun/Siantar) were read daily, but these proved to be of little use as sources of information about the local scene.

FREQUENTLY CITED ABBREVIATIONS AND ACRONYMS

BAPOST	Badan Penuntut Otonom Sumatera Timur; Body to Demand East Sumatran Autonomy
BHL	Barisan Harimau Liar; Wild Tiger Legion
DPRD	Dewan Perwakilan Rakjat Daerah; Regional People's Representative Council
DPRD-GR	Dewan Perwakilan Rakjat Daerah-Gotong Rojong; Mutual Help Regional People's Representative Council
HKBP	Huria Kristen Batak Protestan; Batak Christian Protestant Church
IPKI	Ikatan Pendukung Kemerdekaan Indonesia; League of Supporters of Indonesian Independence
KRSST	Kebangunan Rakjat Simalungun Sumatera Timur; The Awakening of the Simalungun People of East Sumatra
Masjumi	Madjelis Sjuro Muslimin Indonesia; Council of Indonesian Muslim Associations
NST	Negara Sumatera Timur; State of East Sumatra
NU	Nahdatul Ulama; Muslim Teachers' Party
Parkindo	Partai Kristen Indonesia; Indonesian Christian [Protestant] Party
Partindo	Partai Indonesia; Indonesian Party
PKI	Partai Komunis Indonesia; Indonesian Communist Party
PNI	Partai Nasional Indonesia; Indonesian Nationalist Party
PSI	Partai Sosialis Indonesia; Indonesian Socialist Party

One of the most serious problems facing the post-revolutionary Indonesian political elite has turned out to be the maintenance of mutual understanding between themselves and the mass of the peasant population. The attempt to build up a modern national state out of a plurality of distinct regional cultures has been hampered by the difficulty of communication between people still largely absorbed in those cultures and the metropolitan-based nationalist leadership more oriented to the international patterns of intelligentsia culture common to ruling groups in all the new Bandung countries . . .

In such a situation, the individuals and groups who can communicate both with the urban elite and with the rural followers of a particular local tradition perform an altogether critical function. It is these groups and individuals who can "translate" the somewhat abstract ideologies of the "New Indonesia" into one or another of the concrete idioms of rural life and can, in return, make clear to the intelligentsia the nature of the peasantry's fears and aspirations. Analyses of the creation of viable nations in Asia and Africa which simply focus on the political elite, as those of political scientists have tended to do, or simply on the peasant village, as those of anthropologists have tended to do, are necessarily incomplete. What is needed, in addition, is an analysis of the links between the two—i.e., of regional leadership. A vigorous, imaginative regional leadership, able to play a cultural middleman role between peasant and metropolitan life, and so create an effective juncture between traditional cultural patterns and modern ones, is in many ways the most essential prerequisite for the success, in democratic form, of the nationalist experiment both in Indonesia and elsewhere.

Clifford Geertz, "The Javanese Kijaji:
The Changing Role of a Cultural Broker"

INTRODUCTION: THE STUDY OF LOCAL
POLITICS IN A NEW STATE

The Problem of National Integration

In the halcyon days of nationalist movements and early postindependence politics, covering roughly the first decade and a half following the Second World War, the mood of those in the West who wished the new Asian and African nations well was generally optimistic. There seemed to be ample reason for optimism. In most of the new states considerable unity had been generated as a by-product of widespread and deeply felt anticolonialism, and most of the nationalist movements had been, or were on the verge of becoming, victorious in the struggle for independence. Perhaps most importantly, in Western eyes, everywhere in the new states there seemed to be a genuine commitment to some of our most deeply held values: independence, popular sovereignty, representative institutions of government, the rule of law, economic and social progress. With such value commitments, and with national leadership already tested in the fires of revolution and anticolonial politics, the tasks ahead seemed, if not easy, at least not overwhelming in their magnitude.

More recent events have made us more skeptical of the future of the new states, less hopeful that there can be created in Asia and Africa political institutions and practices that are both stable and responsive and at the same time capable of creating the appropriate conditions for economic and social development. In Southeast Asia, Burma, Thailand, and Indonesia have all experienced military takeovers in one form or another; North Vietnam is communist, and the future of the other Indochinese states is highly problematic. Multiracial Malaysia's once seemingly stable and democratic coalition government has been shattered, perhaps beyond repair, in the wake of the 1969 elections; Singapore's dominant party shows signs of increasing authoritarianism; and democratic institutions in the Philippines continue to rest precariously on a narrow foundation of privilege. In South Asia, there is a continuation of military government in Pakistan and concern for the future of democracy in India and Ceylon. Africa has witnessed a series of army takeovers, and in a few states there is the clear possibility of national disintegration. In the wake of these events, we hear less of political development—in the positive sense of emerging democracy—and more of political decay, less of representative government as the means of resolving conflict and building a better society and more of authoritarian solutions to problems that seem otherwise intractable.

One of the most critical of these problems, delineated so sharply by the Nigerian civil war and recurring events in the Congo, but present in various forms nearly everywhere in the postcolonial world, is that of national unity or integration. Most of the new states are built on fragile foundations of national loyalties that emerged only recently, during the last stages of the colonial period and the independence movement. In many cases, notably in Africa but also in parts of South and Southeast Asia, the territorial boundaries of the contemporary states were determined in whole or in part by the exigencies of colonial politics. There is little or no memory of precolonial political systems encompassing the same, or substantially the same, area as the present state (although it has been a common feature of nationalist mythology to assert the existence of such units in order to provide a historical basis for contemporary legitimacy). Instead, many new states contain a diversity of peoples, each of which in the precolonial period was characterized by a distinctive language, religion, culture, social structure, and territorial control. While not entirely isolated from neighboring peoples, each of these societies constituted a separate social and political system, whether in the form of the primitive band or the more sophisticated traditional state.

Colonialism, in many ways disruptive of the traditional integration of

these small-scale societies, was a less than efficient instrument of reintegration on a supralocal level. Such techniques as indirect rule, for example,
tended to encourage localistic and particularistic loyalties, while the processes of social change in the period, e.g. the spread of Western education and
a money economy, undermined the principles of legitimacy of the traditional political systems. Moreover, colonial government was essentially
administrative government with little opportunity for political participation
given to the indigenous peoples either on a local basis or in terms of the
whole territory under colonial rule. The emergence of twentieth-century
nationalist movements represented in part an attempt to overcome local
particularisms and was on the whole successful because of the central importance of a single issue: anticolonialism. With the colonial power removed from the scene, however, particularistic loyalties have reemerged
and now constitute a major threat to the continued viability of the new
states.

In addition to the threat posed by the renewed strength and assertiveness of subnational loyalties, most of the new states are also confronted
with an integrative problem in terms of the relationship between the new
national elite and the rest of the population. This problem has its roots in
the colonial period, when the processes of urbanization and education, the
creation of a modern sector in the economy, and the requirements of colonial
administration combined to create a new elite in many respects alienated
from traditional society but equally ill at ease in colonial society. It was this
elite, or some segments of it, that led the fight for national independence.
In their new positions of authority, however, they find themselves separated
by a series of almost unbridgeable gaps from the people whom they claim to
lead. As Edward Shils has written,

> In almost every aspect of their social structures, the societies on which
> the new states must be based are characterized by a "gap." It is the gap
> between the few, very rich and the mass of the poor, between the
> educated and uneducated, between the townsman and the villager, be-
> tween the cosmopolitan or national and the local, between the modern
> and the traditional, between the rulers and the ruled. It is the "gap"
> between a small group of active, aspiring, relatively well-off, educated

and influential persons in the big towns and an inert or indifferent, impoverished, uneducated and relatively powerless peasantry.[1]

The problem of national integration facing most of the contemporary new states has, then, two major dimensions: (1) a horizontal dimension, which involves a meshing together of disparate social groups—kinship, ethnic, linguistic, religious, racial—within a framework of national loyalties and institutions; and (2) a vertical dimension, which involves the closing of the cultural and political gap between an urban, Western-educated, nationalist political elite on the one hand and the masses of the largely traditional and rural population on the other.[2]

Looking to the future, there are obviously two directions in which a society can go in terms of integration along either of the above dimensions: it can become more integrated, leading to a state of affairs in which loyalties toward the nation are taken for granted and the gaps between elite and mass have diminished, or it can become less integrated, leading to a state of affairs in which civil disorder, secessionist movements or smoldering rebellions are the order of the day and it becomes impossible for the national government to pursue any goals beyond that of attempting to secure the physical survival of the nation. For the future of the new states, then, the critical question is, what are the conditions under which these polities are likely to become more or less integrated?

In some respects Indonesia's integrative problems are less severe than

1. Edward Shils, "Political Development in the New States," pt. 1, *Comparative Studies in Society and History,* 2 (1960), 281.

2. For a definition of national integration similar to mine but with somewhat different terminology, see James S. Coleman and Carl G. Rosberg, Jr., eds., *Political Parties and National Integration in Tropical Africa* (Berkeley and Los Angeles University of California Press, 1964), esp. pp. 8–9: "For our purposes national integration is regarded as a broad, subsuming process, whose two major dimensions are (1) *political* integration, which refers to the progressive bridging of the elite-mass gap on the vertical plane in the course of developing an integrated political process and a participant political community, and (2) *territorial* integration, which refers to the progressive reduction of cultural and regional tensions and discontinuities on the horizontal plane in the process of creating a homogeneous territorial political community." A useful summary of definitions of national integration may be found in Myron Weiner, "Political Integration and Political Development," *Annals of the American Academy of Political and Social Science, 358* (1965), 52–54.

those of other new nations.[3] Unlike neighboring Malaysia, Indonesia is not racially divided, although it contains minority communities of Chinese, Indians, and others; unlike India, Indonesia has not been divided over the question of language—the national language, *bahasa Indonesia,* is the property of no single group and is spoken as a second language throughout the archipelago; unlike Pakistan, separated into eastern and western regions by more than a thousand miles of India, the Indonesian archipelago from Sabang on the northern tip of Sumatra to Merauke on the southeastern edge of West Irian is a contiguous territory. Moreover, the commitment to national independence pervaded all levels of Indonesian society during the long years of revolution from 1945 to 1949 and has served as a powerful cohesive force.

On the other hand, Indonesia shares many of the integrative challenges of other new nations. Its boundaries, and indeed the very idea of an Indonesian nation-state, are a creation of Dutch colonialism. Ethnically, Indonesia contains over three hundred different groups speaking more than two hundred and fifty distinct languages,[4] of which ten groups claim one million or more members. Of these, the Javanese, comprising perhaps forty-five million of a total Indonesian population of slightly over one hundred million, are by far the largest group. Ethnic differences have contributed to another pattern of cleavage in Indonesian society, the division between the central island of Java (more precisely its central and eastern provinces) and the Outer Islands, the largest of which are Sumatra, Kalimantan (Borneo), and Sulawesi (Celebes). The Javanese, numerically dominant, concentrated on densely populated, resource-poor Java, and consuming most of the foreign exchange earned elsewhere in the archipelago, have been regarded with much suspicion and hostility by the peoples of the less populous, foreign exchange-producing Outer Islands. Religion is also a divisive factor. Over

3. For an analysis of the integrative problem in several new states, see Clifford Geertz, "The Integrative Revolution, Primordial Sentiments and Civil Politics in the New States," in Clifford Geertz, ed., *Old Societies and New States* (New York, The Free Press of Glencoe, 1963), pp. 105–57; see also Rupert Emerson's classic *From Empire to Nation* (Cambridge, Mass., Harvard University Press, 1960), pt. 2

4. Hildred Geertz, "Indonesian Cultures and Communities," in Ruth McVey, ed., *Indonesia* (New Haven, Conn., Yale University Southeast Asia Studies, by arrangement with HRAF Press, 1963), p. 24.

90 percent of the population is Muslim, but the Muslims (especially in Java) are divided into two quite distinct groups, those for whom Islam constitutes the central focus of religious life and those for whom it is merely one of a number of elements in a composite, syncretistic religion. In some parts of the country there are also substantial Christian (both Protestant and Catholic) minorities.

In addition to the horizontal cleavages based on ethnic, religious, and regional differences, there has also been a considerable gap between elite and mass in postindependence Indonesian political life. Despite the unifying forces of nationalism and the experiences of years of revolution, there is undeniably a profound difference between the way of life of the national elite and that of the vast majority of the population. Herbert Feith, in a study of the parliamentary democracy period, divided the population into three groups: political elite, including the top decision-makers; political public, "persons outside the political elite who nevertheless saw themselves as capable of taking action which could affect national government or politics"; and the majority of Indonesians, whose political influence is minimal. The top group comprises civilian and military bureaucrats, politicians, and some nongovernmental professionals and businessmen and numbers altogether no more than five hundred persons. This group "was steeped in the all-Indonesian modern urban culture which had grown up around the nationalist movement and its members were correspondingly less closely allied to the cultures of their respective ethnic groups."[5] According to Hildred Geertz, the elite possesses a distinctive "metropolitan superculture," the content of which is most highly developed "in the areas of political ideology, artistic styles and material culture." Higher secondary or university education, colloquial use of the Indonesian language, relatively high consumption of imported luxury goods, foreign travel, and commitment to such goals as "egalitarianism, socialism, economic development, and the advancement of the Indonesian nation" are the major components of the life style of the elite.[6]

The distinctiveness of the elite culture and its heavy dependence on

5. Herbert Feith, *The Decline of Constitutional Democracy in Indonesia* (Ithaca, N.Y., Cornell University Press, 1962), pp. 108–13.

6. H. Geertz, p. 36.

foreign models make it difficult for the Indonesian villager to see himself and the elite member as belonging to the same society. As James Mysbergh has written, the ruling elite and the rural society "no longer have a common frame of reference and often regard one another without real comprehension. Many of the elite have an idealized theoretical concept of the 'rakjat' (people) but no real identification with the workers and peasants nor understanding of their actual problems. Their attitude, partly based on the utopian ideals of the revolution, is that it is their duty to work for the people's welfare and to lead and instruct it, but their approach is paternalistic." To most villagers, the contemporary elite is seen as a continuation of the old aristocracy and is accorded respect on the basis of a traditional acceptance of "autocratic power and a hierarchical system, which imply privilege rather than mutual obligations." Former patterns of elite–mass integration are not wholly operative in the present, however, for the new elite's Western education and cosmopolitan way of life constitute a major barrier to mutual understanding. Where "the old aristocracy . . . commanded respect and homage within the peasant's own cultural pattern, . . . the Westernized elite today seems to him sometimes almost as alien as the Dutch."[7]

Political Organization and Leadership in the Integrative Process

This study seeks to explore the problems posed by the existence of particularistic, subnational loyalties and an elite–mass gap in Indonesia through an analysis of the integrative role of political organization and leadership. What forms of political organization, what kinds of political leadership, are needed to transform Indonesia and other newly independent states into viable nations? Discussion of this question to date has centered primarily around the suitability of democratic versus authoritarian solutions to the integrative problem or, in some formulations, of competitive two- or multiparty systems versus one-party dominance of political life.[8]

7. James Mysbergh, "The Indonesian Elite," Far Eastern Survey, 26 (1957), 39.

8. Much of the debate, focused on one-party systems, has dealt with Africa. See, e.g. the volume edited by Coleman and Rosberg cited above, n. 2; Martin L. Kilson, "Authoritarian and Single-Party Tendencies in African Politics," World Politics, 15 (1963); Ruth Schachter Morgenthau, Political Parties in French-Speaking West

In the immediate postindependence period it was often assumed by both Western scholars and nationalist politicians that representative institutions and competing political organizations could provide a framework within which internal differences would be harmonized or adjusted, and decisions made and implemented with regard to the great issues of social and economic development. In the ensuing years the breakdown of anticolonial unity, the inability of the new governments to get on with developmental tasks, and increasing immobilism have led many to seek a more authoritarian framework of political organization. The existence of an elite–mass cleavage along the lines described by Shils has tended to favor authoritarianism and dependence on charismatic personalities, for it has encouraged many political leaders to believe that they must be the guiding forces in their societies. In the absence of shared values and regular channels of elite–mass communication, it is asserted that the leaders alone know and are able to express the true "general will" of their people, who, as individuals and as members of subnational primordial groupings, are too backward and inexperienced in the ways of a modern (or modernizing) society to be aware of and to act upon their own best interests.[9] In Pakistan, for example, dissatisfaction with parliamentary rule produced a pattern of military dominance at the center and "basic democracies" in the villages, said to be a transitional, tutelary phase in the ultimate democratic development of the country; in Ghana parliamentary government was replaced by one-party rule under Kwame Nkrumah's charismatic leadership, which was in turn replaced by a no-party military regime; in Indonesia a period of parliamentary democracy

Africa (London, Oxford University Press, 1964); Aristide R. Zolberg, *Creating Political Order, The Party States of West Africa* (Chicago, Rand McNally, 1966). For an article dealing with the relationship between the mass party and national integration at the local level see Aristide R. Zolberg, "Mass Parties and National Integration: The Case of the Ivory Coast," *Journal of Politics, 25* (1963).

9. See also the view of Lucian Pye that national leaders in the new states "have few guides as to how the public may be divided over particular issues . . . Forced to reach for the broadest possible appeals, the individual leader tends to concentrate heavily on nationalistic sentiments and to present himself as a representative of the nation as a whole rather than of particular interests within the society." *Politics, Personality, and Nation Building: Burma's Search for Identity* (New Haven, Conn., Yale University Press, 1962), pp. 27–28.

was replaced by Guided Democracy, an uneasy coalition between President Sukarno and the army, with the political parties' power drastically reduced. This was in turn replaced by a military-dominated government without the presence of a charismatic personality or the effective participation of the political parties and other voluntary organizations.

In each of these three cases, and in many others as well, a principal justification for the transformation of parliamentary into authoritarian political systems has been that national unity requires the centralization of authority in a few hands or in a single individual.[10] The symbols of democracy have not been discarded, but their emphasis has shifted from a concern for participation to a concern for leadership, as in Sukarno's repeatedly stated definition of the essence of his regime as democracy with leadership.

Are Ayub Khan, Nkrumah, Sukarno, and other leaders who have called for more centralized, more authoritarian, and more "personalistic" regimes correct? Does national unity in the new states require the suppression of representative institutions and autonomous political organizations such as parties and interest groups, the concentration of power in a few hands at the center, and/or the establishment of a single, nationwide political organization that can mobilize a diverse population for the tasks of development? Or, alternatively, does the authoritarian solution lead to the very opposite of what its proponents desire—a weakening of the fabric of national loyalties, an increasing sense of alienation from the regime and the nation, and finally, a heightened probability of national disintegration?

Postindependence Indonesia provides a particularly suitable setting for an analysis of answers to these questions. Like many other new states, Indonesia contains a multiplicity of cleavages, of both the horizontal and vertical varieties, which constitute grave obstacles to effective national integration. Moreover, the political elite, or at least a substantial segment of it, has been aware that these problems exist and has attempted to deal with them, first by the establishment of a parliamentary government, in which political parties played a central role, and later by reliance on the charisma and leadership abilities of President Sukarno backed up by the coercive power

10. See the statements of African and Asian leaders in Paul E. Sigmund, ed., *The Ideologies of the Developing Nations* (rev. ed. New York, Praeger, 1967).

of the army. How effective have these two almost diametrically opposed approaches been, and what role, if any, can political parties be expected to play in the creation and maintenance of an integrated polity and society in Indonesia?[11]

The Locality as a Research Site

The problem with which this study deals is national integration, but the data and much of the analysis derive from fieldwork in a single subnational locality, the regency of Simalungun and the municipality of Siantar in North Sumatra. What is the utility of studying local politics in order to understand national integration? The answer to this question may be found in a conceptualization of the integrative problem in new states as consisting of an elite–mass gap and a series of "horizontal" primordial cleavages.

From the former perspective, potential closure of the gap depends upon the relationships that develop between the national elite, concentrated for the most part in the capital city, and the great majority of the population who live in many localities throughout the country. These relationships may take various forms, depending upon the objectives of the elite, its internal cohesion and capacity to realize its objectives, the strategies adopted to promote national unity (e.g. the establishment of a single-party system, the formulation of a national ideology), and the responses elite activities generate at the local level. Failure to develop policies explicitly designed to strengthen national unity will, of course, also affect the nature of the elite–mass relationship. In any event, it is at the level of the locality that one can best perceive and evaluate the impact of national policy (or its absence) with regard to a closure of the elite–mass gap. At the national level one is restricted to formal statements of policy and intent, to the analysis of intraelite politics, and to the more dramatic varieties of evidence of national disunity—revolution, rebellion, parliamentary immobilism, and

11. Since the field work for this study was carried out, Sukarno's Guided Democracy regime has been replaced by the "New Order" government of General Suharto. A brief discussion of the present government's efforts with regard to Indonesia's integrative problems is provided in Chapter 7.

so on. Less dramatic responses—the gradual strengthening or weakening of the ties between elite and mass, which may ultimately lead to system viability or breakdown—are hidden from view at the center.

With regard to the second dimension of the integrative problem—primordial cleavages and the development of national loyalties—the study of politics at the local level is also instructive. For it is one thing to discover that primordial loyalties are a central political problem in a new state, and quite another to understand the dynamic interplay of primordial and other loyalties and emergent forms of political organization. Have primordial loyalties been increasing or decreasing in importance during the colonial and postcolonial periods? What effects have processes of social and political change, where these have occurred, had on the relative strength of primordial versus other kinds of loyalties? What are the effects of ideologies that deny the existence or at least relevance of primordial cleavages and of those that are incorporative and tolerant of differences within a loose national framework? And finally, what obstacles, if any, does the persistence of local loyalties present for ultimate integration into the nation-state? Important insights, if not definitive answers, to these questions may be found through detailed examination of the patterns of social cleavage and political organization at the local level, as these have developed over time. A number of such studies, moreover, either within a particular country or in several countries, will provide a substantial empirical basis for comparative analyses and generalizations.[12]

Presuming that the usefulness of local case studies for the comparative analysis of national integration has been established, then, let us turn to questions of methodology and selection of data to be examined at the local level. I have already indicated that my primary concern is with

12. It is worth noting that to date rather more anthropologists than political scientists have recognized the need for case studies of local political life within the framework of the political system of the new nation–state. See the writings of Lloyd Fallers, e.g. *Bantu Bureaucracy* (Cambridge University Press, 1956), and "Political Sociology and the Anthropological Study of African Politics," *Archives Europeenes de Sociologie*, 4 (1963), 325–29; Ronald Cohen, "Political Anthropology: The Future of a Pioneer," *Anthropological Quarterly*, 38 (1965), 125–30; and works of F. G. Bailey, e.g. *Politics and Social Change: Orissa in 1959* (Berkeley, University of California Press, 1963).

organization and leadership, for it is here that interaction takes place, both between the national elite and the local population and among various segments of local society.

With regard to the problem of primordial and other types of horizontal cleavages and their articulation with the organizational system in the Indonesian setting, there has been very little detailed description or analysis.[13] Since contemporary patterns of loyalties are the result of complex processes of social change with deep roots in the precolonial and colonial periods of Indonesian history, my analysis will begin with an exploration of the historical dimensions of group development in the locality, and will attempt to tie together changes resulting from primarily local events and those that must be seen as part of wider networks of social interaction. In this discussion the development of ethnic and religious affiliations as bases for individual identity and group loyalties will be stressed, as will the effects of the sense of affiliation with socioeconomic and regional groups and with the emerging national polity. In the postrevolutionary period the relationship between the cleavages within the locality and the political party system will be examined through analyses of the objectives and strategies of the various parties and organizations, voting behavior in the 1955 elections, the nature of party membership, recruitment of leadership, and patterns of factionalism within the local party organizations.

With regard to the elite-mass gap, it has been argued by at least two students of Indonesian politics that even at the level of the locality there has been almost no interaction between the urban-based governmental and political elite and the predominantly rural population. In an attempt to assess the extent of the elite-mass cleavage, J. D. Legge has utilized the social background approach in a comparative analysis of the membership of twelve regency legislatures in East Java and West Sumatra and the provincial legislature of East Java. On the basis of his data, Legge argued that

13. The best analysis of the 1955 elections, which touches on these problems, is Herbert Feith, *The Indonesian Elections of 1955* (Ithaca, N.Y., Cornell University Modern Indonesia Project, 1957). See also the collection of articles edited and introduced by G. William Skinner, *Local, Ethnic, and National Loyalties in Village Indonesia: A Symposium* (New Haven, Conn., Yale University Southeast Asia Studies, 1959); and Clifford Geertz, "The Javanese Kijaji: The Changing Role of a Cultural Broker," *Comparative Studies in Society and History*, 2, 228–49.

Membership of representative councils has reflected the narrowness of Indonesia's political elite. Even at the *kabupaten* [regency] level council members could hardly be regarded as representative of the rural community which formed the great mass of constituents, and at the provincial level the connection was still more tenuous. By far the greatest single occupational group to be found on councils has been formed by civil servants, a fact which is reminiscent of the local bodies established during the colonial period. Other groups were small traders, religious leaders, teachers, labor leaders, and industrial workers. Only an isolated few have come from the peasantry.[14]

With reference to the whole of regency government, Legge asserts that "it serves the interests of the elite, which has never belonged to, or has escaped from, the *desa* [village]."[15] Legge's conclusions are supported by the anthropologist G. William Skinner, who writes that

in moving from local up into regional levels of the socio-political structure, the villager almost immediately and universally encounters leaders and officials, groups and causes, which are predominantly town- and elite-oriented. The administrative officials are town-based, often not from the local area, and of markedly superior educational attainment and social status. Organizations based at regional levels are largely urban in character, and their leaders are seldom farmers . . . Above the local level, the villager is hard put to find leaders who genuinely identify themselves with the values of the rural population.[16]

The difficulty with the Legge-Skinner approach to elite–mass relationships, whether applied in Indonesia or elsewhere, is that it assumes what is at best only a hypothesis, i.e. that occupation and education, by which elite status is defined, determine political attitudes and behavior. Such an assumption is not very meaningful because it depends on a generally discredited theory of functional representation, which asserts that only a

14. John D. Legge, *Central Authority and Regional Autonomy in Indonesia: A Study in Local Administration 1950–1960* (Ithaca, N.Y., Cornell University Press, 1961), p. 134.

15. Ibid., p. 94.

16. Skinner, p. 5.

peasant can represent a peasant.[17] In fact, there is no a priori reason why, for example, a lawyer cannot represent a predominantly working-class district in an American state legislature, or why an Indonesian civil servant cannot represent a rural constituency. The important point is not who or what the individual legislator or party leader is, in terms of education or occupation, but rather what constituency he represents and what the nature of his relationship is with that constituency.

Social background studies, while certainly relevant, are clearly not central to an analysis of the problems of elite–mass integration in a new state. What is central is an explication of local political leadership and organization in terms of (1) the kinds of social groups which are (or are not) represented in the political process, (2) the kinds of organizations, local and supralocal, with which these groups affiliate or which claim to represent them, (3) the nature of the leader–follower relationship within each organization, and (4) the nature of the relationship between local and national leaders, organizations, and processes. The case study method, which permits intensive analysis of organizational life within a fairly small geographic area, is admirably suited to the exploration of these topics.

The Choice of a Locality

Under the present system of territorial administration in Indonesia, the island of Sumatra is divided into six provinces or first-level self-governing regions.[18] The provinces are divided into regencies and municipalities,

17. Hans Daalder criticizes European studies of the social background of parliamentarians, ministers, and party members for a determinism "which sees too direct a link between the social origins of politicians and class bias, in their politics." "Parties, Elites and Political Developments in Western Europe," in Joseph LaPalombara and Myron Weiner, eds., *Political Parties and Political Development* (Princeton, N.J., Princeton University Press, 1966), pp. 70–71.

18. According to Law No. 1 of 1957, a basic law on regional government, Indonesia is divided into first-, second-, and third-level self-governing regions, supplanting the former administrative levels of province, residency, regency, district, subdistrict (the lowest level of the central administrative hierarchy), and village or village complex. In practice the new system has been put into effect only at the first and second levels (corresponding respectively to the former provinces and regencies), and no

called second-level self-governing regions, which are further divided into subdistricts and villages. The province of North Sumatra, extending from the primitive island of Nias off the west coast to the great rubber and tobacco plantations of the former East Coast Residency, contains eleven regencies and six municipalities.[19] The regency of Simalungun (population approximately 525,000) is located about two hours' drive south and west on a paved all-weather road from the provincial capital of Medan, and is bordered on the north and east by the plantation areas of Asahan and Deli/ Serdang, on the west by the regency of Karo, and on the south by the waters of mountain-ringed Lake Toba. Approximately in the center of the regency is the municipality of Pematangsiantar (also called P. Siantar or Siantar), a market and administrative center and the second largest city of North Sumatra, with a population of about 113,000.[20]

---

decision has as yet been made concerning the third level. In early 1964 it was announced that all residency and district level administrative offices were to be abolished (they had in any event become largely nonfunctioning), leaving the present arrangement as follows:

> Province (first-level self-governing region)
> Regency or municipality (second-level self-governing region)
> Subdistrict
> Village or village complex

Law No. 1 is available in Departemen Penerangan Republik Indonesia, *Almanak Lembaga-Lembaga Negara dan Kepartaian* [Department of Information, Republic of Indonesia, *Almanac of State Institutions and Parties*] (Djakarta, 1961), pp. 163–89. It is quoted in English translation in Legge, Appendix C, pp. 258–69.

19. The regencies are: Deli/Serdang, Langkat, Karo, Simalungun, Asahan, Labuhan Batu, North Tapanuli, Dairi, Central Tapanuli, South Tapanuli, and Nias. The municipalities are: Medan, Pematangsiantar, Tandjung Balai, Bindjai, Tebingtinggi, and Sibolga. See Departemen Dalam Negeri dan Otonomi Daerah, *Ichtisar Daerah Administrasi Seluruh Indonesia* [Department of the Interior and Regional Autonomy, *Summary of Administrative Regions Throughout Indonesia*] (Djakarta, 1962), pp. 42–45.

20. Simalungun population from Pemerintahan Daerah Tkt. II Simalungun, *Lapuran Tahun 1963* [Government of the Second-Level Region of Simalungun, *Report for 1963*] (P. Siantar, 1963), p. 4. Figure for Pematangsiantar supplied by the Head of the Census Section, Municipality of Pematangsiantar, July 1963. Pauline D. Milone ("Contemporary Urbanization in Indonesia," *Asian Survey*, 4 [August

Simalungun/Siantar, while in no sense typical of Indonesia as a whole—no single region could typify the immense diversity of contemporary Indonesia—manifests a great many of the country's cultural and political cleavages in unusually distinct, if sometimes eccentric, form. At the level of ethnic division there are four major Indonesian groups—Simalungun Bataks, North Tapanuli Bataks, South Tapanuli Bataks, and Javanese—plus a sizable overseas Chinese population.[21] Ethnicity, however, is only one aspect of sociocultural diversity. In addition, the people of Simalungun/Siantar are divided by religion (Islam, Protestantism, Catholicism, and animism), socioeconomic differences (urban and plantation workers, plantation squatters, wet- and dry-rice farmers, traders, a white-color class), and regional sentiments (indigenous people of East Sumatra versus migrants). Ideological cleavages related to the national party system and to the struggle for independence have complicated still further the grounds on which men differ in their values and attitudes toward politics and government, and the goals for which they are willing to wage political combat.

A further aspect of diversity in Simalungun/Siantar lies in the different combinations and patterns of cleavages and loyalties that have developed in various parts of the region in the course of the twentieth century. There are in fact several "local environments" in contemporary Simalungun, each of which has responded somewhat differently to the political developments of

---

1964], 1005) gives the population of Siantar as 114,870 and ranks it twenty-first of all Indonesian cities. The largest city in North Sumatra is Medan, with a population of approximately 500,000. The prefix *pematang* in the Simalungun Batak language indicates the capital of a traditional kingdom; while the formal name of the municipality is Pematangsiantar, it is usually referred to simply as Siantar.

21. The role of the Chinese community in Simalungun/Siantar politics is beyond the scope of this study. In general the Chinese in the region have operated politically on two levels. First, as individuals, many of the wealthier Chinese have developed mutually beneficial personal relationships with important government officials. Second, at the group level, their interests have been represented by trade associations and by Baperki (Badan Permusjawaratan Kewarganegaraan Indonesia, Consultative Body for Indonesian Citizenship). The Chinese did not directly participate, either individually or collectively, in partisan politics in the region, although it was widely believed that they were a major source of funds for the local Communist Party leadership.

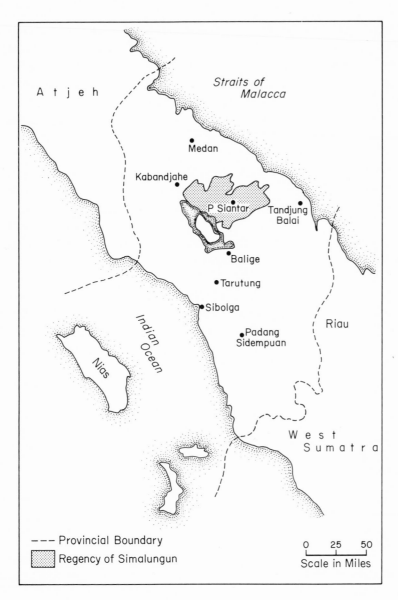

Map 1. The Province of North Sumatra

the postrevolutionary period. The major distinctions to be made among localities include: Lower Simalungun, a multiethnic area where there has been extensive plantation development, comprising six subdistricts (the administrative level below the regency); Upper Simalungun, seven subdistricts unaffected by the plantation economy and containing a large majority of Simalungun Bataks; the Road to Parapat area, four subdistricts somewhat akin to Lower Simalungun because of a partial intrusion of plantation agriculture but with a majority North Tapanuli Batak population; and the municipality of Siantar, an urban area with a multiethnic population and an economy largely dominated by petty trade.[22]

Taken together, the social, cultural, economic, and political cleavages of contemporary Simalungun/Siantar and their various combinations in four distinct subregions provide an excellent setting for an examination of the problem of national integration. Detailed examination of political organization and leadership in a region containing so many of the conflicts which affect Indonesia as a whole should yield insights and hypotheses relevant to other regions, to the national political process, and indeed, to other new states.

22. With the exception of Siantar, these regions are not formal administrative units but rather informally delineated geographic areas recognized by the residents as possessing the specific characteristics mentioned above.

1. THE TRANSFORMATION OF TRADITIONAL SIMALUNGUN

From the perspective of this study, postindependence political development in the region of Simalungun and Siantar is largely a story of the efforts of political parties and other national power centers to secure local influence and/or mass support. The success or failure of these efforts has depended not simply on the will and organizational skill of those who have sought support. The local social and cultural environment, shaped by decades of colonial rule, military occupation, and nationalist revolution, has been a critical variable, affecting not only the prospects of partisan success but also the internal characteristics of emergent political organizations, the nature of their leadership, and, ultimately, their capacity to mitigate the integrative problems of the new nation. Because of this intimate relationship between environment, organization, and integrative capacity, it is necessary to sketch out in some detail the principal characteristics of traditional society and government in Simalungun and Siantar and their transformation during three crucial periods in the twentieth century: the colonial period, the Japanese occupation, and the Revolution.

Traditional Society and Government in Simalungun

As recently as the last decade of the nineteenth century, Simalungun was an ethnically homogeneous society. Its inhabitants, numbering no more than 75,000, were all Simalungun Bataks, one of several Batak subgroups indigenous to North Sumatra. The Simalungun Bataks of the region spoke a common language, possessed a common culture, lived in small villages (often considerably distant from each other), grew dry rice, and were organized politically into several autocratic but loosely governed primitive states.

The kinship system of the Simalungun Bataks, like that of other Batak subgroups, was (and is) patrilineal, with each individual belonging to a series of ever-wider lineages and clans and descent ultimately traceable to a mythical first Batak. The fundamental unit of social organization among the Simalungun Bataks was the nuclear family. Loyalties and patterns of social interaction above the nuclear family level, however, were oriented primarily toward the multiclan village in which the individual resided and on which he depended for material and psychic sustenance, and only secondarily toward his lineage or clan.

Several factors seem to be involved in the Simalungun Batak emphasis upon the village rather than the kinship unit. Among these are the absence of a ruling or landowning clan and the variety of clans and lineages residing in a single village. By the late nineteenth century, and perhaps much earlier, considerable territorial mixing of clans and lineages had occurred throughout Simalungun. Although members of one clan tended to predominate in a given area, no village was exclusively inhabited by a single clan or lineage. There was thus a relatively small number of clan- or lineage-mates upon whom one could call during a harvest or in times of crisis, necessitating the development of nonkinship, village-based relationships and patterns of assistance. Moreover, in the nineteenth century there was relatively little intercourse among villages; each village unit was reasonably self-sufficient economically, regional markets were still underdeveloped, and it was not even necessary to seek wives outside the village.

This discussion of the strength of village loyalties and the tradition of village self-sufficiency is particularly relevant to an understanding of precolonial politics and government in the region. Politically, traditional Simalungun was divided into several small kingdoms, each of which consisted of a number of villages and larger territorial units which recognized the authority of a paramount ruler (radja) and paid tribute to him. The pattern of authority was basically pyramidal rather than hierarchical, with each subordinate unit duplicating on a small scale the larger systems of which it was a part.[1] Structural instability—the endless repetition of a cycle

    1. On the distinction between pyramidal and hierarchical primitive political systems, see A. Southall, *Alur Society* (Cambridge, W. Heffer and Sons, 1953).

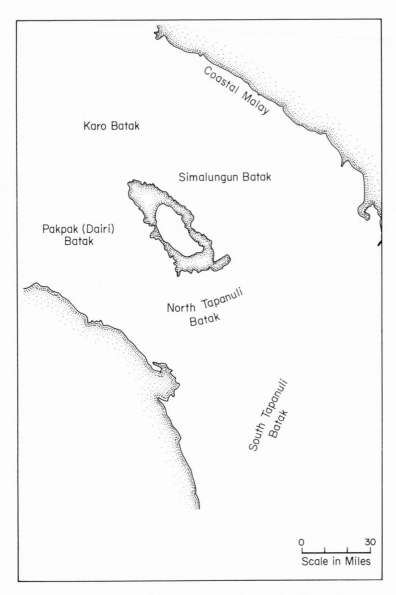

Map. 2.   Ethnic Groups of North Sumatra (original areas of settlement)

Source: Clark E. Cunningham, *The Postwar Migration of the Toba-Bataks to East Sumatra,* p. 4.

of emergence, growth, decline, and fall—was endemic in the kingdoms of Simalungun and seems to have been related to the tenacity of village loyalties and traditions which constantly undermined the authority of supravillage rulers and over a period of generations contributed to the dissolution of old constellations of power and the creation of new ones.

The origins of the kingdoms of Simalungun are shrouded in legend and mystery. But, whatever the earlier patterns of development may have been, it seems probable that the kingdoms of the late nineteenth century began and grew as the result of the emergence (often through migration into the area) of an aggressive and expansionist leader in one village who brought more and more villages under his control.

At the time of the first sustained Dutch penetration of Simalungun four kingdoms—Siantar, Tanah Djawa, Pane, and Dolok Silau—exercised hegemony over the greater part of the region. Each of the four kingdoms had its central village, or *pematang,* where the radja and his officials resided; the inhabitants of the pematang (usually the largest village in the kingdom) and a number of smaller neighboring villages were directly under the authority of the radja.

Within the pematang and its satellites the radja's rule was apparently quite autocratic. He was acknowledged to possess supernatural power as an attribute of his office and was considered to be a god residing on earth, qualities that served to legitimize any arbitrary actions he might take. The radja had, it is said, life and death power over his subjects and commanded their complete obeisance; they prostrated themselves in his presence and used a special "high" language when speaking to him.[2]

Outside the directly ruled territory of the radja the structures of government and the relationship of subordinate rulers to the radja varied considerably from kingdom to kingdom, due to differing historical circumstances and processes of growth. Several kingdoms contained relatively autonomous subunits whose rulers, called *tungkat,* exercised rather wide

2. Just how arbitrary and oppressive the radja were is a matter of some debate. Dutch writers and Simalungun Batak former revolutionaries interviewed by the author considered them to be extremely so, while other Simalungun Bataks felt that the tales of cruelty and oppression were much exaggerated. In most cases, the latter group argued, the radja and other traditional rulers were constrained by respect for the limitations imposed on their authority by the *adat* (custom and customary law).

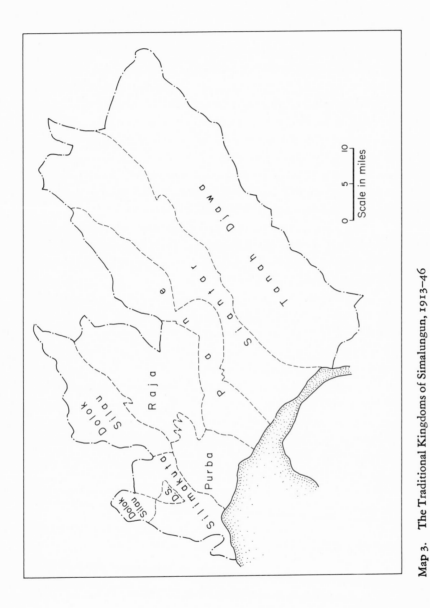

Map 3. The Traditional Kingdoms of Simalungun, 1913–46

Source: The General Agricultural Condition of Simeloengoen (P. Siantar, Gunseibu-Kezaibu 2602 [1942]).

authority in their own areas, while recognizing the sovereignty of the radja. Each tungkat had his own pematang (with its satellite villages) in which he exercised direct authority; he also ruled indirectly over a number of other villages within his region. There were also villages and clusters of villages that seem to have had a great deal of autonomy from both radja and tungkat. Until the coming of the Dutch the relationships between these various levels of authority were apparently never very stable. Conflict among radja was also common, usually involving attempts at expansion of the territory of one kingdom to include villages under the authority of another radja.

The traditional status hierarchy in Simalungun was, for the most part, based on the political rather than on the kinship system. The radja, tungkat, hereditary village headmen, heirs apparent, and members of their immediate families, holding all governmental authority and possessing supernatural power, formed the top level of a three-tiered stratification system. Non-hereditary officials constituted a subclass of this aristocracy. At the second level was the majority of the population of all clans and lineages (including members of the ruler's clan and lineage not in the line of succession), who all had the same rights and obligations toward their rulers. At the bottom of the system were the slaves of the aristocracy, individuals captured in war, and the children of illegitimate unions and of criminals who had been put to death. The most important aspect of this stratification system was the clear differentiation between an aristocracy born to rule and the common people who had no share in authority. This characteristic of traditional social structure, unique to the Simalungun Bataks among all of the ethnic groups residing in the region in the post-1950 period, was to have significant implications for the adaptability of the group to the politics of independent Indonesia.[3]

The Colonial Period: Patterns of Social Change

THE COMING OF THE DUTCH

Dutch penetration of Simalungun brought an end to the processes of growth, decline, amalgamation, and disintegration of the traditional king-

3. The Javanese may be cited as having a stratification system similar to that of the Simalungun Bataks; as noted below, however, the Javanese migrants did not bring their aristocracy with them to Simalungun.

doms. The campaign to extend Dutch rule throughout the Indonesian archipelago brought colonial power in force to Atjeh on the northern tip of Sumatra, to Tapanuli through the ports on the west coast, to the fertile lowlands of the East Coast, and, in the 1880s and 1890s, to Simalungun. With few exceptions the Dutch met little resistance from the traditional rulers. The famous *Korte Verklaring* (Short Declaration), in which the radja "admitted that his territory was under Dutch rule, undertook not to enter into political relations with foreign powers, and . . . agreed to comply with all such rules and orders regarding his State as Government should prescribe,"[4] was signed by all of the rulers of Simalungun in 1907.

The colonial government used this broad grant of power to effect many changes in the traditional kingdoms. In order to make the radja more responsible for the governing of their rather loosely constructed kingdoms, it was thought necessary to rationalize the traditional governments by establishing clear lines of hierarchical authority and by determining the geographical boundaries of each kingdom and its subdivisions. Seven kingdoms were recognized by the Dutch in the area of Simalungun. These were divided into districts, roughly comprising the territories headed by tungkat, and further subdivided into villages or village clusters, again more or less in accord with traditional boundaries.

The position of the old aristocracy in the new order was somewhat ambiguous. At first, the Dutch objective was to rule indirectly and to abstain from continuous interference with traditional government except in matters related to the protection of what were considered basic human rights. But, as the Dutch government moved beyond the doctrines of protection and regularized traditional administration and toward a more positive welfare policy, the indigenous rulers were increasingly restricted in their authority and bypassed in the implementation of policy. Perhaps most importantly, new district towns rather than the pematang of the kingdoms became the centers of an expanding colonial administration. Civil servants, many of whom were not Simalungun Bataks, were posted to these towns to implement government policy in such areas as agricultural improvement, public health, forestry, and so on. During most of the colonial period there were thus two governments in Simalungun, that of the increasingly active colo-

4. J. S. Furnivall, *Netherlands India* (Cambridge, University Press, 1944), p. 237.

nial power and that of the increasingly restricted traditional kingdoms.

To the extent that any power remained in the hands of the traditional rulers, its locus shifted upward to the radja. In rationalizing the governmental hierarchy the Dutch had stabilized the position of the radja as final authority in his kingdom and supported him in any disputes with his subordinates.[5]

Dutch colonial power thus transformed the traditional political systems of Simalungun from loosely articulated and irregularly ruled kingdoms built upon and continually undercut by particularistic village loyalties to an artificially stable system of seven kingdoms with limited authority, rationalized and hierarchical levels of administration, and clear-cut geographical boundaries. This transformation of traditional government was, however, but one aspect of the political development of Simalungun in the early twentieth century. Of perhaps more fundamental importance were the impact of a modernizing economy and the structures and processes that accompanied it, and the introduction of the world religions of Christianity and Islam.

THE IMPACT OF THE PLANTATION ECONOMY

The most profound changes produced by the colonial period occurred in the kingdoms of Pane, Siantar, and Tanah Djawa (the present areas of Lower Simalungun, the Road to Parapat, and Siantar municipality), in large part as the result of the development of a plantation economy. In 1906 a representative of the British firm Harrisons and Crosfield, which had extensive plantation acreage in Malaya, introduced the high quality, high yield *Hevea*

---

5. As one informant put it:
   In the old days, the tungkat were fairly powerful. If united they could often overcome the will of the radja. Before the Dutch, for example, if a *tuan huta* [headman] didn't like a subordinate official and wanted to replace him, and the tungkat agreed but the radja didn't, the tungkat would usually win. The radja was dependent in many ways on the support of his tungkat, with whom he shared authority in adat matters. After the Dutch came, whenever there was a dispute between a radja and a tungkat, the Dutch supported the radja and the radja won.
   Interview with Bandar Alam Purba Tambak, former radja of Dolok Silau and in 1964 head of the Agrarian Service, Regency of Simalungun.

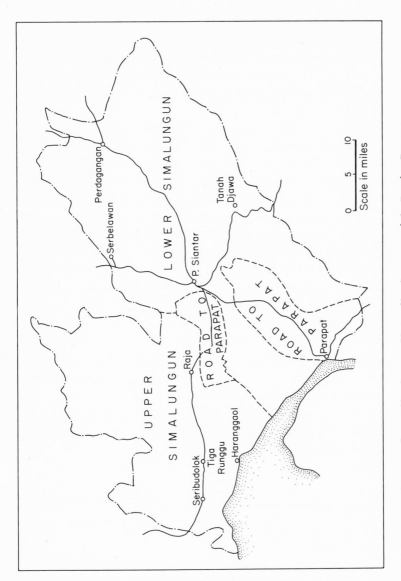

Map 4.   Lower Simalungun, Upper Simalungun, and the Road to Parapat

Source: Pemerintahan Daerah Tkt. II Simalungun, *Lapuran Tahun 1963*, p. 2.

brasiliensis rubber tree to East Sumatra.[6] Rubber quickly established itself as the principal plantation crop in Simalungun, followed by tea, sisal, coffee, and palm oil. In 1922 there were twenty rubber, fourteen tea, two sisal, and ten "mixed" plantations, cultivating rubber, tea, coffee, and oil palms. Most of the plantations were owned by large syndicates whose capital was Dutch, British, and/or American.

Underpopulation in East Sumatra and the unwillingness of the indigenous peoples of North Sumatra to work on the plantations required the European planters to import contract laborers from Java. By 1920, according to the colonial official J. Tideman, there were 44,000 Javanese contract laborers in Simalungun and perhaps another 20,000 Javanese whose contracts had expired and who had settled in villages near the plantations or in the expanding towns. The Javanese represented approximately 37 percent of the total population of Simalungun in 1920 and 43 percent in 1930.[7] By 1939 estate laborers and their families alone numbered 114,573 of a total population of 369,099, or 31 percent; unfortunately no figures are available on the number of Javanese ex-laborers at this time. [8]

The great majority of Javanese who became plantation laborers in Simalungun were from the poorest and most disadvantaged peasant segment of Javanese society. In *The Religion of Java,* Clifford Geertz distinguishes three main cultural types among the ethnic Javanese "grouped according to their world outlook—according to their religious beliefs, ethical preferences, and political ideologies." These three groups are the *"abangan,* representing a stress on the animistic aspects of the overall Javanese syncretism and broadly related to the peasant element in the population; *santri,* repre-

6. G. C. Allen and Audrey G. Donnithorne, *Western Enterprise in Indonesia and Malaya* (London, George Allen and Unwin, 1957), pp. 118–19.

7. For 1920, see J. Tideman, *Simeloengoen: het land der Timoer-Bataks in zijn vroegere isolatie en zijn ontwikkeling tot een deel van het cultuurgebied van de oostkust van Sumatra* [Simalungun: The land of the Eastern Bataks in its former isolation and its development into a part of the plantation area of the east coast of Sumatra] (Leiden, S.C. van Doesburgh, 1922), pp. 84, 195–209; for 1930, see *Census of 1930 in the Netherlands Indies; 4: Native Population in Sumatra* (Batavia, Dept. van Economische Zaken, 1935), p. 26. Population of Siantar not included.

8. *The General Agricultural Condition of Simeloengoen* (P. Siantar, Gunseibu-Kezaibu 2602 [1942]), p. 16. Population of Siantar not included.

senting a stress on the Islamic aspects of the syncretism and generally related to the trading element (and to certain elements in the peasantry as well); and *prijaji*, stressing the Hinduist aspects and related to the bureaucratic element..."[9]

It was primarily the first of these groups, the abangan, who came to Simalungun. The society from which they had come was relatively atomistic and weak in social organization and integration. The kinship system in Java, as Hildred Geertz has written, "is bilateral and nucleating . . . the nuclear family of parents and young children stands essentially on its own and usually in a separate house, and obligations between kinsmen are minimal." Moreover, "there is a very high divorce rate . . . and children frequently live in a series of different family groups during the course of their childhood. There are no corporate kin groups. . . . Above the household there are no organized groupings for economic, ritual or other purposes." In Java only the hamlet unit provided a measure of social integration, and even that was in most cases weak and unable to command the loyalties of its inhabitants.[10]

Life on the plantations was turbulent and confusing for the Javanese, intensifying social disorganization and disintegration. Particularly in the early years, sanitary facilities were minimal and there was much overcrowding in the barracks-like *pondok* in which the workers were housed. Attempts to develop a sense of community within the pondok were not very successful, as new workers were constantly arriving and old ones were being transferred to other parts of the plantation.[11]

9. Clifford Geertz, *The Religion of Java* (Glencoe, Ill., The Free Press, 1960), pp. 4, 6.

10. Hildred Geertz, "Indonesian Cultures and Communities," in Ruth McVey, *Indonesia*, pp. 47–48. For a more extended treatment of the Javanese kinship system, see Hildred Geertz, *The Javanese Family* (New York, The Free Press of Glencoe, 1961).

11. A reflection of the importance of a sense of community among the Javanese may be seen in the nature of labor–management disputes in Simalungun, of which well over half in the early 1960s were concerned with attempts by the management to transfer workers from one part of a plantation to another. Interviews with officials of PPN (Government Estates Administration) and Goodyear Tire and Rubber Company.

Cut off from their traditional political and cultural leaders, the prijaji, it was difficult for the abangan plantation workers to develop an indigenous elite. Their life centered around the plantation and its activities; they were legally subjects of the Dutch government and not of the traditional Simalungun kingdoms, and their affairs were regulated largely by the plantation managers, who even involved themselves in the selection of pondok heads. The pattern of social stratification that developed was also plantation-oriented, comprising two principal status groups, the ordinary workers and the foremen; individuals who possessed special skills, such as artisans, were somewhere in between. Relationships between foremen and workers and between pondok heads and residents were at best uneasy, as these potential leadership groups were often seen as instruments of higher authority rather than as spokesmen for the workers. Since wages were low and there was little opportunity for capital accumulation it was hard to break out of plantation society.

At the end of their contract period many Javanese returned to Java, but a substantial number remained in Simalungun, moving (with Dutch assistance) to their own villages near the plantations, where they became subjects of the radja (but continued to be protected by Dutch officials from any interference by their nominal Simalungun overlords). Some gravitated to the growing towns, such as Serbelawan, Perdagangan, or Siantar, where they became artisans, unskilled laborers for the Chinese, or petty traders, and lived clustered together in their own neighborhods. For the children of most Javanese, whether in the pondok, villages, or towns, there were few educational opportunities that might have encouraged the development of a modern elite. Almost no Javanese received enough education to become civil servants, although a few (principally the sons of foremen and town Javanese) became teachers in the so-called *wilde scholen* (unaccredited private schools) in the 1930s.

The growth of a plantation economy in Simalungun and the importation of large numbers of workers presented a major problem to the planters and to the Dutch government: How were the newcomers to be fed? The indigenous Simalungun people, practicing slash-and-burn dry-rice cultivation, barely produced enough food for themselves. In order to increase the supply of rice the Dutch made some attempts to convert the Simalungun Bataks to wet-rice *(sawah)* cultivation in the river valleys and lowlands around the plantations, but were largely unsuccessful; in any event there were simply too few people in Simalungun to produce the necessary quantities of rice. The problem was partially alleviated by the opening of the road to the rice fields of Tapanuli which permitted easier transport of rice to Simalungun. But the valleys of mountainous Tapanuli were already becoming densely populated and there was little land available for the opening of new fields, and this source provided only a limited amount of rice for the plantation workers.

In order further to ease the problem of food supply the Dutch encouraged the migration of large numbers of North Tapanuli Bataks from their homeland to Simalungun. Small groups of migrants began to enter Simalungun at about the time the traditional rulers signed the Short Declarations with the Dutch. With few exceptions they settled along the river valleys in Lower Simalungun, Siantar, and the Road to Parapat, where it was possible to construct extensive irrigation systems (see Table 1–1). In 1912 there were 1,760 North Tapanuli Bataks in Simalungun; by 1920 there were over 20,000 and by 1930 almost 50,000.[12]

Several factors contributed to the willingness of the North Tapanuli

Table 1–1. Irrigated Rice Fields (Sawah) in Simalungun, 1913–42

Year	Total Sawah (hectares)
1913	720
1918	3,700
1923	7,097
1928	7,959
1933	8,865
1942	9,723

Source: A. Pandiangan, "Persawahan di Kabupaten Simelungun" [Wet-rice Cultivation in the Regency of Simalungun], in *Kenang-Kenangan Pekan Pertundjukan Simelungun 10 Mei 1952–25 Mei 1952* [A Souvenir of the Simalungun Exhibition Fair, May 10, 1952–May 25, 1952] (P. Siantar, 1952), p. 82.

12. Figures for 1912 and 1920 from Tideman, pp. 186, 187; for 1930, from *Census of 1930 in the Netherlands Indies,* p. 31.

Bataks to leave their villages and journey to a strange land where, only a few years before, the few among them who visited Simalungun feared for their lives. Population pressure was certainly the key factor, and the traditional practice in North Tapanuli of young men leaving their villages of birth to found new villages in less populated areas encouraged emigration. The *rust en orde* (peace and order) established by the Dutch in Simalungun removed the fear of being killed or sold into slavery by the traditional rulers, and Dutch encouragement and assistance in building irrigation systems were also important, as was the improved system of roads.

For the most part the immigrants came from the region of North Tapanuli known as Toba, on the southern shore of Lake Toba around the present town of Balige, but a considerable number were from the Silindung Valley, where the town of Tarutung is now located, and other regions were represented as well. Many of the migrants were already Christians, as German missionaries from the Protestant Rhenish Mission Society had been working in Tapanuli since 1861 and had been particularly successful in the Toba and Silindung areas.[13] The missionaries encouraged migration to East Sumatra, seeing the migrants as an aid in converting the peoples of that region to Christianity.

The legal position of the North Tapanuli migrants vis-à-vis the Simalungun radja was for some years uncertain. At first they were considered, like the plantation workers, subjects of the Dutch government, but in 1918 it was decided that all Indonesian inhabitants of Simalungun (except the plantation workers) would henceforth be subjects of the radja. This caused a certain amount of discontent among the North Tapanuli Bataks, who considered themselves superior to the Simalungun people and did not wish to recognize the radja as overlords. As in the case of the Javanese villagers, however, the Dutch served as mediators between the newcomers and the Simalungun aristocracy (whose authority was in any event quite weak in the towns and plantation districts by this time), and there was little actual interference in village affairs by the radja or their subordinates. In particular there was no interference with the determination of who was to live in the new villages and how much land the newcomers were to be given; these matters were controlled by the Dutch.

13. Dr. T. Muller Kruger, *Sedjarah Geredja di Indonesia* [A History of the Church in Indonesia] (Djakarta, 1959), pp. 182–85.

One unintended consequence of the immigration of North Tapanuli Bataks to Simalungun was the partial breakdown of their traditional forms of social organization. Although the North Tapanuli Batak kinship system was almost identical to that of the Simalungun Bataks, the relationship between kinship and village organization was quite different. In the North Tapanuli setting, kinship was the basis of hamlet organization and land was owned in common by members of the founding lineage. In the first years of the migration some attempt was made to establish the new villages in Simalungun on a kinship basis similar to that of North Tapanuli villages. Two factors prevented such a development: (1) individuals of many different clans were involved in the migration and were mixed together in the new villages, so that there were no localized lineages; and (2) no lineage could claim ownership of the newly opened land, which was legally regarded as the territory of the traditional kingdoms, rights of usage being given to individual migrants. The basic unit of social organization in the Tapanuli highlands, the localized lineage, thus could not be preserved in Simalungun and had to be replaced by other institutions. At the level of village organization, a voluntary association, the *dongan sahuta* (village association, literally "friends of one village"), to which most villagers belonged, performed some of the functions of the localized lineage (assisting in adat ceremonies, providing financial help in times of crisis). In small villages there was usually only one dongan sahuta, which included the whole village, while in the larger villages and towns there might be several, each of which included a cluster of houses or the residents of one street.

The dongan sahuta never became a focus for the loyalties of its inhabitants as had the multiclan village units of the Simalungun Bataks. Instead the lineage remained strong and there was frequent communication with lineage mates in other parts of Simalungun and North Tapanuli. Broader kinship groupings also took on a new significance. In Tapanuli, Edward Bruner has commented, "the localized lineage is a meaningful corporate group, but the higher level patrilineal segments are merely descent categories."[14] In Simalungun, as in other parts of the East Coast to which the North Tapanuli Bataks migrated, the clan, consisting of a number of line-

14. Edward Bruner, "Kinship Organization among the Urban Batak of Sumatra," *Transactions of the New York Academy of Sciences*, ser. 2, 22 (1959–60), 119.

age segments with a common patrilineal name, became an important solidary unit. Where there was a substantial number of individuals with a common clan name, and particularly in the town of Siantar, clan organizations were formed whose principal duties were to organize and coordinate adat cere-monies and to provide a measure of social security for their members, tasks they shared with the dongan sahuta. Where the number of clan mates was too small to form an effective organization, two or more clans that traced descent from a common ancestor joined together for the same purpose.

Beyond the loyalty to clan, region of origin also became an important aspect of self-identification and identification of others for North Tapanuli Bataks in Simalungun. As a clan in North Tapanuli is generally located in a single, if often vaguely defined, area, an émigré could easily be identified by his clan name as, for example, *orang Toba* or *orang Silindung* (a Tobanese or a man from Silindung). As a migrant he developed a certain loyalty to his place of origin and an affinity with others from his region.[15] No comparable loyalty to his adopted home emerged among the North Tapanuli Bataks in Simalungun, although several factors have tended to undermine the im-portance of both clan and regional identification, particularly in the late colonial and postcolonial periods. Among these factors are the frequency of intermarriage between people from different regions, the pressures on North Tapanuli Bataks throughout East Sumatra to be united against other ethnic groups which, it is felt, threaten their position in the area, and the role of Christianity in providing a sense of unity among North Tapanuli Bataks and a sense of the separateness of the group from other Sumatran peoples. It is worth noting that before World War II North Tapanuli migra-tion went no farther than Simalungun; the Muslim Malay sultans to the northeast were hostile to Christian Bataks and devised various means of keeping them out.[16] North Tapanuli Bataks, in their homeland and in

15. Differences among the various regions of North Tapanuli are slight, consisting principally of minor dialect variations and differences in adat, but they seem to have been meaningful enough to generate a sense of distinctiveness on the part of each regional group.

16. Clark E. Cunningham, *The Postwar Migration of the Toba-Bataks to East Sumatra* (New Haven, Conn., Yale University Southeast Asia Studies, 1958), pp. 87–88.

Simalungun, thus saw themselves as an island of Christianity in a sea of Islam, and their faith provided them with a measure of unity. To some extent this sense of unity was reflected organizationally in the supraregional HKBP (Huria Kristen Batak Protestan, Batak Christian Protestant Church), whose churches have been important centers of social life in the village and partially bridge regional differences.[17]

Not all of the North Tapanuli Bataks who migrated to Simalungun in the colonial period were wet-rice farmers. As a part of their attempt to interest the people of North Tapanuli in Christianity, the missionaries had been very active in establishing schools at the village level. According to Cunningham, "The *zending* school, or regional mission school, emphasized religious instruction, but also included practical reading, writing, and arithmetic. This school became a fixture in the community, serving to make the Christian Batak one of the most literate groups in Indonesia and paving the way for the great influx of Bataks into clerkships, and administrative, educational, and technical professions."[18] Missionary emphasis on education was a fortuitous development for the Dutch government and the European planters in Simalungun who needed personnel to fill a wide variety of white-collar jobs. As there were no plantations in Tapanuli, few positions requiring education were available there, and many North Tapanuli Bataks gravitated to Simalungun, where they became, after about 1930, the predominant white-collar group. Some of them were even hired by the radja or tungkat, who were themselves usually uneducated but were required by the Dutch to keep records of government transactions.

URBANIZATION AND THE GROWTH OF A MONEY ECONOMY

The introduction of the plantation system, in addition to stimulating the immigration of large numbers of Javanese and North Tapanuli Bataks to Simalungun, also led indirectly to an influx of two other major groups,

17. The HKBP was founded in 1930, with headquarters in Pearadja (Tarutung). While not the only North Tapanuli Batak church, it is by far the largest, with nearly 750,000 members (of a total Sumatran Protestant population of almost 1,200,000) in 1958. See Muller Kruger, pp. 190–98 and appendix. Until 1963 Simalungun Batak Protestants were also members of the HKBP.

18. Cunningham, p. 51.

Muslim Bataks from South Tapanuli and Chinese, both of whom were attracted by the growth of towns and the expansion of trade. Both the North Tapanuli Bataks who sold their rice and the Javanese who bought it were part of a new money economy in Simalungun, and the South Tapanuli Bataks and Chinese saw an opportunity to cash in on the new wealth.

Although some South Tapanuli Bataks became rice farmers, the majority settled in the growing towns of Perdagangan, Serbelawan, and Siantar. Census data for both 1920 and 1930 indicate a South Tapanuli population of about 6,000, representing in the latter year 3 percent of the total Simalungun population.[19] The South Tapanuli Bataks, Islamized since the eighteenth century or earlier and including a large and active trading class, fit very closely Herbert Feith's description of the Islamic-entrepreneurial political culture in Indonesia.[20] Their kinship system is similar to that of other Batak groups, consisting of exogamous clans inhabiting particular areas. The effect of Islamization, however, has been to reduce the importance of kinship and regional affiliations and to place the Muslim Bataks within the framework of a wider community, *ummat Islam* (Islamic world or community), which includes other santri groups such as the Minangkabau and Coastal Malays. This enlargement of the group with which South Tapanuli Bataks identify themselves was particularly apparent among the migrants in Simalungun, many of whom dropped their clan name, using only a given (Muslim) name. South Tapanuli Bataks were thus often in-

19. For 1920, see Tideman, p. 187; for 1930, *Census of 1930 in the Netherlands Indies,* p. 30.

20. Feith distinguishes between two main "political cultures" in Indonesia, the Javanese-aristocratic and the Islamic-entrepreneurial. The latter "is a product of the maritime commercial towns and states of coastal Sumatra, North Java, Kalimantan and Sulawesi, of thorough Islamization, of a relatively slight Dutch impact, and of the revival of entrepreneurship in the present century." Its main features, in contrast to the Javanese-aristocratic political culture, are a respect for economic pursuits, support for an Islamic state, less anti-Dutch but more anti-Chinese sentiment, a readiness "to accept and incorporate influences stemming from the modern West," and a lesser sympathy for socialist ideas. Herbert Feith, *The Decline of Constitutional Democracy in Indonesia,* pp. 31–32. Because of the South Tapanuli Bataks' commercial orientation and the strength of their Islamic beliefs, Geertz' term santri may also be used to distinguish them (and other locally resident Sumatran Muslims) from the abangan (peasant animistic with an overlay of Islamic belief) Javanese in Simalungun.

distinguishable from the smaller migrant groups of other Sumatran santri with whom they mixed in the marketplace and the mosque and with whom they lived in the santri *kampung* (wards) of the towns. Social intercourse between Muslim and Christian Bataks in Simalungun was almost non-existent apart from work and commercial relationships, as the latter were infidels who ate pork (the principal ritual food in North Tapanuli) and, what is worse, allowed pigs to wander loose in their villages.

Besides the trading element there was also a significant group of Muslim Bataks who became white-collar workers for the government, the plantations, and the radja. In the last half of the nineteenth century South Tapanuli pilgrims in the Middle East had been strongly influenced by the Islamic reform movement with its stress on modern education. Moreover, German missionaries, whose work in South Tapanuli predated their entrance into North Tapanuli, had also established schools, and some of their students were Muslims. Many of the migrants from South Tapanuli to Simalungun had thus acquired at least a rudimentary Western-style education. Until 1930 the Muslim Bataks seem in fact to have been the predominant educated group in Simalungun, but were thereafter outdistanced by the North Tapanuli Christians.

South Tapanuli religious teachers also migrated to Simalungun, where they established Islamic schools and several Islamic educational and social organizations. The most important of these were Muhammadijah, founded in 1927, and Aldjam'ijatul Waslijah, founded in 1930.[21] By the end of the colonial period, Aldjam'ijatul Waslijah had established an extensive network of branches and schools throughout Lower Simalungun and in Siantar city, while most of the Muhammadijah schools were located in Siantar.

The influx of Chinese into Simalungun was greatest before World War I and declined thereafter, probably in response to the economic slump in

21. HAMKA (H. Abdulmalik Karim Amrullah), *Sedjarah Islam di Sumatera* [A History of Islam in Sumatra] (2d ed. Medan, Pustaka Nasional, 1950), p. 42. On the growth of Muhammadijah in Simalungun and East Sumatra generally, see *Peringatan 30 Tahun Muhammadijah di Daerah Sumatera Timur* [In Commemoration of 30 Years of Muhammadijah in the Region of East Sumatra], (Medan, 1957) and HAMKA, *Kenang2-an Hidup* [Memoires], (Kuala Lumpur, 1966).

the early 1920s and the Great Depression. In 1920 there were about 10,000 Chinese in Simalungun and another 3,000 in the city of Siantar; by 1939 there were 6,339 Chinese in the city and only 3,060 outside Siantar, most of whom were in Perdagangan, Serbelawan, and Tanah Djawa.[22] Tideman divided the Chinese into two groups, "a well-to-do commercial class, which forms the predominant element in the busy commercial district of the capital city" and in other towns in Lower Simalungun, and a smaller group of unskilled laborers, only a few of whom worked on the plantations.[23] The Chinese were outside the authority of the radja and, following the Dutch practice of "like over like," were headed by a Chinese "lieutenant" who was directly responsible to the Dutch government. Perhaps the most important role the Chinese played in the economy of Simalungun was as middlemen in the rice trade and moneylenders to the farmers, whose collateral was their rice crop.

Urban development was another important component of social change in the colonial period and, like the immigration of South Tapanuli Bataks and Chinese, it was an indirect result of the introduction of the plantation system. The largest of the new towns—Siantar, Tanah Djawa, Perdagangan, and Serbelawan—were located near the plantations and expanded around a pematang core. Each town varied from the others in its ethnic composition, but, as indicated above, most included substantial numbers of South Tapanuli Bataks and Chinese as well as some Javanese and North Tapanuli Bataks. The development of Siantar city deserves special attention, not only because this city came to be the center of Dutch administration, the market economy, and the political life of Simalungun, but also because the changes that were taking place in Siantar were also occurring, on a smaller scale, in the other towns of the region.

In 1907 Siantar consisted of probably fewer than a thousand Simalungun Bataks. Its growth since that time may be attributed to its central position as a crossroads, linking together Tapanuli, Karo, and the East Coast, and its location in the center of the areas of plantation and sawah development. By 1930 the Simalungun Bataks were a tiny minority and the main lines of the

22. For 1920, Tideman, p. 209; for 1939, *The General Agricultural Condition of Simeloengoen,* p. 16.
23. Tideman, p. 209.

contemporary pattern of ethnic division were established (see Tables 1–2 and 1–3). Residential segregation and a measure of occupational differentiation of ethnic groups were characteristic of town life in Siantar from the

Table 1–2. Population Growth in Siantar

Year	Indonesians	Europeans	Chinese	Other Asians	Total
1920	6,096	203	2,874	287	9,460
1930	9,711	163	4,964	490	15,328
1939	17,731	n.a.	8,506	401	26,638
1950	34,913	132	12,512	970	48,427
1963	91,681	66	16,334	929	109,010

Source: 1920, 1930, and 1950 data from Madja Purba, "Pematangsiantar, Setengah Abad" [Pematangsiantar, a Half-Century] in *Kenang-Kenangan Pekan Pertundjukan Simelungun*, p. 33. Figures for 1939 from *The General Agricultural Condition of Simeloengoen*, p. 16. Figures for 1963 were computed from Bagian Sensus Kotapradja Pematangsiantar, *Daftar Ichtisar Penduduk Kotapradja Pematangsiantar Achir Djuni 1963 Mengenai: Agama, Pekerdjaan, dan Kewarganegaraan* (Census Section, Municipality of Siantar, A Summary List of the Inhabitants of the Municipality of Siantar as of the end of June 1963, concerning: Religion, Occupation, and Nationality) which lists the total population in 1963 as 112,687. The total of 109,010 was arrived at by adding the figures for each racial group.

Table 1–3. Ethnic Affiliations Among the Indonesian Population of Siantar, 1930

Ethnic Group	Percent of Population
North Tapanuli Batak	31
Javanese	24
South Tapanuli Batak	23
Minangkabau	5
Simalungun Batak	5
Other Indonesian	12
Total	100 (9,192)

Source: Adapted from *Census of 1930 in the Netherlands Indies, 4: Native Population in Sumatra* (Batavia, Dept. van Economische Zaken, 1935).

early years of its growth. The first migrant groups, the North and South Tapanuli Bataks, settled on the southern and northern banks of the Bolon River respectively (probably because of their respective points of entry— the North Tapanuli Bataks came via Parapat and Tanah Djawa, the South Tapanuli Bataks via Perdagangan); these two settlements came to be called *Kampung Kristen* (Christian ward) and *Kampung Melaju* (Malay, indicating Muslim, ward). When substantial numbers of Javanese came to the city, they settled in their own quarter *(Kampung Djawa,* Javanese ward, now called *Kampung Bantan)* on the Muslim side of the river. The Chinese also lived to the north of the Bolon in their own kampung, where they built shops and a central market with Dutch assistance. The Chinese quarter quickly became the center of economic life in the city and in Simalungun as a whole. A small group of Europeans lived clustered together in the vicinity of the Dutch government buildings, between the South Tapanuli Bataks and the Chinese, and the indigenous Simalungun people remained in the pematang. With some modification, this pattern still exists today.

Occupational differentiation among ethnic groups, while it existed and played a role in ethnic separatism, was not nearly as clear-cut as residential segregation. In the first decade of Siantar's development, ethnic-occupational lines of division were fairly sharp—the North Tapanuli Bataks in Kampung Kristen were engaged mostly in sawah agriculture and were in, but not of, the urban community, the South Tapanuli Bataks were petty traders, the Javanese were unskilled laborers, the Chinese monopolized the central market, and the Simalungun Bataks were isolated in the pematang, the land available to them for swidden agriculture constantly being infringed upon by the growth of the town. Subsequent developments produced major changes in this pattern. The growth of Dutch administration, both for Siantar and for Simalungun, created a civil servant class composed of North and South Tapanuli and a few Simalungun Bataks. An expanding population reduced the amount of land available for farming within the city limits and more and more people of all ethnic groups turned to petty trade. Under the influence of a few Coastal Malays who had come to Simalungun as traders and Muslim religious teachers, most of the Simalungun Bataks in Siantar were converted to Islam and at least partially integrated into the Islamic-entrepreneurial culture. This contact between Simalungun

Batak Muslims and Coastal Malays established a bond between the two groups that was to become a focus for political organization in the post-independence period.

SOCIAL CHANGE IN UPPER SIMALUNGUN

Plantation and urban development and their consequences were not evenly distributed throughout Simalungun. Their impact was felt most strongly in the areas of Lower Simalungun and the Road to Parapat and in the city of Siantar; by contrast, in the kingdoms of Raja, Dolok Silau, Purba, and Silimakuta (the present area of Upper Simalungun), few plantations were opened, migration was on a very small scale, and the slow growth of a market economy had only a limited impact on the life of the ordinary villager. What social change did occur in this area was caused primarily by the interplay of three factors: Christianity, education, and improved communications.

Early in the twentieth century the Rhenish Mission Society, fresh from its successes in North Tapanuli, decided to expand its activities to Simalungun. Fluent in the North Tapanuli Batak language and accompanied by assistants and teachers from that area, the missionaries hoped to use their knowledge and experience to convert large numbers of Simalungun Bataks in a short period of time. But, unwilling to master the Simalungun language and unable to convert members of the traditional aristocracy (who must have seen Christianity as an attack on their own authority, which was rooted in the possession of supernatural powers) progress was slow. As in Tapanuli, the Christian missionaries in Simalungun concentrated on the development of educational facilities as a means of conversion. The first schools were built in Raja, Purba, and Silimakuta; by the end of the colonial period there were perhaps 25–30 church-run, three-year elementary schools with a total of 1,000 pupils in Upper Simalungun.[24] After 1910 some of the graduates of

24. Unfortunately there are no figures available on the number of schools in the colonial period; the earliest total is for 1953 (29 schools with 1200 students) given in 60 *Tahun Indjil Kristus di Simalungun* [60 Years of the Gospel of Christ in Simalungun] (P. Siantar, Pimpinan Pusat Geredja Kristen Protestan Simalungun [Central Leadership of the Simalungun Christian Protestant Church], 1963), p. 73. As no new schools were built during the Japanese occupation (1942–45) or the

these schools became teachers and a few were sent to Tapanuli or Java for further education. In 1929 the first Simalungun minister was ordained.[25]

It was through the schools that the missionaries had the largest impact on Simalungun society, creating a new (albeit very small) class of educated and semieducated individuals. This group constituted a new elite whose status was based on secular learning and acceptance of Christianity and was unrelated to traditional authority. Ministers and teachers were the most mobile members of this group, and their contacts with other ethnic groups, particularly the North Tapanuli Bataks, were the most frequent. Ethnic consciousness grew rapidly among the educated Simalungun Bataks, who disliked having to learn the North Tapanuli language and resented having North Tapanuli Bataks as their superiors within the church and educational hierarchies. The first formal expressions of this resentment were the decision taken by a 1928 church conference to drop the North Tapanuli Batak language in favor of the Simalungun language in all churches and church schools, and the formation by the church of an advisory committee consisting of teachers and lay leaders, whose tasks were the preparation of schoolbooks, a grammar of the Simalungun language, religious texts, a hymnal, and a church periodical (all in the Simalungun language). Later efforts included the decision to build a Simalungun museum in Siantar and attempts to gain a degree of autonomy for Simalungun Bataks within the HKBP church. An ethnic organization, Simalungun Sapanriahan (Simalungun Unity), founded in 1936 to advance Simalungun Batak culture and language, was led by Simalungun officials of the Dutch government and the church-affiliated teachers and had strong anti-North Tapanuli Batak overtones.

While ethnic consciousness was growing among the educated Simalungun Bataks, improved communications were helping to stimulate similar de-

---

Indonesian Revolution (1945–49), these figures probably describe accurately the immediate prewar situation.

25. Roman Catholic missionaries were also active in Upper Simalungun from the beginning of the century, but did not move inland from their base at Haranggaol on Lake Toba until the 1930s, when a church was built near Pematang Raja. By this time most of the accessible villages in Raja had become Protestant and the Catholics made little progress. They finally returned to Haranggaol, where the largest concentration of Catholics in Simalungun is still located.

velopments among the uneducated. The construction of the road from Siantar to Seribudolok (begun in 1906) was an important event, facilitating considerably communication between the government and the radja and between the missionaries and the common people, and bringing the Simalungun people into more direct contact with the North Tapanuli Bataks whose rice fields lined the road to Siantar and with the other groups that had moved into Simalungun. Another important consequence of the development of modern educational and communications facilities was the creation of a large group of Simalungun Batak primary school graduates whose education and exposure to urban life in Siantar left them dissatisfied with village life but unable to advance in the city. Lacking funds, they could not acquire the further education (for the most part, only the sons of the aristocracy and a few individuals selected by the missionaries received more than three years of schooling) which would prepare them for positions as clerks in government or plantation offices. Lacking already successful urban relatives who could give them a start in commerce, they were hesitant to move to the city. As they were not members of the aristocracy, there was little hope for them to enter the traditional structures of government. Frustrated at every turn, these young men spent most of their time in the coffee shops of Raja, Tiga Runggu, Haranggaol, and other towns, brooding over the barriers placed before them but doing little to organize resistance to the radja or the Dutch.

The Emergence of Nationalist Organizations and Leadership

Most of the organizations that appeared in Simalungun during the colonial period were ethnic or religious in form and content and did not directly enter the political arena. Ethnic and religious loyalties and cleavages were not, however, the only sources of organizational development in Simalungun/ Siantar. Toward the end of the colonial period there emerged a group of individuals of a variety of ethnic groups and religious affiliations, largely urbanites, who were most intensely in contact with the non-Indonesian elements of what J. S. Furnivall called the plural society in the Dutch East Indies—the Europeans, who were the highest status group and held political power, and the Chinese, who were dominant in the local economy. Among those Indonesians who followed urban occupations, i.e. the petty traders, schoolteachers, entrepreneurs, and government and plantation officials, there was daily interaction and common exposure to the frustrations inherent in a society in which Indonesians were at the bottom of the social, economic, and political ladders. There was common exposure also to new ideas and attitudes, to the concept of independence from colonial rule, to ideas of an Indonesian state and a restructuring of Indonesian society and economy.

After some sporadic and unorganized attempts at agitation in the 1920s, organizations with specifically political purposes and nationalist orientation began to take root in Simalungun in 1931 with the formation of branches of Partindo (Partai Indonesia, Indonesian Party) and Indonesia Muda (Young Indonesia). Partindo at the national level was the principal successor organization to the Partai Nasional Indonesia (Indonesian Nationalist Party), which had been founded by Sukarno and others in 1927 and subsequently outlawed by the Dutch. Partindo's leadership "aimed at complete independence on a basis of non-cooperation but was considerably more moderate in the methods it advocated than the PNI had been." Released from jail in 1931, Sukarno joined Partindo in July 1932 and "was made chairman by unanimous acclaim. Under his leadership the party immediately adopted a firmer nationalist line, and its growth accelerated enormously. By mid-1933 it had 50 branches and 20,000 members . . ."[26]

The early Partindo leadership in Simalungun consisted for the most part of educated and semieducated men who had traveled widely and come into contact with nationalist figures in Medan and Java in the 1920s. Its membership was drawn largely from the small traders, the schoolteachers, and the journalists; few civil servants were represented, as this group enjoyed the benefits of relatively high status and a reasonable wage and were fearful of Dutch reprisals. Severely restricted in their freedom to organize and agitate against the Dutch government, the active nationalists constituted only a small elite group in Siantar and had even fewer adherents in the other towns of Simalungun. Branches of Partindo were established in Serbelawan and Perdagangan, where the membership consisted mostly of South Tapanuli Bataks and a few Javanese, and in Tanah Djawa, where it was led by North Tapanuli Bataks.

26. George McT. Kahin, *Nationalism and Revolution in Indonesia* (Ithaca, N.Y., Cornell University Press, 1952), pp. 92, 94.

Unable to form a mass movement and completely shut out of the political institutions of the colonial government (the Dutch-appointed Indonesian members of the Siantar city council, the only body in which the nationalists might have been represented, were nonparty civil servants and professionals), the leadership of Partindo in Simalungun concentrated on nationalist education and the creation of cadres through Indonesia Muda, efforts that were particularly successful in the private schools but left untouched the uneducated youth and the rural population. In 1934 Partindo was dissolved by the Dutch, and there followed a three-year hiatus in organizational activity in Simalungun. In 1937 Gerindo (Gerakan Rakjat Indonesia, Indonesian People's Movement) was founded in Java by former Partindo leaders. Its members were militant nationalists but in the situation of the late 1930s were intensely aware of the threat of Japanese fascism and more disposed than Partindo had been to cooperate with the Dutch.[27] Gerindo in Simalungun was similarly a continuation of Partindo, with the same leadership, and was active until the end of the colonial period. Its membership in the region on the eve of the Japanese occupation was less than 250.

Japanese Occupation

Despite considerable social change in Simalungun during the colonial period—the growth of ethnic and religious differentiation and consciousness, the emergence of towns and of urban elites based on trade and education, the introduction of nationalist ideas and the development of an embryonic nationalist movement—the colonial government effectively managed to keep the lid on growing tension and discontent. Dutch power in the 1930s was supreme and unassailable. The colonial system had achieved a high degree of stability and there was no question as to the locus of ultimate authority, even in "indirectly" ruled territories such as Simalungun. The destruction of colonial authority came not as a result of indigenous opposition but because of the inability of the Dutch to withstand the military power of an aggressive and expansionist Japan. On March 9, 1942, after limited and ineffective resistance, the Dutch government in Java surrendered

27 Ibid., p. 96.

to the invading Japanese forces. Four days later the Japanese were in Sima-lungun, where they remained for nearly four years.[28]

The installation of a Japanese military administration in Simalungun brought with it several changes in governmental structure and personnel. All Dutch men and women, including government officials and plantation administrators (and nationals of other countries hostile to the Axis Powers) were ultimately interned, although some were kept on until they could be replaced by Japanese or Indonesians. A few high officials were replaced by Japanese, while most other government and plantation jobs formerly held by Europeans were given to Indonesians. The traditional kingdoms of Simalungun remained intact in form but were largely bypassed by the Japanese, who appointed their own administrative personnel at the district level for rice collection, labor recruitment and civil defense. The judicial system, in which separate courts had been provided for Europeans, for Indonesians under the authority of the traditional kingdoms, for Indo-nesians outside the territory of the kingdoms, and for non-Indonesian Asians, was reorganized into a single and uniform system.[29] In Siantar the city council was dissolved and the office of Municipal Secretary, second highest administrative post in the municipality and formerly held by a Dutchman, was given jointly to an Indonesian and a Japanese "adviser." The city's wards were divided into "blocks" or neighborhoods under block leaders for the purpose of distributing rice and sugar rations.[30] By de-veloping their own governmental structures and staffing them with carefully selected individuals, the Japanese hoped to be able to exercise more effec-tive control over the population and to mobilize it for participation in the war effort.

At the beginning of the Occupation the Japanese were widely regarded

28. The date March 13 is given in Madja Purba, "Pematangsiantar, Setengah Abad" [Pematangsiantar, A Half-Century], in *Kenang-Kenangan Pekan Pertun-djukan Simelungun 10 Mei 1952–25 Mei 1952* [A Souvenir of the Simalungun Ex-hibition Fair, May 10, 1952–May 25, 1952] (P. Siantar, 1952), p. 34.

29. M. L. Siagian, "Peradilan didaerah Kabupaten Simelungun" [Justice in the Regency of Simalungun], in *Kenang-Kenangan Pekan Pertundjukan Simelungun,* pp. 44–45. Japanese residing in Indonesia were beyond the jurisdiction of the new court system.

30. *The General Agricultural Condition of Simeloengoen,* p. 103.

as liberators; in a few months, however, the atmosphere of jubilation changed to one of deepening discontent. The heavy-handedness of Japanese administrators, the fear of the Japanese secret police, and the oppressiveness of forced labor practices were in part responsible for the change of attitude, but perhaps more fundamental was the poverty which came to affect all strata of the population. Before the war it had been necessary to import rice in large quantities to feed the plantation workers and the growing urban population of East Sumatra. Wartime conditions in Southeast Asia precluded large-scale importation of rice, forcing the Japanese to lower rice consumption in Simalungun in order to feed their own troops and to provide a minimum supply of rice to Indonesians in other parts of East Sumatra. In order to increase rice production, the Japanese encouraged Indonesians to settle on the plantations, areas that had been inviolable during the colonial period. In many cases the Japanese ordered the clearing of overage rubber and other trees and the replanting of the area with rice and other food crops. This work was carried out by Javanese plantation laborers who were then resettled in villages on the newly cleared land. Jungle land, also under concession to the plantations but still unexploited, was turned into rice fields by villagers (mostly Javanese and North Tapanuli Bataks) who took advantage of the Japanese disregard for plantation rights and their policy of increasing food supply.[31] According to figures published by the regency government in 1952, sawah land in Simalungun increased by 31 percent between 1942 and 1944.[32] The total increase in irrigated rice fields, and in land utilized for food production in general, was certainly much higher than these figures suggest, as most of the incursions onto plantation land were organized by the villagers themselves and were not reported in government statistics.

At the outset of the occupation, in Simalungun as elsewhere in Indonesia, the Japanese adopted a harsh attitude toward indigenous organizations both of the political and nonpolitical variety. In Simalungun Gerindo was

31. Karl J. Pelzer, "The Agrarian Conflict in East Sumatra," *Pacific Affairs, 30* (June 1957), 155–56. See also Cunningham, *The Postwar Migration of the Toba-Bataks,* pp. 89–90.

32. A. Pandiangan, "Persawahan di Kabupaten Simelungun" [Wet-Rice Cultivation in the Regency of Simalungun], *Kenang-Kenangan Pekan Pertundjukan Sime-*

banned and the nationalistically inclined weekly newspapers of Siantar ceased publication. The Christian churches were subject to continual harassment and their schools were taken over by the government. The advisory committee of the Simalungun division of the HKBP church was dissolved and its magazine was banned.[33] Many prominent nationalist figures throughout East Sumatra were arrested for anti-Japanese activities.[34]

After the first year of occupation the Japanese attitude toward the nationalist leaders began to change. Increasing numbers of Indonesians, needed for the war effort, were recruited into such organizations as Heiho,[35] a military-cum-labor auxiliary force of the Japanese Army, and Gyugun or Peta, an army established for internal defense. Just how many youths in Simalungun received military or paramilitary training is not known, but the number was certainly considerable. The official history of the Revolution in North Sumatra, published by the Ministry of Information, asserted, doubtless with some exaggeration, that "all the people were forced to drill and to know how to receive commands in a military manner."[36] The

---

lungun, p. 82. Earlier figures may be found in Table 1–1. Madja Purba (p. 17), writes that only one major sawah development project was carried out by the Japanese in Simalungun. This project was located in Huta Baju, district Tanah Djawa, and eventually encompassed 3500 hectares.

33. See T. Muller Kruger, *Sedjarah Geredja di Indonesia*, p. 192; and 60 *Tahun Indjil Kristus di Simalungun*, pp. 30–31.

34. Kementerian Penerangan Republik Indonesia, *Republik Indonesia, Propinsi Sumatera Utara* [Ministry of Information of the Republic of Indonesia, *Republic of Indonesia, Province of North Sumatra*] (Medan, 1953), p. 20. This is the official history of the Revolution in North Sumatra.

35. Hei: soldier; Ho: second-class reserve; M. A. Aziz, *Japan's Colonialism in Indonesia* (The Hague, Martinus Nijhoff, 1955), p. 229 n. Heiho was established in Sumatra in May 1943 and was open to elementary school graduates between the ages of 18 and 30. Japanese recruitment propaganda in Sumatra emphasized the "opportunity for the youth of Indonesia to join in devoting their energies to defend Greater East Asia against the colonialists." O. D. P. Sihombing, *Pemuda Indonesia Menantang Fasisme Djepang* [Indonesian Youth Challenges Japanese Fascism] (Djakarta, 1962), pp. 138–39.

36. *Republik Indonesia, Propinsi Sumatera Utara*, p. 19. Aziz (p. 230 n.) lists the number of Peta soldiers in Java at the time of the Japanese surrender as 37,000,

military atmosphere of the Occupation was in sharp contrast to the colonial period when formal military training was unavailable to most Indonesians in Simalungun/Siantar.

In order to facilitate recruitment into their military organizations and to develop support in general for the war, the Japanese began to rely heavily on nationalist leadership and propaganda. The support of prominent East Sumatran nationalist leaders was enlisted by offering them a role in the training of recruits. As a result of this policy nationalist leaders were provided with a core of armed and trained supporters, and national consciousness among the youth of the region increased markedly. An opportunity for intensive nationalist indoctrination was provided by the creation of camps where specially selected youths were given intensive military training. In terms of the revolutionary and postrevolutionary leadership it produced for Simalungun, perhaps the most important of these camps was TALA PETA, located at Gunung Rintis in the East Sumatran regency of Deli/ Serdang. TALA PETA provided a sort of advanced training for those who had shown leadership capacity in the smaller camps and civil defense organizations which had been established throughout East Sumatra.[37] Only a few Japanese participated in the actual training of cadres which was led by such prominent nationalist leaders as Saleh Umar, Jacub Siregar, and Abdullah Jusuf, who emphasized nationalist indoctrination and the techniques of guerrilla warfare.[38] Many young men from Simalungun, particularly Simalungun Bataks, received training at TALA PETA, where they

---

and Gen. A. H. Nasution writes that the Japanese were able "in a period of about a year to organize 50–60 battalions in Java and about the same number in Sumatra-Malaya." See his *Tentara Nasional Indonesia* [Indonesian National Army], *1* (Bandung/Djakarta, 1963; originally published in 1956), 85.

37. "The objective of TALA PETA was to create cadres who were disciples of Japan. Another intention of TALA PETA was to carry out preparations for a guerrilla organization which it was hoped would help the Japanese army in the mountains when and if the Allied army landed, that is, a sort of total defense advance force which it was hoped by Japan could forge a pro-Japanese popular spirit in defense and supply." *Republik Indonesia, Propinsi Sumatera Utara,* pp. 20–21.

38. Interviews with Abdullah Jusuf, A. Djulan Purba, and Djatongam Saragih (political leaders in Simalungun who received training at TALA PETA).

became the nucleus of an armed guerrilla organization that was to play an important role in the impending revolution.

At the mass level, one of the most important results of the policy of cooperation with Indonesian nationalism was that it permitted the widespread dissemination of nationalist ideas and popular identification with nationalist leaders throughout the archipelago. A principal instrument of this dissemination was the radio. "The Japanese considerably built up the archipelago's radio network, making sure that many of the villages and every city square had receiving sets. . . . At prescribed hours the population was required to listen to their official broadcasts, including the frequent speeches of Sukarno."[39] In Simalungun, radio sets were mostly restricted to the wealthier inhabitants of the towns, but were supplemented by loudspeakers (particularly on the plantations) and by word-of-mouth communication of the content of nationalist speeches by itinerant merchants and other townspeople who maintained contact with the villages.

Revolution

By early 1944 Indonesians in Simalungun and Siantar, as elsewhere, were becoming increasingly aware that the Japanese were losing the war. As the situation in the Pacific deteriorated, the decision was made in Tokyo, announced on September 7, 1944, to grant independence to Indonesia.[40] On March 1, 1945, the Japanese intention to establish a body for the Investigation of Indonesian Independence was announced by the authorities in Java.

39. Kahin, p. 108. See also Willard H. Elsbree, *Japan's Role in Southeast Asian Nationalist Movements 1940–1945* (Cambridge, Mass., Harvard University Press, 1953), p. 123. Elsbree writes that "in 1944 the Communications Bureau of the Sumatran Military Administration began the task of providing radios for every three thousand inhabitants." Elsbree's source for this information was Office of Strategic Services, *Programs of Japan in Sumatra, with Biographies,* comp. Research and Analysis Branch (Honolulu, Hawaii, 1945), p. 15. The lateness of the date given would indicate that the effectiveness of the radio as an instrument of nationalist indoctrination was somewhat lower in Sumatra than in Java.

40. The limited nature of the projected grant of independence, even as late as July 1945, is discussed in Benedict R. O'G. Anderson, *Some Aspects of Indonesian Politics Under the Japanese Occupation: 1944–1945* (Ithaca, N.Y., Cornell Modern Indonesia Project, 1961), pp. 34–35.

A Central Advisory Council and a Sumatran Investigating Committee for the Preparation of Independence were subsequently established, but because of the shortness of time and the difficulties of communication between Java and Sumatra and within Sumatra, neither of these bodies played an important role in the events surrounding the capitulation of the Japanese and the onset of the Revolution.

On September 21, the Japanese in North Sumatra publicly announced their surrender to the Allies, stating that they were under instructions to maintain civil and military authority in the region until the arrival of British troops. Despite their instructions, the Japanese were hesitant to interfere directly with the nationalist leaders. On October 3 the declaration of independence of the Republic of Indonesia, proclaimed in Djakarta on August 17, was announced in Medan by the newly appointed Republican governor of Sumatra. The next day Madja Purba, the highest ranking Indonesian official of the Japanese administration in Simalungun, received a wire from the governor requesting him to form a government in the regency. Purba's task was simplified considerably by the fact that the Japanese, in the final days of the Occupation, had elevated Indonesians to newly created positions of "vice-head" of most important governmental departments, thus creating a kind of embryonic Indonesian government which could easily be taken over by the Republic.[41]

The last months of 1945 and the beginning of 1946 were a period of party and organization building in Simalungun. All four of the national political parties which were to develop significant support in the region—PNI (Partai Nasional Indonesia, Indonesian Nationalist Party), PKI (Partai Komunis Indonesia, Indonesian Communist Party), Masjumi (originally an abbreviation of Madjelis Sjuro Muslimin Indonesia, Council of Indonesian Muslim Associations), and Parkindo (Partai Kristen Indonesia, Indonesian Christian [Protestant] Party—emerged during the early revolutionary period. Because of communication problems each party was more or less autono-

41. *Republik Indonesia, Propinsi Sumatera Utara*, pp. 21–22. The elevation in rank did not occur until after August 9. Anderson (p. 12), compares a similar situation in Java to a relay race, in which "the two bureaucratic directorates ran things side by side until the baton of power was finally relinquished to the Indonesian leadership."

mous of its parent organization on Java throughout the Revolution. Party organization was minimal and concentrated at the regency level, and few attempts were made to enroll party members in the districts and villages. Emphasis was placed instead on guerrilla organization, and many revolutionaries served as both party and guerrilla leaders; because of the circumstances of the period the latter role was by far the more influential. The party leadership's tasks were to provide political guidance to their affiliated youth groups and to provide liaison between the youth and the government. In fulfilling the latter function, the leadership was not entirely successful. Competition developed among armed youth groups,[42] many of which were independent of or only loosely controlled by the newly established political parties and the Indonesian army, a situation that undermined the fragile hold of the new Republican government on the instruments of authority. The period was thus one of chaos, confusion, and not a small degree of lawlessness in Simalungun.

In part the confusion stemmed from the fact that the Revolution in Simalungun began in a vacuum, without any preexisting leadership or organization that could command the allegiance of a majority of the population and channel the revolutionary fervor of the youth. Neither the traditional rulers nor the officials of the new government could fill this vacuum. The radja and lesser aristocrats (who in any event had no claim on the loyalties of non-Simalungun Bataks) had been discredited by years of cooperation with the Dutch and Japanese (and were considered by many to be "feudal" oppressors). Moreover, it was widely reported at the time of the Japanese surrender and the Republican takeover that several of the traditional rulers were organizing a reception committee for Allied troops and were arranging for food to be taken to the Dutch imprisoned in internment camps, thus further arousing the hostility of the revolutionaries.[43]

42. The word "youth" as used here is a translation of the Indonesian *pemuda;* it signified a revolutionary state of mind rather than a specific age group, though the members of most armed groups were in fact young. On the revolutionary youth, see John R. W. Smail, "On the Style of the Indonesian Revolutionaries," Paper no. 89, International Conference on Asian History, University of Hong Kong, August 30–September 5, 1964.

43. Interviews with former revolutionaries in Simalungun, and *Republik Indonesia, Propinsi Sumatera Utara,* p. 22. An attempt was made in January 1946 at a

The new government of Simalungun consisted largely of rather colorless longtime administrators who, while capable of running a government, could not lead a revolution. Madja Purba, for example, was a 1932 graduate of a school for civil servants in Bukittinggi, had been employed by the Dutch government in Simalungun until 1942, and had continued to work under the Japanese. He had not been active in the prewar nationalist movement and, in 1963, did not even know who its leaders in the region had been.

From the beginning of the Revolution there was thus considerable mutual distrust and suspicion between radical revolutionaries and more moderate elements in the local political leadership. In part this distrust stemmed from the fact that moderates and radicals measured each other in terms of different conceptions of status. The moderates, some of whom were active in party and organization politics and others not, were found most often in the ranks of the civil servants, professionals (ministers and other religious leaders, teachers, doctors), and local entrepreneurs. Many of them were graduates of or had at least been exposed to advanced Dutch schools, were somewhat Westernized, and had achieved positions of respectability in the prewar world. The civil servants of this group had not participated in the nationalist movement during the colonial period and on the whole tended to take a wait-and-see attitude toward the Revolution; while not in favor of a return of Dutch power (it would have meant demotion for many of them), they were reluctant in the ambiguous political situation of 1945–46 to take any positive action that might have unpleasant consequences. Other moderates, however, such as the leaders of the Muslim educational and social organizations who became active in Masjumi and the North Tapanuli Christians who led Partai Kristen Indonesia, were firmly committed to the nationalist cause.

The revolutionary youths, in contrast to the moderates, had on the whole little formal education, spoke no Dutch, and were far removed socially from the world of the prewar Siantar elite. They were imbued with revolutionary

---

meeting of the Komite Nasional for East Sumatra and the traditional rulers to persuade the latter to democratize their governments. Although an agreement was reached, the sultans and radja apparently made no changes in their administrations. Ibid., p. 76.

fervor and determined to strike out against the returning Dutch and those Indonesians whom they felt to be sympathetic to the Dutch. In their eyes the moderates were not willing to make sacrifices for the Revolution; the moderates, on the other hand, tended to dismiss the youths as mere adventurers. Where the one group was most concerned with the maintenance of order, the other wanted to make a revolution.

In the eyes of large sections of the Simalungun public, the militant revolutionary groups had as much or more claim to the legitimate exercise of power in the region as the civil bureaucracy, as it was the revolutionaries who possessed the special skills required for the creation and defense of an independent Indonesia. Even in remote villages it became common practice to address the young revolutionaries as *bapak* (father), an honorific used to denote the higher status of the person being addressed. The new government's ability to coordinate and oversee the activities of the revolutionary groups was thus severely attenuated by the special position of the latter as the chief bearers of the dominant revolutionary values. Moreover, the government for a time had no armed forces beyond a small police force and was therefore powerless, even if it had the will, to impose itself on the armed youth.

The scattered outbursts of violence in Simalungun during this period reflected the conflicts between these various groups and the transformation of values that was taking place throughout Indonesia. One such incident, resulting from the growing conflict between revolutionary youth and the traditional elite, was the East Sumatran Social Revolution, which virtually destroyed the remnants of the traditional kingdoms in a single night. On March 3, 1946, four Simalungun radja and many lesser officials and members of their families were assassinated, and a number of others were captured and imprisoned. Although the Social Revolution was directed primarily against the traditional aristocracy, it also affected civil servants, doctors, and other conspicuously well-to-do and Westernized individuals. Neither a popular uprising nor a spontaneous expression of mass hatred, the Social Revolution was rather a well-planned, carefully executed series of assassinations organized by a few armed youth groups whose identity is still unclear.[44] The motives behind the outburst can be found in the frustrations generated

44. The consensus among informants who were active revolutionaries or civil servants at the time was that the most important role in both the planning and

during the colonial period centering on the lack of social mobility, for which the youth blamed the traditional aristocracy as much as the Dutch.

In the wake of the Social Revolution, the radical youths vastly increased their influence in East Sumatran politics and lines of cleavage, not only within the ethnic Simalungun community but in the larger society as well, hardened. Differences and conflicts among the various revolutionary groups in the region were perhaps inevitable. A large number of organizations existed and there were great disparities among them in terms of financial support and the availability of weapons and supplies. Ethnic, religious, and/or ideological diversity contributed further to the potential for conflict.[45]

Revolutionary activity in Simalungun lasted only until the first Dutch "police action" in July 1947. On July 30, Dutch troops attacked Simalungun; after sporadic fighting the revolutionaries and many Republican government officials fled the regency, regrouping in Tapanuli where they formed a Republican Government of the Regency of Simalungun in exile. A sizable group of civil servants, teachers, and others elected to stay in Simalungun and accept employment from the Dutch government. After several months of Dutch occupation a State of East Sumatra (Negara Sumatera Timur, NST) was formed.[46]

---

execution of the Social Revolution in Simalungun was played by Barisan Harimau Liar (Wild Tiger Legion), an organization led by Simalungun Bataks and based on a nucleus of revolutionaries who had been trained at TALA PETA during the Japanese occupation. Procommunist and other youth groups were probably also involved.

45. For an account of East Sumatran politics in this period see Kahin, pp. 178–83. In Simalungun radical youth leaders obtained control of the government in April; within a month, however, they were ousted by the newly organized Indonesian army and allied guerrilla groups, and relative calm prevailed for the remainder of the Republican period.

46. On the Dutch "police action" and NST, see *Republik Indonesia, Propinsi Sumatera Utara*, pp. 146–53, 215–29; Djabatan Penerangan Republik Indonesia, Propinsi Tapanuli-Sumatera Timur, *Perdjuangan Rakjat Tapanuli-Sumatera Timur* [Information Service of the Republic of Indonesia, Province of Tapanuli-East Sumatra, *Struggle of the People of Tapanuli-East Sumatra*] (1950), pp. 110–16; and Henri J. H. Alers, *Om een rode of groene Merdeka, 10 jaren binnenlandse politiek Indonesie 1943–1953* [For a Red or Green Independence, 10 Years of Internal Politics in Indonesia 1943–1953] (Eindhoven, Uitgeverij Vulkaan, 1956), pp. 155–56.

Although Indonesians of all ethnic groups remained in Simalungun after the Dutch takeover and worked for the new government, only those Simalungun Bataks who supported the claims of the traditional aristocracy were strongly committed to NST. Among most members of other ethnic groups, opposition to NST, rooted in a number of factors, was profound. North Tapanuli Bataks and Javanese on and around the plantations, for example, feared that a continuation of Dutch influence in the region would facilitate the efforts of European plantation owners to reclaim land they had been using since the Japanese occupation; South Tapanuli Muslims were opposed on religious grounds; and Simalungun Batak former revolutionaries feared reprisals under a regime controlled by the aristocrats. Finally, not least important as a factor in the widespread opposition to NST was the deeply held commitment to independence from colonial rule within the framework of the Indonesian Republic proclaimed in 1945.

On December 27, 1949, after negotiations at The Hague in which representatives from the Netherlands, the Republic of Indonesia, and the Dutch-created states participated, sovereignty was formally transferred to a federal Republic of the United States of Indonesia, of which NST was a member state. Without broad backing and under pressure from the returning revolutionaries, who held mass demonstrations in cities and towns throughout East Sumatra in late 1949 and early 1950,[47] NST could not endure after the removal of the Dutch props that had created it. On May 13, 1950, the government in Medan agreed to its incorporation into a unitary state,[48] and on August 15, two days before the fifth anniversary of the proclamation of independence, Simalungun again became a part of the Republic of Indonesia.

An Integrative Revolution

The developments described in the preceding sections were not unique to Simalungun. They represented, rather, one instance of a complex process

47. On the movement for the dissolution of NST and the reaction of NST supporters, see *Republik Indonesia, Propinsi Sumatera Utara*, pp. 340–85; *Perdjuangan Rakjat Tapanuli*, pp. 138–68; Alers, pp. 222–23.

48. Kahin, pp. 460–61.

of social and political change occurring throughout the archipelago under the impact of colonial rule (including the Japanese occupation) and the forces colonialism set in motion. While the response in Simalungun was in its particulars unique, similar events, varying in form and intensity, occurred elsewhere. Social change in one region came increasingly to affect developments in other regions, creating entirely new patterns of supralocal social interaction where there had been, in the precolonial period, only intermittent contact. This expansion of the social sphere within which the individual interacts with others, and the formation of new social groups with claims on individual loyalties, has produced in Indonesia what Clifford Geertz has termed an "integrative revolution," defined as a tendency toward "the aggregation of independently defined, specifically outlined traditional primordial groups into larger, more diffuse units whose implicit frame of reference is not the local scene but the 'nation'—in the sense of the whole society encompassed by the new civil state."[49]

In Simalungun/Siantar this aggregative process has been proceeding along several different dimensions for well over half a century. Of primary importance has been the development of a sense of ethnic identity, of membership in a group defined and limited by common language, adat, and, in most cases, assumed kinship ties. In the postrevolutionary period, the most important of these groups have been the Simalungun Bataks, comprising perhaps 30 percent of the local Indonesian population, the Javanese, also about 30 percent, the North Tapanuli Bataks, about 20 percent, and the South Tapanuli Bataks, perhaps 10 percent.[50]

Prior to the twentieth century the ethnic group as a self-perceived, coherent social unit did not exist in Simalungun or in North Sumatra as a whole. Individuals had relations with individuals, lineage groups with lineage groups, and villages with villages, but few regular patterns of interaction existed above this level and there was little sense of belonging to larger social or political units. The Simalungun Batak kingdoms and the Malay sultanates of the East Coast provide a partial exception to this pattern, but they too were fairly small territorial units and it is uncertain to what extent

49. Clifford Geertz, "The Integrative Revolution," p. 153.
50. These are crude estimates, based on census data and on informed guessing.

Table 1-4. Major Ethnic Groups in Simalungun/Siantar, 1963–64

Ethnic Group	Migrant Status	Religion	Area of Residence	Occupation
Simalungun Batak	indigenous	majority Protestant	Upper Simalungun	dry-rice agriculture
North Tapanuli Batak	migrant	Protestant	Lower Simalungun, Road to Parapat, Siantar	white-collar, trade, wet-rice agriculture
South Tapanuli Batak	migrant	devout Muslim (santri)	Lower Simalungun, Siantar	trade, religious education
Javanese	migrant	nondevout Muslim (abangan)	Lower Simalungun, Siantar	plantation, urban labor, wet-rice agriculture

the individual identified himself with their socially distant elites and primarily exploitative governments.

The sense of ethnic distinctiveness and ethnic community felt by members of the various ethnic groups in postrevolutionary Simalungun began to grow during the colonial period when economic change, improved communications, missionary activity, and other developments brought individuals of diverse cultural backgrounds into contact with each other for the first time. Simalungun Bataks, for example, resented the invasion of their homeland by outsiders who did not speak their language, did not follow their adat, and were not members of one of the four Simalungun clans. North Tapanuli Bataks, confronted by other groups, realized that they too possessed a common language and adat despite regional differences among them. Their sense of community was further strengthened by their common status as agricultural pioneers and by their ability to trace an assumed kinship connection with any other North Tapanuli Batak.[51] In Siantar city they congregated in their own neighborhoods on the east side of the Bolon River, and in the rural villages they also lived apart from other groups. South Tapanuli Bataks, who came to Simalungun primarily as traders, similarly lived in separate neighborhoods in Siantar and in the smaller towns of the region. The Javanese, brought by the Europeans to work on the great rubber and tea estates, formed a still more isolated enclave, separated from the Sumatran peoples not only by adat and linguistic differences and by residential segregation but also by their employment as contract laborers, a status considered inferior by all other groups.

Principles of inclusion and exclusion, of what constitutes the "we" and "they" of ethnic affiliation, vary from group to group. The North Tapanuli Batak sees his identity in terms of his own lineage segment, the larger patrilineage of which it is a part, the still larger territorial group that makes up a subdivision of North Tapanuli, and finally all North Tapanuli Bataks

51. North Tapanuli Bataks claim that all the Batak peoples are descended from a single common ancestor, and thus it is possible to trace kinship connections to the clans of South Tapanuli, Simalungun, and Karo. Published North Tapanuli Batak genealogies normally relegate these groups to a minor position, however, and individuals of other Batak subgroups are not in fact very interested in, and some deny, their common ancestry.

(who form a single language group).[52] The Simalungun Batak places less emphasis upon extended family relationships, more on village of origin (which usually contains individuals from several lineages) and on membership in the total Simalungun group, defined primarily as a linguistic-cultural entity.[53] For the South Tapanuli Batak devotion to Islam is an integral part of his identity, setting him off from other Batak subgroups, and kinship is relatively less important. Like his northern neighbors, the South Tapanuli Batak also identifies himself by region of origin, among which there are minor adat and linguistic differences. Finally, among the Javanese, who have no extended family system, the sense of a distinctive identity is related to the use of the Javanese language, the symbols of popular Javanese culture such as the *wajang* and *ketoprak*,[54] and to Javanese mysticism.

Social relationships in the contemporary period have tended to be within rather than among the major ethnic groups. For such strata as rural villagers and plantation workers, this pattern is to some extent imposed by residential separation and by lack of facility in the Indonesian language, the principal vehicle of communication among peoples of different ethnic origins (approximately 50 percent of the regency population is literate in

52. For an analysis of the importance of the lineage segment, the patrilineage, and so forth, as determinants of villagers' loyalties in North Tapanuli, see Edward M. Bruner, "The Toba Batak Village," in Skinner, ed., *Local, Ethnic, and National Loyalties,* pp. 52–64. On the effects of urbanization (in Medan) on North Tapanuli Batak social structure, see Edward M. Bruner, "Kinship Organization among the Urban Batak of Sumatra," *Transactions of the New York Academy of Sciences,* ser. 2, 22 (1959), and Edward M. Bruner, "Urbanization and Ethnic Identity in North Sumatra," *American Anthropologist,* 63 (1961).

53. At the 1964 Seminar on Simalungun Culture (Seminar Kebudajaan Simalungun) there was some discussion as to whether the principle of inclusion should mean membership in one of the four Simalungun Batak clans—Purba, Saragih, Damanik, and Sinaga—or whether people of other clans who had become Simalungun Bataks linguistically and culturally should be included. Most participants in the seminar seemed to favor the latter alternative.

54. Wajang is traditional Javanese theater, performed either by leather puppets or by human actors, and with plots based on Javanese versions of the Indian Mahabharata and Ramayana epics. Ketoprak is a modern Javanese-language drama and variety show.

Indonesian).[55] Among the more educated, particularly the civil servants and the politicians but also the merchant and entrepreneurial classes, work group associations assume greater importance, but even here social relationships are largely within one's own ethnic group. There is no coherent social elite, based on wealth, education, high governmental or political status, or other values, that overarches ethnic differentiations. Instead, stratification patterns based on occupation and education have developed differently for each ethnic group and the individuals who fill the various status categories within each group associate rather more with each other than they do with people of similar attainments in other groups. For the North Tapanuli Bataks these elites include the entrepreneurs, self-employed professionals, civil servants, church leaders, and schoolteachers; for the South Tapanuli Bataks, the religious leaders and teachers, merchants and civil servants; for the Javanese, the schoolteachers and politicians; and for the Simalungun Bataks, the church leaders, civil servants, and schoolteachers. For many Simalungun Bataks the traditional aristocracy, though now shorn of all its power and position, retains high status.

The development of religious loyalties, simultaneously intensifying ethnic cleavages within Simalungun/Siantar and opening channels of communication beyond the region, constitutes a second dimension of the integrative revolution. Between South and North Tapanuli Bataks, in fact, the critical cleavage has not been adat and linguistic differences (although these differences exist) but rather the conversion of the former group to Islam and the latter to Christianity. The adat-language gap between South Tapanuli Bataks and Javanese has also been intensified by religious differences, the former group being much more thoroughly Islamized than the latter. Between the North Tapanuli and Simalungun Bataks, the common acceptance of Christianity and common membership in a single Protestant church has not contributed markedly to a diminution of ethnic animosity, in part because of the dominant position of North Tapanuli Bataks in the church hierarchy from 1907, when the first missionaries came to Simalungun, until 1963,

55. Bagian Sensus, Pemerintahan Daerah Tkt. II Simalungun, *Daftar Penduduk Kabupaten Simalungun* [Census Section, Government of the Second-Level Region of Simalungun, *List of the Inhabitants of the Regency of Simalungun*].

when the Simalungun Protestant Christian Church became a fully independent body.

The introduction of Christianity and Islam also widened the scope of primordial loyalties, however, by giving the peoples of Simalungun/Siantar a set of values and institutions which they shared with groups in other parts of the Indonesian archipelago. The devout Muslims of Simalungun had much in common with other Muslim communities in Sumatra, the north and south coasts and the western part of Java, Kalimantan, Sulawesi, and indeed throughout the Islamic world. The bond of religious community was further strengthened by the growth of Islamic social and educational organizations, the institution of the *hadj* (pilgrimage to Mecca) and by the concept of ummat Islam (the Islamic community or world). The Indonesian Protestant community included not only North Tapanuli and Simalungun Bataks, but also Niasians, Ambonese, Minahasans, and even some Javanese. Conferences among the leaders of the various Protestant churches, the establishment of a common theological seminary in Djakarta (then Batavia) in 1934, the creation of the Dewan Geredja Indonesia (Indonesian Council of Churches) in 1950, and the growth of such organizations as the Indonesian Christian Women's Association provided an institutional framework for the development of supraethnic religious loyalties. Finally, Roman Catholicism, both as a set of religious beliefs and as an institution, provided a link between such disparate groups as the small Simalungun Batak Catholic community and their coreligionists in Flores, East Nusatenggara. Like the Muslims, Indonesian Christians have also been a part of worldwide religious communities and have been affiliated with international religious organizations.

A third aspect of the integrative revolution, so far less pronounced than those described above, has been the development of supraethnic regional loyalties. In the 1950s many Simalungun Bataks felt a sense of common cause with the other indigenous peoples of East Sumatra, the Karo Bataks and Coastal Malays, in opposition to the predominance of Tapanuli Bataks in the provincial government (and military establishment) and in various second-level governments of East Sumatra. When regional animosities were directed against them, the migrant peoples, including both Tapanuli Bataks and Javanese, were also able briefly to work together for the preservation of the North Sumatran province. Neither of these blocs has been able to form a more enduring community, however, as ethnic and religious differences have been too deep and pervasive. Since 1960, in fact, Simalungun Batak cooperation with Karo Bataks has declined as a result of the struggle to acquire positions of influence within the provincial military establishment and in civilian government.

The impact of the plantation economy in Simalungun/Siantar has contributed a fourth dimension to the integrative revolution, i.e. the emergence of a rudimentary sense of a common fate among the relatively detraditionalized plantation workers and squatters of Lower Simalungun. Javanese, North Tapanuli Bataks, and smaller proportions of other ethnic groups have shared a common socioeconomic status and a common opposition to plantation administrators and the army and police officers and government officials who have opposed their claims and demands in the postindependence period. In time it is possible that the sense of shared interests the plantation environment has fostered among individuals of widely varying religious and ethnic backgrounds will develop into a profound and enduring alliance, but this does not yet seem to have occurred. Patterns of residential segregation, linguistic barriers, and the continued importance of traditional ethnic stereotypes and hostilities all militate against the reintegration of these groups into a cohesive social class, as does the fact that both the Javanese and (especially) the North Tapanuli Bataks in Lower Simalungun have continued to maintain (and place a high value upon) relationships with members of their respective ethnic groups in other parts of Sumatra, in Java, and indeed throughout the archipelago. Both groups are thus imbedded in an extensive network of ethnic-based social relationships, which tends to intensify their sense of ethnic identity and distinctiveness and to reduce the integrative effect of a common socioeconomic status.

Finally, superimposed upon all of these diverse cleavages and loyalties, there has also developed an identification with the Indonesian nation. The sense of common membership in a nation spreading far beyond the borders of Simalungun/Siantar first began to emerge in the early decades of the twentieth century. Members of a new elite, based on the attainment of modern education and commercial or government employment and including, in varying proportions, individuals from every ethnic group in the

region, traveled to Medan, Padang, Java, and elsewhere. In their travels and
in their relationships with one another they discovered a common hostility
to the foreigner and, eventually, a common desire to assert their independence from the Dutch within the framework of the colonially demarcated
boundaries of the Dutch East Indies.

Of course, not all members of the local elite were equally committed to
the goal of national independence or to the same postindependence political
objectives. Among those individuals active in prewar secular nationalist
organizations, the fire of opposition to the Dutch burned strong and the ultimate objective was the creation of a secular state. Among a large part of the
Muslim leadership opposition to colonial rule was also strongly felt, but the
postindependence objective was an Islamic state. Among other groups and
individuals the nationalist movement was less popular. Simalungun Batak
and Coastal Malay Muslim leaders saw national independence as a direct
threat to the authority of their patrons in the Dutch-supported traditional
kingdoms and sultanates, and many Simalungun Bataks of all religious per-
suasions retained their loyalties to the aristocracy despite the appeals of nationalist politicians. Many North Tapanuli Bataks who were well placed in
the plantation or government administrations or were prominent in the
church hierarchy tended to view nationalist organizations with mixed emo-
tions and were doubtful as to their future in an independent, predominantly
Muslim Indonesia.

Despite the small size and the internal divisions of the nationalist elite
and the reluctance of many locally prominent individuals to identify themselves with the nationalist cause, the impact of nationalism on local society
was profound. The events of the four-year revolution against the restoration
of Dutch rule were of crucial importance in strengthening among the elite
and extending to the population as a whole the sense of belonging to a
common nation. Although guerrilla organizations were commonly formed
along ethnic and religious lines, members of all groups supported and participated in the Revolution. By 1950 the active opponents of independence
were defeated and discredited and Simalungun was officially a part of the
Republic of Indonesia. Among the members of the new political and governmental elite the idea of nationhood had by then taken deep root. In local
society as a whole, through the medium of the revolutionary leadership, it

had gained widespread acceptance in at least rudimentary form. During the period of this study intensive and repeated interviews were conducted with a great many party politicians (from both legal and banned parties), government officials, army officers, religous leaders, and others at the regency/ municipality, subdistrict, and village levels. Among this elite an attitude of hostility (or resignation) toward the Djakarta regime was common, but antinational or separatist sentiment was rare in the extreme. As of 1964, at least, national loyalties seemed well established.

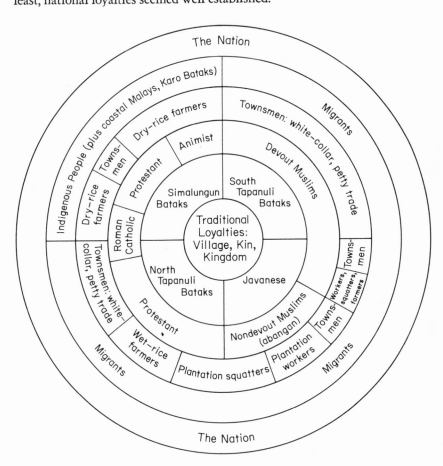

Figure 1.1   The Integrative Revolution in Simalungun/Siantar

The integrative revolution, then, has taken several forms in Simalungun/ Siantar. Loyalties to village, lineage group, and kingdom, while still operative, have been aggregated into ethnic, religious, regional, and socioeconomic ties most of which reach beyond the borders of the region and whose "implicit frame of reference is not the local scene but the 'nation.'" Beyond these essentially subnational loyalties, moreover, there has also developed an explicit and widespread sense of membership in the new Indonesian nation. In 1950, at the conclusion of the revolution, these several distinct and yet related loyalties constituted the basic ingredients with which a political party system was to be built.

2. THE INDONESIAN PARTY SYSTEM, 1950–64

The development of local party systems in Indonesia, as suggested in Chapter 1, has been fundamentally affected by two variables: (1) the local social and cultural environment, and in particular its patterns of cleavage and consensus; and (2) the role of political parties in the national and local governmental processes. Accordingly, this chapter begins with a discussion of the changing patterns of national and local authority in which the political parties have operated, then turns to an examination of the major national parties active in Simalungun/Siantar in 1963–64, their objectives, strategies, and organization.

National Politics and the Development of the Party System

As in many other new Asian and African nations, the history of the party system in Indonesia is a chronicle of decline, of the increasing governmental irrelevance of structures that in the early days of independence played a central role in the political life of the nation.[1]

Initial developments in Indonesian politics suggested a healthy future for

1. For detailed analyses of postindependence national politics in Indonesia, see Herbert Feith, *The Decline of Constitutional Democracy in Indonesia;* Daniel S. Lev, *The Transition to Guided Democracy: Indonesian Politics, 1957–1959* (Ithaca, N.Y., Cornell University Modern Indonesia Project, 1966); and Herbert Feith, "The Dynamics of Guided Democracy," in Ruth McVey, *Indonesia.*

the party system. The adoption of a democratic provisional constitution in 1950 and the prominent position it gave to the new parliament encouraged the proliferation of political parties and assured them an important place in the national political process. National elections for both the parliament and a constituent assembly, with seats to be distributed on the basis of proportional representation, provided a further stimulus to party growth and the extension of party branches to all parts of the country. The years 1954–55, immediately preceding the elections, were a period of intense campaigning throughout the archipelago. Four parties emerged from the elections as major forces on the national scene: PNI, with 57 out of 273 parliamentary seats; Masjumi, also with 57 seats; NU (Nahdatul Ulama, Muslim Notables' Party), 45 seats; and PKI, 39 seats. Another twenty-four parties and organizations were able to win one or more parliamentary seats. Among the more important of the smaller parties, in terms of their influence in the national arena, were PSI (Partai Sosialis Indonesia, Indonesian Socialist Party); Parkindo; and Partai Katholik (Catholic Party).

Through the first half of the decade of the 1950s parliament was the dominant governmental structure in Indonesian political life. Within the parliament party politicians, claiming to articulate the interests of a broad range of social groups—farmers, workers, devout Muslims of both modernist and traditional-syncretist varieties, nondevout Muslims, Protestants, Catholics, and others—dominated the decision-making process. Legitimation for parliamentary and party dominance could be found in the acceptance among the elite and the political public of the concept of popular sovereignty and the view that the interests of the people were expressed through the parties and organizations of which they were members and for which they cast their votes. The preeminent symbol of the regime (by no means, however, universally accepted by the political elite) was Pantja Sila. Its five principles (nationalism, internationalism or humanitarianism, representative government, social justice, and belief in God), were coined by Sukarno in 1945 and intended to "contain within it the political interests of the Islamic and Christian, gentry and peasantry, nationalist and communist, commercial and agrarian, Javanese and 'Outer Island' groups in Indonesia" on a loose, pluralistic basis.[2] While hardly a model of democratic

2. Clifford Geertz, "Ideology as a Cultural System," in David E. Apter, ed., *Ideology and Discontent* (New York, The Free Press of Glencoe, 1964), p. 68. See

practice—parliamentary institutions were operative for less than a decade and national elections were held only once—the period clearly represented an attempt to deal with the multiform problems of a new nation through a set of structures that permitted and encouraged autonomous political organizations, a free press, and a competitive, bargaining political process in which the interests of all groups could be represented.

Parliamentary democracy did not, however, usher in a new era of national unity, social justice, and economic progress for the Indonesian people. All of the major substantive issues of the 1950s, including economic development, administrative reorganization, modernization and rationalization of the armed forces, internal security, and decentralization of authority to provincial and local government, were dealt with by "a posture of meeting challenges by buying off the hostility of the challengers" rather than through consistent, problem-oriented policy-making.[3] Ideological hostilities, particularly between the secular nationalists and the proponents of an Islamic state, increased during and after the 1955 election campaign, making intra-elite cooperation on even ostensibly nonideological matters difficult to achieve. As the decade wore on, parliament and the party system seemed to more and more Indonesians a barrier to the realization of the kind of society for which the Revolution had been fought, rather than an instrument through which such a society could be created.

Opposition to parliamentary government, at first reflected largely in a growing but inarticulate dissatisfaction with the direction in which the country seemed to be going, soon found an effective protagonist in the person of President Sukarno. A radical nationalist whose life had been devoted to the politics of revolutionary opposition, Sukarno had been obliged to take a back seat as a ceremonial president under the 1950 constitution. Dissatisfied with his own role and with the decline in revolutionary fervor of the post-1950 period, he was quick to capitalize on parliamentary immobilism and inability to resolve major problems. The events of 1956

---

also J. M. van der Kroef, "Pantjasila: The National Ideology of the New Indonesia," *Philosophy East and West* (October 1954).

3. Feith, *The Decline of Constitutional Democracy*, p. 570. The discussion in this paragraph is based largely on Feith's analysis, pp. 556–78.

through 1958—accelerating inflation and a generally deteriorating economic situation, a series of rebellions by regional military commanders supported
by several prominent party leaders, continued inability of cabinet government to resolve the outstanding foreign policy question of the postrevolutionary period, the "return" of West Irian (Dutch New Guinea) to Indonesian control—brought support for parliamentary government to its nadir
and support for the kind of personal leadership offered by Sukarno to its
zenith.

The parliamentary system was officially ended by a presidential decree of
July 5, 1959, which abolished the 1950 constitution in favor of a return to
the Constitution of 1945, in which executive rather than legislative authority was predominant. In the new regime political power was divided informally between President Sukarno, whose chief responsibilities were in the
areas of ideological formulation, foreign policy, and the organization of
government, and the army, which concentrated on "regional government,
state enterprises, mostly ex-Dutch, and matters directly connected with civil
security."[4]

To Sukarno and his supporters, the most pressing problem of the day,
the sine qua non for national development of all kinds, was national unity.
The party system of the past and the immobilism it bred, the Western-
derived model of democracy which was nothing but "50 percent plus one
democracy" and "free-fight liberalism," were held to be directly responsible
for the confusion and disorder of the 1950s. Under Sukarno's "Guided
Democracy," emphasis was placed on traditional village modes of decision-
making—*musjawarah* (discussion leading to unanimity) and *mufakat* (agreement or consensus)—within governmental bodies comprising not only the
political parties but also "functional groups" such as labor, farmers, youth,
women, and the military, which were said to reflect the specific interests of
the people. Ideally, the membership of all deliberative and decision-making
structures was to be based on the principle of NASAKOM, an acronym ex-
pressing the unity of nationalists, religious people, and communists.

The political parties were further shaken by the effects of a 1959 presi-

4. Feith, "Indonesia," in George McT. Kahin, ed., *Governments and Politics of
Southeast Asia* (2d ed. Ithaca, N.Y., Cornell University Press, 1964), p. 243.

dential edict on the "simplification" of the party system,[5] as a result of which all but ten parties were dissolved, either because they were too small to fulfill the requirements of size or because they were unwilling to cooperate with the new order. In the former category were many small "personalistic" parties and parties of only ethnic and/or regional significance, while the latter group included the largest Muslim party in Indonesia, Masjumi, and the small but influential Indonesian Socialist Party (PSI). Those parties that remained (with the partial exception of PKI, which provided mass support for the President, thereby giving him more freedom of action vis-à-vis the army) were emasculated, charged with building support for the regime among their membership but permitted only a very limited role in the governmental process.

Guided Democracy thus represented a far-reaching transformation of political life in Indonesia and of the approach to the problems of national integration. If, in the parliamentary period, national unity was to be created and maintained by an open political process in which various interests found a forum in the legislative arena, it would be achieved under Guided Democracy through the leadership of Sukarno as the personification of the nation's identity and the spokesman for all of its interests. The promulgation and propagation of a unifying national ideology was central to this effort, as was the weakening or destruction of the organizations and leadership held responsible for the disunity of the 1950s.

The Party System and the Local Governmental Process

As the importance of political parties in the national government has changed a great deal in the period since independence, so also has the role of parties in local government varied considerably. From 1950 to 1956 legislative institutions, through which the parties could exert influence in the governmental process, existed only at the national level. Local government in these years continued to operate in the administrative tradition of colonial rule, with all authority exercised by regional bureaucrats appointed

5. *Penetapan Presiden No. 7/1959 tentang Sjarat-sjarat dan Penjederhanaan Kepartaian,* available in Departemen Penerangan Republik Indonesia, *Almanak Lembaga-Lembaga Negara dan Kepartaian* (Djakarta), pp. 423–26.

from and responsible to Djakarta. All parties thus had as their primary objective the development of as extensive a base of support as possible for the
purpose of increasing their representation in parliament. At the various
subnational levels, the role of party branches was almost wholly limited to the
creation of mass support for the benefit of the national organizations in
Djakarta.

The events of the postelection years altered this objective in several ways.
In 1957 a new law on regional government established first- and second-
level self-governing regions in Indonesia corresponding respectively to the
former provinces and regencies/municipalities.[6] Simalungun and Siantar,
formerly a single administrative unit, had been separated in 1956 and each
was now given the status of second-level self-governing region.

Legislative authority in the new regions was vested in regional legislatures,
called Dewan Perwakilan Rakjat Daerah (Regional People's Representative
Councils).[7] Membership in the legislatures was allotted on a provisional
basis (until local elections could be held) in proportion to each party's vote
in the 1955 parliamentary elections. Executive power in the new governments was exercised by a Regional Head *(Kepala Daerah)* and a Regional
Executive Council *(Dewan Pemerintah Daerah),* of which the Regional
Head was ex officio chairman. The members of the Regional Executive
Council were to be elected by and from the regional legislature, on the basis
of proportional representation of the parties in the legislature, and were
collectively responsible to it. Until further legislation could be passed, the
Regional Head was also to be chosen by the legislature (with central gov-
ernment approval) and could be dismissed by it.

From 1956 through 1959, at least, party leaders took the new legislatures
seriously. Leading party figures sought legislative positions and began
actively to press for solutions to problems of concern to their constituents

6. *Undang-undang No. 1 tahun 1957 tentang Pokok-pokok Pemerintahan
Daerah,* available in *Almanak Lembaga-Lembaga Negara dan Kepartaian,* pp. 163–
89. Translated excerpts are in J. D. Legge, *Central Authority and Regional Autonomy,*
appendix C, pp. 258–69.

7. The DPRD were actually established in late 1956 under the authority of Law
No. 14 of 1956. Until 1959 they were called DPRDp (Transitional Regional People's Representative Councils).

through legislative action. While many sessions were devoted to questions of legislative organization, the selection of administrative personnel, and responses to instructions from the provincial government, the legislators also discussed the reorganization of the tax structures of the regency and municipality, improvements in the distribution of foodstuffs and in market organization, the decline in water and electricity supply in the municipality, provision of better medical facilities in outlying parts of the regency, agricultural development, relationships between plantation administrators and workers and squatters, disputes between Muslims and Christians, and so on.[8] In addition, party leaders pushed for a more rapid devolution of authority to enable them to act upon rather than merely to discuss these problems.

In the next few years events beyond local control combined to diminish the power of the legislatures, the parties, and indeed of civilian government in general. At about the time that the Simalungun and Siantar legislatures convened for their first sessions, the North Sumatran provincial army commander, Col. Maludin Simbolon, announced that he was severing all relations with the central government and temporarily assuming authority over civilian government in the province.[9] Within five days the coup was reversed and the rebels were forced to flee to the highlands of Tapanuli. A state of war and siege, under which the military assumed many of the powers of the civilian government, was proclaimed and remained in effect until May 1, 1963.

In Simalungun/Siantar the impact of the state of war and siege was relatively mild. The major changes were that the regency and municipality army commanders became the de jure superiors of the Regional Head, army officers were placed on the plantations to ensure uninterrupted production, political party activity in the villages was restricted, and the military attempted to exercise control over party-affiliated labor, farmer,

8. These subjects were found in a survey of the official minutes (risalah) of plenary sessions of the legislatures, only scattered numbers of which were available for the 1956–59 period, or were mentioned to the author in interviews with legislators.

9. On Simbolon's coup and its aftermath, see John R. W. Smail, "The Military Politics of North Sumatra, December 1956–October 1957," unpublished paper, Cornell University, n.d.

youth, and women's organizations through the establishment of bodies for cooperation between the army and labor, the army and women, and so on. Civilian government functioned much as it had before, and the army did not interfere with routine administration or legislative activities, but the military had in fact become the most powerful force in the political life of North Sumatra.

At the same time repercussions of events in Djakarta were being felt in Simalungun. The implementation of Guided Democracy meant a reversal of the limited trend toward regional autonomy and democratization, and party leaders found themselves in a less promising position than they had been in even before the creation of the regional legislatures. Presidential Edict No. 6 of 1959 withdrew from the legislative branch the right to dismiss the Regional Head, who was restored to his pre-1957 position as both representative of the central government and the chief executive of his region. The Regional Head also became ex officio chairman of the legislature, thus weakening the autonomy of that body. The Regional Executive Council was abolished and replaced by a Daily Government Board (Badan Pemerintah Harian), whose members, nominated by the legislature but selected by the governor of the province with the advice of the regency/municipality Regional Head, were responsible only to the latter. Finally, the lawmaking power of the legislature was further weakened by a provision of the edict that gave authority to the Regional Head to "delay a decision of the Regional Representative Council . . . when in his opinion it conflicts with the main lines of state policy, the general interest, or legislation of a higher level."[10]

The legislature did retain a measure of influence over the selection of the Regional Head, since it nominated candidates for this position. However, during the period of Guided Democracy, even after the return to full civilian authority in 1963, effective control over the selection of the Regional Head was in the hands of the army. The selection of the Regional Secretary, the second most important administrative post in the region, was much more of a local process in which the party branches had greater influence. In two such elections witnessed in Simalungun/Siantar in 1964, the prenomination

10. Article 15, paragraph 2, in Legge, p. 273.

bargaining was confined to the Regional Head, members of the legislature, and the parties they represented, with no evidence of outside intervention.

In 1961 the regional legislatures throughout Indonesia were reorganized and restyled DPRD-GR (Dewan Perwakilan Rakjat Daerah-Gotong Rojong, Mutual Help Regional People's Representative Councils) to conform to the pattern of representation of functional groups adopted by the national parliament and designed by the Sukarno-army coalition to limit the influence of the parties. In the new legislatures half of the members were to represent political parties and half functional groups. In practice, since most voluntary associations in Indonesia are affiliated with political parties, the new legislatures were still dominated by the parties, although not as exclusively as they had been.

Even excepting the power of the military, the question of legislative versus executive control of government in Simalungun/Siantar during the period of this study was, in the final analysis, largely an academic one. For much of the postindependence period local government had neither the funds nor the authority to govern effectively. With monetary inflation, bureaucratic expansion, and the unwillingness of the central government to increase the taxing power of the regions, the Regional Heads and other officials spent much of their time in Medan and Djakarta seeking subsidies that would enable them to meet the routine costs of administration. No funds were available to carry out development projects or even in some cases to maintain facilities such as roads and markets. In Siantar city local autonomy was somewhat broader than in the regency. As in Simalungun, however, many important government officials were neither appointed nor dismissed locally, and the municipality's fiscal authority was insufficient to meet development needs.

Thus, even during the 1957–59 period of greatest legislative power in local government, few decisions of importance for Simalungun/Siantar could be made at the local level. After 1959, when the balance of local authority shifted back to "one-man rule" by the Regional Head, the legislative bodies existed in a kind of limbo, unsure of their functions and of their raison d'etre. Except on those infrequent occasions when a Regional Head or a Regional Secretary was to be chosen, there was little of significance to discuss. The annual debate on the budget estimates for the coming year, particularly in the regency, was usually conducted in an atmosphere of grim hopelessness.

In the light of these developments, party objectives and strategies became increasingly future- rather than present-oriented and directed more toward influence within the civilian and especially the military bureaucracy than toward legislative control. The reorganized regional legislatures, despite their relative powerlessness, continued to attract the most prominent party leaders, as they provided a measure of status and a small income to the party leaders who served as legislators. A few legislators (particularly in Siantar, where local government had more authority) dedicated themselves to making the new bodies work. Most, however, wanted simply to maintain or improve their party's relative strength in case the legislatures again became important structures of decision-making. Party-building in the villages, the major activity of leaders of all parties in the early and mid-1950s, was of less significance in the 1960s, although the degree of activity varied from party to party. To the extent that it continued, party-building among the villagers was based primarily on the hope of a further reversal in the national power structure in which the parties would again become influential, and only secondarily on the desire to affect current policy-making. In the fluid political situation of the mid-1960s, anything seemed possible and the party leaders wanted to be prepared for all eventualities.

Political Strategies and Objectives

It is customary to classify political parties in Indonesia by ideological orientation into two broad categories: (1) secular parties, represented in Simalungun/Siantar in 1963–64 primarily by PNI and PKI and secondarily by Partindo (Partai Indonesia, a 1958 split from PNI), the army-created IPKI (Ikatan Pendukung Kemerdehaan Indonesia, League of Supporters of Indonesian Independence), and the "national-communist" Partai Murba (Proletarian Party); and (2) religious parties, represented primarily by Parkindo and Masjumi and secondarily by Nahdatul Ulama and Partai

Katholik.[11] This classificatory scheme, while in many ways an oversimplification of the similarities and differences among the parties, is useful for our purposes because it suggests the fundamentally different responses of various party elites to the problem of national integration. The secular parties, with ideologies based on variants of nationalism and/or Marxism, have for the most part denied the relevance of ethnic, cultural, and religious cleavages for contemporary politics, condemning such cleavages as dysfunctional for the creation of a unified, modern nation. The Muslim parties, while similarly opposed to ethnic divisions, have viewed the nation as a single Islamic community containing a few non-Islamic minorities. Their political goal has been to make nation and ummat (the Muslim community) coterminous. The Christian parties, Parkindo and Partai Katholik, fit neither of these categories. As the representatives of small (but, like the constituencies of the larger parties, ethnically diverse at the national level) minority groups, their raison d'etre has been self-protection. For them, national integration is a function of the authoritative institutions of government within which conflicts are resolved or adjusted by bargaining among religious and other groups.

In order to build mass support in Simalungun/Siantar in the early 1950's and to maintain and strengthen that support in the succeeding years each of these parties had to come to terms with the problems posed by the local social and cultural environment. Each party's electoral and organizational strategy thus reflected both an attempt to create local political loyalties in its own ideological image and a response to the patterns of cleavage of the region.

11. Banned in 1960, Masjumi was not formally active in Simalungun/Siantar in 1963–64. Because of its major importance in the region throughout the 1950s and the continued hold which it had on its supporters during the research period, it is included in the following analysis. IPKI, Partindo, and Murba were parties without significant mass support in the region and are treated here only peripherally. Other parties, active in the region during the 1950s but no longer in existence by 1963, included KRSST (Kebangunan Rakjat Simalungun Sumatera Timur, The Awakening of the Simalungun People of East Sumatra), a Simalungun Batak party described in Chapter 6, and also such nationally and locally small parties as Partai Buruh (Labor Party) and Partai Sosialis Indonesia (Indonesian Socialist Party).

THE SECULAR PARTIES

From the early days of the Republic, the primary goal of PNI and PKI in Simalungun/Siantar was to become the predominant party in the region. Predominance was measured by the leaders of both parties in terms of electoral support (of particular importance before 1955, but a continuing consideration), influence within numerically and strategically important social groups, and (especially after 1956) influence in the structures and processes of local government.

In their quest for mass support, PNI and PKI faced a formidable obstacle: their respective philosophies, Marhaenism and Marxism-Leninism, were imported ideologies of little obvious relevance to the great bulk of the populace. The Indonesian Nationalist Party's Marhaenist ideology evolved as an attempt to transfer the élan and symbolism of the struggle against the Dutch to the postindependence problems of nation-building. In an analysis of the party system as of 1950, Herbert Feith described PNI ideology as follows:

> PNI ideology was centered in the Revolution. It was the formulation par excellence of the mood of nationalist political messianism characteristic of the old revolutionary fighters. . . . [Marhaenism] was a political creed stressing national unity and national culture and socialist or collectivist economics. It affirmed the importance of democratic rights and opposed dictatorship, but condemned liberalism and individualism, declaring them to be offshoots of capitalism. Based on an eclectic selection of ideas from Western and Asian nationalists, Western socialists, and traditional Indonesian social thought, Marhaenism reflected both the PNI's attachment to the symbols of the nationalist Revolution and the difficulties which the party faced in establishing a highest common factor of ideological orientation.[12]

In stressing national unity and national culture, Marhaenism specifically denies a legitimate role to ethnic and religious cleavages, and parties based on such cleavages, in Indonesian political life. Among the leadership, especially at the regency/municipality, provincial, and national levels, the na-

12. Feith, *The Decline of Constitutional Democracy*, pp. 139–40.

tional idea is certainly the most "common factor of ideological orientation."

PNI's strength has not, however, been due solely to its nationalist orientation. In East and Central Java, where the bulk of party members and supporters are concentrated, PNI has been heavily supported by the traditional Javanese aristocracy, in the postindependence period entrenched in the lower echelons of the government bureaucracy, who react negatively to the worker-peasant-oriented PKI and the religious parties but may have little awareness of or interest in the nationalist content of party ideology. Because its base is largest and most firmly established in Java, PNI has thus become strongly identified on the national scene with the interests of the Javanese, and particularly the Javanese bureaucratic elite.

The Indonesian Communist Party, like PNI, opposed traditional ethnic and religious divisions and at the same time drew most of its support from the ethnic Javanese. Unlike PNI, however, PKI ideology was phrased primarily in terms of class conflict (i.e. the proletariat and peasantry allied with elements of the "national bourgeoisie" in opposition to the forces of feudalism and imperialism and the "compradore bourgeoisie").[13] At the same time, for tactical reasons, PKI stressed its adherence to nationalist slogans and symbols and, in East and Central Java, relied heavily on a blending of Marxist ideology with the traditional "folk religion" of the ethnic Javanese.[14]

In an attempt to make their ideologies relevant to the Simalungun/Siantar context, leaders of both PNI and PKI developed a basic strategy that relied primarily on appeals to the most uprooted and detraditionalized groups in the region—the plantation and urban workers and the squatters on plantation land. Many of the strengths and weaknesses of PNI and PKI in Simalungun/Siantar in 1963–64 were directly related to their reliance on the support of these groups.

Organizationally, these secular parties corresponded in some respects to Maurice Duverger's model of the mass party. Both parties placed great emphasis on membership recruitment (either into the party itself or into its

13. Donald Hindley, *The Communist Party of Indonesia, 1951–1963* (Berkeley and Los Angeles, University of California Press, 1964), pp. 29–59, esp. pp. 37–38.

14. C. Geertz, "The Integrative Revolution," in C. Geertz, ed., *Old Societies and New States*, p. 133.

subsidiary organizations) and both possessed a "strongly articulated" or highly developed and hierarchically ordered complex organization. In terms of the basic elements of party organization, PKI approximated the model of a party whose basic structural unit is the cell (although the lowest active organizational unit was in most cases the party subsection, which corresponded to the PNI's subbranch and was territorially rather than functionally based), with daily contact among members, a high degree of party discipline, and selection of local leaders by appointment from above. PNI, on the other hand, fitted more closely the model of a branch party, emphasizing quantity at the expense of quality and headed by elected leadership councils which directed the implementation of party policy in the subdistricts and villages.[15]

In the regency, PNI and PKI leaders concentrated most of their efforts and expended the greatest part of their funds in the area of Lower Simalungun. This was so for a number of reasons. Perhaps most obvious is the fact that 72.6 percent of the regency electorate in 1955 (73.1 percent of total regency population) was located in this area. Clearly, to be the majority party in Simalungun a party must be dominant in Lower Simalungun. The importance of this region extends beyond the percentage of the regency electorate it represents, however, because of what has been described as the "high national-level political effectiveness"[16] of the plantation workers and squatters who make up a probable majority of the (adult male) population there. Strikes, still resorted to on occasion despite their illegality, well-organized movements of squatters onto just-cleared plantation land (a favorite tactic of PKI, used less by PNI), or actions such as the PNI-inspired workers' takeover of the British plantations in Simalungun in 1964, have high political visibility and effectively display the power and influence of their perpetrators. Moreover, a party with a large following on a particular plantation has influence with the plantation administration, a situation that can provide a variety of benefits, not the least of them financial, to the party and/or its leadership.

Both PNI and PKI made extensive use of subsidiary organizations (called *gerakan massa,* or mass movements, by PNI) to develop a base of support

15. Maurice Duverger, *Political Parties, Their Organization and Activity in the Modern State* (New York, John Wiley & Sons, 1963), pp. 23–26, 41–47, 63–90.
16. Feith, *The Decline of Constitutional Democracy,* p. 125.

in the plantation areas. The important role PKI accorded to these organizations was derived from the general strategic program of the party, the "national united front" policy, adopted by the party leadership in 1951, when D. N. Aidit became first secretary. According to Donald Hindley, the Aidit leadership conceived of the national united front policy

> as entailing unity in two separate spheres and of two distinct qualities: the unity of the masses directly led and controlled by the Party and its mass organizations, a disciplined unity embracing the truly revolutionary classes [proletariat, peasants, and petty bourgeoisie]; and the unity, in the form of friendship and cooperation, between PKI and the non-Communist political forces. . . . In the implementation of this policy, PKI has faced three main and inseparable tasks: (1) to build PKI into a disciplined, mass party; (2) to attract, mobilize, organize and lead the three most revolutionary classes—and to do the same for any other elements in society which might prove susceptible; and (3) to gain the tolerance and cooperation of as many as possible of the political forces that are not anti-Communist.[17]

For PNI, on the other hand, development of mass organizations in Simalungun represented not so much one aspect of a coherent and detailed

Table 2–1. Membership in
PNI and PKI Mass Organizations in Simalungun

Type of Organization	PKI	PNI
Labor	45,000	4,092
Farmers	20,517	12,200
Youth	1,500	2,500
Women	*	489
Culture	*	100

Sources: PNI figures from Dewan Tjabang PNI Kabupaten Simalungun, *Laporan Umum* (PNI Branch Council, Regency of Simalungun, *General Report*), July, 1963, p. 15. PKI data from organization chairmen except for Youth data, which was obtained from the Political Affairs Office, Regency of Simalungun, and dated 1961.
*Data not available.

17. Hindley, p. 49.

strategic plan as it did a response to the organizational threat of PKI. The gerakan massa of both PNI and PKI in Simalungun/Siantar included parallel labor unions, plantation workers' unions, and farmers', youth, women's, and cultural groups.[18] By organizing such a wide variety of groups, both PNI and PKI hoped to make party-related activities the focus of a "comprehensive pattern of social integration" as they had become on Java.[19]

Each of the PNI gerakan massa maintained a hierarchical structure of branch organizations roughly parallel to that of the party, with horizontal as well as vertical formal lines of command, i.e. the executive leadership of the party at each level had responsibility for the supervision and direction of gerakan massa activities within its territorial jurisdiction in cooperation with the gerakan massa branch organizations at the next highest level. In practice, organization leaders in the subdistricts and villages took their orders from regency gerakan massa officials, who were in turn directly integrated into or closely allied with the regency party leadership responsible for the planning of organizational drives and other activities. With the exception of the youth group Pemuda Rakjat, PKI subsidiary organization leaders, in line with national party policy, denied formal partisan affiliation. In practice these leaders, at the regency/municipality as well as subdistrict levels, seem in fact to have been largely autonomous of the local party or-

18. PKI mass organization in Simalungun included SOBSI (Sentral Organisasi Buruh Seluruh Indonesia, Central All-Indonesian Workers' Organization) and its affiliated member unions, of which SARBUPRI (Sarekat Buruh Perkebunan Republik Indonesia, Plantation Workers' Union of the Republic of Indonesia) was by far the largest, BTI (Barisan Tani Indonesia, Indonesian Farmers' Front); Pemuda Rakjat (People's Youth); GERWANI (Gerakan Wanita Indonesia, Indonesian Women's Movement); and LEKRA (Lembaga Kebudajaan Rakjat, People's Cultural Institute). The most important of the PNI gerakan massa in Simalungun were PETANI (Persatuan Tani Nasional Indonesia, Indonesian National Farmers' Union); KBM (Kesatuan Buruh Marhaenis, Marhaenist Labor Union), all of whose members were affiliated with KBP (Kesatuan Buruh Perkebunan, Plantation Workers' Union); KBKB (Kesatuan Buruh Kenderaan Bermotor, Motor Vehicle Workers' Union); Wanita Demokrat Indonesia (Democratic Women of Indonesia); Pemuda Marhaenis (Marhaenist Youth); and LKN (Lembaga Kebudajaan Nasional, National Cultural Institute).

19. Clifford Geertz, "The Javanese Village," in Skinner, ed., Local, Ethnic, and National Loyalties, p. 37.

ganization, receiving instructions directly from their provincial-level organization and/or party superiors.

The specific organizational technique most favored by PNI and PKI cadres was to gain the support of locally influential leaders by convincing them of the practical advantages for themselves and their followers of affiliation with a nationally powerful organization. The propaganda of gerakan massa leaders in Lower Simalungun stressed mainly these advantages. Among the workers the protection available through membership in the union was most emphasized. At recruitment meetings the most frequent theme of the speakers was that the organization would ensure job security and oppose arbitrary actions of the plantation administrators against the workers (e.g. firing, demotion, moving a worker from one part of the plantation to another). Since most of the plantations are run by the state, it was difficult for the PNI-affiliated labor union (which emphasized the identity of its policies with the government's, and particularly Sukarno's, programs) to use such traditional goals of labor unions as demands for higher wages in its propaganda to potential members. An attack on plantation wage policy could easily be interpreted as an attack on the state.[20] PKI's labor federation was less bound by this restriction, but was careful to distinguish opposition to Sukarno (which it abjured) from opposition to the "bureaucracy" (whose plantation policies it attacked).

Among the farmers living on the borders of the plantations, the greatest needs are for more rice fields and for acceptance by the government of their claims to land they have already taken from the plantations. PKI and PNI farmers' organizations were instrumental in organizing local irrigation committees, representing their interests before local government officials (to secure permits and equipment for the construction of new sawah), defending squatters' rights in the courts, and on occasion illegally proceeding with the acquisition of new land and the building of rice fields. Without the support of a supravillage organization the farmer felt powerless in the face of the plantations and the government; with support he was willing to take action to defend and improve his economic position.[21]

20. On this point, see E. D. Hawkins, "Labor in Transition," in Ruth McVey, *Indonesia*, esp. p. 270.

21. This observation is also made by Karl Pelzer in "The Agrarian Conflict in East Sumatra," *Pacific Affairs*, 30 (June 1957), 154.

Besides these pragmatic means of winning support, PNI gerakan massa propaganda in Lower Simalungun emphasized the nationalist roots of the party's ideology and revolutionary history. This propaganda had three purposes: (1) to minimize the fissiparous tendencies of ethnic and religious cleavages; (2) to vilify the PKI, its chief competitor in the plantation areas, as the agent of an international conspiracy more dedicated to the interests of world communism than to the Indonesian nation; and (3) to provide a firm basis of ideological commitment in order to ensure continued allegiance to the organization and to the party. PNI also stressed its belief in the importance of religion and the right of every individual to worship as he pleases (much of the propaganda of the religious parties termed the PNI antireligious), accusing the Communists in turn of atheism. More specific inculcation of Marhaenist ideology was confined to indoctrination sessions for local leaders, the distribution of party pamphlets, and speech-making tours of the local branches by regency leaders. It may be added that in the selection of speakers and the assignment of cadres to specific subdistricts much attention was paid to the ethnic makeup of the audience or potential membership; it was generally realized, for example, that North Tapanuli Batak cadres would have little success among Javanese workers and that Javanese cadres were unable to organize Batak farmers.

In contrast to the PNI mass organizations, the Communist Party affiliates went to great lengths to deny any connection with PKI or adherence to communist ideology. Their propaganda, although phrased in familiar communist terminology, was oriented largely toward local issues and grievances in an attempt to recruit and hold members. At the same time, every effort was made to indoctrinate the local noncadre leadership and membership with the views of PKI on national and international issues. Even at the village level, resolutions condemning domestic "counterrevolutionaries," the Peace Corps, or government policies opposed by PKI were frequently prepared and forwarded to Djakarta. Criticism of opposition organizations was much more subdued, in conformity with national PKI policy which proscribed open attacks against those organizations regarded as potentially friendly or useful. PNI was much less inhibited in this regard.

PNI and PKI party organizations, as distinct from the mass movements, played considerably different roles in the implementation of the common worker-squatter strategy. Both parties maintained branches at the regency and subdistrict levels, called branch and subbranch by PNI, and section and subsection by PKI. Below the subdistrict, the basic PNI unit was the territorially organized *ranting,* which required a minimum of fifteen members (for this reason many PNI ranting encompassed more than one village), while PKI's basic unit was the *kelompok* (group), organized on either territorial or functional lines and with a membership not exceeding ten.

To become a member of PNI in Simalungun was a fairly simple process, requiring only that the applicant register his name with his local ranting, state his acceptance of the party's ideology and program, and agree to submit to party discipline. Though the party constitution calls for the payment of dues,[22] there were few attempts to collect them in the regency (with the exception of occasional solicitations for special purposes) and little was required of the ordinary member in the way of party work or ideological purity.

In contrast to PNI, PKI membership was difficult to obtain, requiring (1) a period of candidacy (varying with the class origins of the applicant, his previous membership in another party, and so on) during which the candidate member was given ideological training and party tasks whose execution was carefully watched; (2) recommendations from persons who were already PKI members; and (3) endorsement by the next highest party committee. Having joined the party, the PKI member was required to maintain a minimum level of party activity or face expulsion.[23] In general, standards for admission and the performance of party tasks and obligations were strictly adhered to by the Communist Party in Simalungun, and membership was accordingly small.

Nationalist Party regency-level leadership concentrated primarily on the expansion of party membership in Lower Simalungun, and there was considerable overlap between the party and gerakan massa membership. In part this was encouraged in order to increase the loyalty of the gerakan massa members to PNI and to imbue them with at least a vague sense of common Marhaenist identity. More important, however, is the fact that the

22. "Anggaran Dasar Partai Nasional Indonesia," in *Almanak Lembaga-Lembaga Negara dan Kepartaian,* p. 442.

23. *Material for the Sixth National Congress of the Communist Party of Indonesia,* pp. 114–21 (ch. 2, art. 5–22).

power base of the dominant faction in the regency leadership was concentrated in Lower Simalungun. These were the former PNI guerrilla leaders, Javanese for the most part, who had lived for long periods in Lower Simalungun, developed extensive contacts there during the Revolution, and were generally respected by the local population (particularly, of course, by the Javanese) as men of stature and influence. Since the early 1950s these leaders had been dependent for their continuation and promotion in regency and higher party office on the support of the subdistrict branches in Lower Simalungun. The expansion of party membership in these subdistricts (producing an increase in the size of Lower Simalungun's delegation at party conferences) was thus of central importance to them.

Such calculations were largely irrelevant to the PKI leaders, whose party positions (in practice, though not according to the party constitution) depended on the decisions of higher party committees rather than on periodic elections. The development of the Communist Party organization in Simalungun/Siantar was in fact only a secondary concern of the higher party leaders, who apparently decided in the early 1950s to maintain only a small party organization in Simalungun and to concentrate on the development of the subsidiary organizations. This decision was probably made on the grounds that an active, proselytizing party organization would serve, in the early stages of the development of support, to alienate more individuals than it would attract because of the strength of religious beliefs in the region.

PNI and PKI party and subsidiary organization activities in Upper Simalungun were much less intensive than in Lower Simalungun. In part the reasons for this comparative neglect were the small size of the population and (for PNI) the lack of interest of the dominant faction within the regency leadership (which controlled the disbursement of party funds) in the growth of the party in that area. More fundamental, however, was the lesser relevance of PNI and PKI ideology and programs to the problems of Upper Simalungun. This was so for two reasons. First, the lack of specific grievances related to conditions of employment (most people are self-employed farmers) or land tenure (there is an ample supply of swidden land) meant that the worker-squatter strategy was inapplicable to the social conditions of Upper Simalungun. Second, there are strong feelings of communal solidarity among the less detraditionalized Simalungun Bataks, who constitute a large majority of the population of the area. Party-based political organization was seen in Upper Simalungun as fundamentally divisive of ethnic unity, felt to be of crucial importance in counteracting the "takeover" of the economic and political life of the regency and municipality by non-Simalungun Bataks. The nationalism of PNI and its emphasis on panethnic unity and the class-oriented ideology of PKI thus had little appeal to the Simalungun Bataks.

Despite these difficulties, PNI was not totally inactive in Upper Simalungun. Its leadership in the locality consisted for the most part of former guerrillas, who sought support in the postrevolutionary period among those Simalungun Bataks opposed to the traditional aristocracy. PKI, on the other hand, had no leadership or organization in the region apart from one sub-section in Silimakuta subdistrict (see Map 5).

The subdistricts along the Road to Parapat, except for a few plantation enclaves populated largely by North Tapanuli Bataks, were also relatively neglected in PNI and PKI councils. In part, as in Upper Simalungun, this was because of a lack of pressing social problems and the seeming irrelevance of party ideologies and strategies. Moreover, PNI's old guard subdistrict leaders in this area, still oriented to and increasingly lost in the dreams of the Revolution, were unable to make the transition from the struggle for independence to the demands of party-building, and until the early 1960s there was a lack of young North Tapanuli Batak cadres capable of revitalizing the subdistrict branches. By 1963–64 the cadre problem had become less severe and new beginnings had been made, particularly in the towns of Pane Tongah, Tiga Balata, Tiga Dolok, and Parapat, where a nucleus of PNI activists was being formed around the party's youth organization and motor workers' union. Both PNI and PKI activities in this area focused primarily on the towns, with the villages remaining relatively isolated from party conflict.

In Siantar city, both PNI and PKI suffered from the fact that the social environment, which emphasizes primordial differences and loyalties, has no functional equivalent of the worker-squatter group and thus severely limits the effectiveness of partisan appeals framed in terms of either secular ideologies or pragmatic interests. PKI strategy in Siantar followed the pattern described for Lower Simalungun, with heavy emphasis on labor union

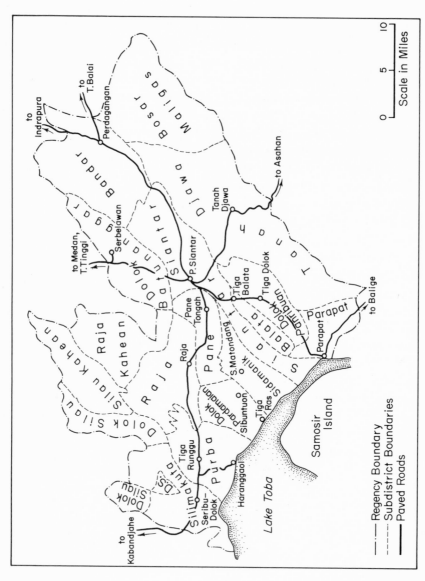

Map 5.   The Regency of Simalungun

Source: Pemerintahan Daerah Tkt. II Simalungun, *Lapuran Tahun 1963*, p. 2

development. PNI's city branch was less concerned than its regency counterpart with the expansion of either party or gerakan massa membership. In large part this neglect was related to the lack of interest of the dominant faction in the city party leadership, whose positions did not depend on the support of gerakan massa members, but rather on a coalition of party leaders each of whom could count on the support of a number of the party's ranting at the biennial Party Conference. These individuals were not willing to risk jeopardizing their leadership by a strengthening of potentially competitive power centers in the party. Consequently, the PNI gerakan massa in the city were considerably less developed than those in the regency. In addition to their activities with party affiliates, both PNI and PKI attempted to infiltrate various nonpartisan organizations such as PGRI (Persatuan Guru Republik Indonesia, Association of Teachers of the Republic of Indonesia), Legiun Veteran (Veteran's Legion), Angkatan '45 (Generation of 1945), and PPDI (Persatuan Pamong Desa Indonesia, Association of Indonesian Village Officials).

The Nationalist and Communist parties also sought to increase their influence in the local governmental process. Since most high-ranking government officials in the region were appointed from Medan or Djakarta, beyond the control of the regency/municipality party branches, party leaders concentrated their efforts on the regional legislatures and executive councils. In the first regional legislatures, established in 1956, seats were allotted on the basis of the 1955 election returns and no party was able to alter the distribution in its favor. In both Simalungun and Siantar PNI and PKI formed an alliance in order to win control of the legislative leadership and of committee assignments. In the regency the PNI-PKI coalition also included the small Labor Party (Partai Buruh). Although this bloc contained only fifteen of the thirty members it was able to gain both the chairmanship (PNI) and the vice-chairmanship (PKI) because of the lack of cooperation between Masjumi and the Christian parties. In Siantar PNI and PKI joined forces with Parkindo, obtaining the chairmanship for Parkindo and the vice-chairmanship for PKI. PNI, which was entitled to a seat on the Regional Executive Council (along with Parkindo and Masjumi), agreed to this arrangement. Between 1956 and 1964 legislative cooperation between PNI and PKI, at times joined by other parties, continued, particularly in

the nomination of Regional Heads and the selection of Regional Secretaries.[24]

Table 2–2. Party Representation in the Regional Representative
Councils (DPRD) of Simalungun and Siantar

	Simalungun		Siantar
Party	*Seats*	*Party*	*Seats*
PNI	9	Masjumi	6
PKI	5	Parkindo	5
Masjumi	5	PNI	2
Parkindo	5	PKI	1
KRSST	3	NU	1
Partai Buruh	1		
Partai Katholik	1		
PSI	1		
Total	30	Total	15

Source: Data on file in offices of DPRD–GR secretaries, Simalungun and
Siantar.

The dissolution of the old regional legislature and its replacement by the
reorganized "mutual help" legislature was a happy event for PNI, which
was able to take advantage of a favorable set of circumstances to increase its
representation in both the city and the regency. Party and functional group
nominees (two for each seat) were submitted to the Regional Heads and
regency/municipality army commanders for approval and recommendations
and then sent to the North Sumatran army commander and the governor
(who was to make the final selection). In Siantar the Regional Head (a PNI
sympathizer) and the municipality army commander (not so much pro-PNI

24. In Siantar, PNI and PKI supported the same candidates for Regional Head in
1960 and 1964 and Regional Secretary (with Parkindo) in 1964. In Simalungun,
PNI and PKI (with Partai Buruh) nominated the same candidate for Regional Head
in 1960 in the first (but not the second) round of nominations and were allied (with
Parkindo) in the selection of a Regional Secretary in 1964.

as anti-PKI), with the backing of their respective provincial superiors, co-operated with the branch PNI chairman in the nomination of functional group representatives. Of the eight functional group seats in the new legislature, three went to PNI, one to Parkindo, one to NU, two were nonparty, and one was left vacant. PNI's overall representation increased from two to five, while PKI continued to hold only one seat. In Simalungun PNI also cooperated (though less closely) with the Regional Head and regency

Table 2–3. Party Representation in the DPRD–GR of Simalungun and Siantar

Simalungun		Siantar	
Party	*Seats*	*Party*	*Seats*
PNI	12	PNI	5
Parkindo	3	Parkindo	4
PKI	3	NU	2
NU	2	PKI	1
Partai Katholik	2	Nonparty	2
IPKI	1	Vacant	1
Nonparty	7		
Total	30	Total	15

Source: Adapted from data provided by secretaries of DPRD–GR, Simalungun and Siantar. These figures are based on the official party representatives plus DPRD–GR members from functional groups affiliated with or dominated by a particular party. In Simalungun, party representation was: PNI, 5; Parkindo, 3; PKI, 3; NU, 2; Partai Katholik, 1; and IPKI, 1. The functional group representatives included 7 PNI members (veterans, youth, women, Generation of 1945, farmers, labor, and national entrepreneurs) and 1 Partai Katholik member (Catholic religious leadership). The unaffiliated group included representatives from the army, police, Muslim religious leadership (who was said to be pro-PNI), Protestant religious leadership, cooperatives, adat, and intellectuals (after 1962 this seat was vacant). In Siantar, party representation was: PNI, 2; Parkindo, 3; PKI, 1; and NU, 1. Functional group representatives included 3 PNI members (youth/women, labor, and cooperatives/national entrepreneurs), 1 Parkindo member (Protestant religious leadership), and 1 NU member (Muslim religious leadership). The police and army representatives were nonparty.

army commander. PNI representation in the regency legislature increased from nine to twelve, while PKI strength dropped from five to three.[25] PNI's representation in the new Siantar Daily Government Board was two out of four (compared to one out of three in the old Regional Executive Council). In Simalungun, where the Daily Government Board was largely ignored by the Regional Head, only two of its four seats were filled in 1964 (by Parkindo and PKI). Candidates for the two vacant seats, both of which were claimed by PNI, were submitted to the Regional Head in 1963, but no further action was taken.

Although PNI was generally more successful in establishing a modus vivendi with the army leadership, both parties sought military support. PNI-army cooperation was based primarily on a common desire to reduce PKI strength in the region rather than on a pro-PNI bias within the army. The army's policy was reflected not only in the selection of legislators, but also in the predominant position of PNI in the bodies for cooperation between the army and the various functional groups and in the army-controlled Veterans' Legion and Generation of '45. Although both PNI and PKI had highly placed supporters within the army during the period of this study, neither could claim exclusive or even substantial army support. On the plantations, for example, neither party obtained the cooperation of the army, which preferred to create a separate labor organization to oppose the party-affiliated unions. And finally, in any relationship between the army and the parties, the latter were distinctly junior partners.

THE RELIGIOUS PARTIES

The objectives, strategies, and form of organization of the religious parties differed in several important respects from those of the Nationalist and Communist parties. In the years immediately preceding the elections all parties conducted extensive campaigns throughout the region. After 1955, however, only PNI and PKI continued actively to organize the population at the village level. The religious parties, by contrast, did not have comprehensive strategic plans and did not conduct drives to recruit new mem-

25. For a more detailed discussion of the selection of legislators in Simalungun, see Chapter 6.

bers. Instead, their leaders devoted most of their political energies to the affairs of local government. Organizationally, the religious parties corresponded roughly to Duverger's model of the cadre party. Although formally similar to the secular parties, their party and subsidiary organizations were weakly articulated and their leaders relatively unconcerned with problems of membership recruitment. The basic unit of party organization, formally the branch, in reality more closely resembled Duverger's caucus, "a group of notabilities for the preparation of elections, conducting campaigns and maintaining contact with the candidates."[26]

The most important reasons for these differences are related to the image each party had of itself in relation to the national and local political processes and to the nature of the local support each sought. PNI and PKI, as we have seen, regarded themselves at least potentially as representing the whole Indonesian people, undifferentiated as to religion or ethnicity. Ultimately, they sought support on the basis of their capacity to build a modern Indonesia which would satisfy the emerging aspirations of people for a better life within the framework of a secular nation-state. Their ideologies, at least within the Indonesian context, were universalistic—they applied to all Indonesians. At the same time, they bore little relation to the powerful ethnic and religious cleavages of the local community. Partisan appeals had to be made on other grounds, by translating ideologies into programs that would strike a responsive chord in Simalungun/Siantar.

The religious parties differed in their approaches to the problem of national integration. Masjumi and Nahdatul Ulama, identifying the interests of the religious community with those of the state, viewed themselves as representing the totality of Indonesian political aspirations within the framework of Islam, while Parkindo and Partai Katholik sought representation on the basis of their minority status.[27] In Simalungun/Siantar, however, none

26. On the cadre party, see Duverger, pp. 17–23, 41–47, 63–90.

27. At the national level Masjumi, representing primarily the modernist wing of Indonesian Islam, received most of its support from the Outer Islands, while NU, like PNI and PKI, has been a predominantly East and Central Javanese party, representing a syncretistic blend of Islam and specifically Javanese religious beliefs and practices. NU was, until 1952, when it established itself as a separate political party, one of several constituent organizations within Masjumi.

of the four religious parties could claim to represent all of the local population. Instead, each sought the support of particular segments of local
society. Parkindo's and Partai Katholik's appeals were of course directed
toward the Protestant and Roman Catholic communities respectively, while
Masjumi and NU competed for the support of the santri Muslims.

Prior to the elections, the objective of each religious party at the local
level was simply to make the party organization and its views as well known
as possible among the people whom it sought to represent in the national
parliament. In large part the local election campaigns of the religious parties
were conducted via the established religious institutions of the community.
HKBP ministers, for example, although they did not become Parkindo
leaders, inserted party propaganda into their Sunday sermons, and church
lay leaders became active campaigners in the districts. Most of the Islamic
social and educational organizations in the region became formally affiliated
with Masjumi, giving that party a virtual monopoly over the services of the
local Muslim religious leadership. NU, on Java an educational organization
with pervasive influence in rural society long before it became a political
party, did not exist in Simalungun/Siantar until 1953 when a local party
branch was formed. Without the support of well-established religious
leadership and organization in the region, the party began its career under
much less auspicious circumstances than did the other religious parties.

The religious parties placed heavy emphasis in their electoral propaganda
on appeals to religious loyalties, with the party represented as the political
arm of the religious community. Without exception, religious party leaders
characterized the secular parties as antireligious, implying that a national
victory for the latter would lead to discrimination against the faithful (including, some of the more flamboyant politicians are reported to have
argued, desecration of graveyards and destruction of churches and mosques).
The point they wished to make was clear: a vote for the religious party was
a vote for the community of believers, and a vote for any secular party was
a vote against that community.

In the years following the elections the religious parties were relatively
inactive, although rudimentary organizations were maintained, particularly
at the regency/municipality and subdistrict levels. Beginning in 1956 the
regency/municipality party organizations took on important new duties—

the nomination of candidates for seats in the regional legislatures (a process that occurred once in 1956 and again in 1960) and the supervision of the activities of their legislative representatives. At the subdistrict level, party leadership councils were maintained so that periodic regency conferences to select new leadership and pass on their policies could be held. In the villages there was normally no formal leadership structure, although one or more individuals regarded themselves and were generally regarded as spokesmen for the party.

While the religious parties were less active in the postelection period than PNI and PKI, they were not blind to the threat presented by the organizational efforts of the secular parties in the plantation subdistricts. In an attempt to counter the influence of PNI and PKI gerakan massa, the religious parties also made use of subsidiary organizations. Parkindo's affiliates in Simalungun/Siantar included women's, youth, and university students' organizations. In 1964 a member of Parkindo's Leadership Council in Siantar city was actively organizing a branch of a new Parkindo labor union among city government employees. Partai Katholik, less active in these areas, had women's, youth, and labor affiliates. NU's most prominent local affiliates were its youth organization and its women's group, and the party was also in the process of building local branches of farmers' and labor groups. Masjumi had been most active among women and laborers.

Some of these organizations were quite large, at least in terms of claimed members. Parkindo's women's group, for example, claimed a Simalungun/Siantar membership of just under 3,000, while its youth movement claimed 1,000 members, and its student group included nearly all of the students in the local Christian university's two faculties, theology and education. NU's Siantar branch of Muslimat NU, a women's group with a membership of 500, was considerably more active than either its PNI or PKI counterpart. In the fields of labor and farming, however, none of the religious parties offered serious competition to the PNI and PKI organizations.

The activities of most of these organizations, in contrast to those of PNI and PKI, had a distinctly nonpolitical cast. Their orientation was rather toward religious education, particularly for the women and youth but also in the case of the labor unions. Thus, when discussing the programs of their affiliates, party leaders stressed the educational aspect and showed little interest in appeals based on the needs of the squatters for more land or of the plantation workers for higher pay, better living and working conditions, job security, and the like. Emphasis was placed on strict adherence to legality in the relationships between the organizations, on the one hand, and the plantations and government, on the other.

At least in the cases of Parkindo and Partai Katholik, another difference between the religious and secular parties was apparent. For PNI and PKI, the party organization was paramount, directing and supervising the activities of its affiliates. Parkindo and Partai Katholik's affiliates, on the other hand, were essentially self-contained organizations, financially independent of the party and communicating only infrequently and on a basis of equality with the party leadership. Parkindo's labor union to some extent represented a departure from this pattern, since it was explicitly created by the national party leadership to provide an alternative for Protestant workers to the secular unions. In Siantar, however, the union was not organized by the dominant party leadership but rather by dissidents who hoped to return to positions of influence within the party by developing a mass base in the union. This use of an affiliate in order to gain positions in the party organization was a common strategy of local PNI politicians, but had not been used by a Parkindo leader before 1964.

NU's relationships with its affiliates more closely paralleled the pattern of PNI, with the regency/municipality party acting as a parent organization directing the activities of its children, and adopting a more positive strategy designed to increase the party and subsidiary organization membership. This greater activity of NU (relative to Parkindo and Partai Katholik, but still very limited compared to PNI or PKI) was largely because NU had not succeeded in obtaining the extensive support of the local religious leadership enjoyed by the other religious parties.

Participation by the religious party leaders in local government was confined for the most part to the regional legislatures. In the Siantar legislature, Parkindo formed an alliance with PNI and PKI in opposition to the Muslim parties and succeeded in obtaining the chairmanship for itself. Masjumi and NU, although outvoted eight to seven in the full legislature, chaired all three of its committees and were able to work closely with the first two municipal Regional Heads (the first, who held office from 1956 to 1958, was a Masjumi supporter and the second, from 1958 to 1959, was pro-NU). Masjumi and Parkindo were also represented in the Regional Executive Council. In the reorganized legislatures the PNI-PKI coalition (with the sometime support of NU and and the police, army, and Muslim religious leadership representatives) was dominant, with Parkindo in the opposition, although there was much cooperation among individual members across party lines. Parkindo and NU each had one seat on the Daily Government Board.

In the first Simalungun legislature the religious parties were unable to unite among themselves or to enter the PNI-PKI-Partai Buruh alliance, and their influence was largely confined to the Regional Executive Council, where Parkindo and Masjumi each had one seat. After the appointment of a new Regional Head in 1960, the three religious parties represented in the reorganized legislature (Parkindo, Partai Katholik, and NU) played a more influential role despite the fact that PNI and PKI held a majority of the seats.[28]

Religious party influence within the military in Simalungun/Siantar was minimal. The decline of Masjumi (several of whose national leaders supported the regional rebellions) coincided with the rise to political power of the army in the late 1950s, and the local branches of NU and Partai Katholik were too small to merit military attention. Parkindo was hampered by its identification with the North Tapanuli Batak Protestant community, of which Col. Simbolon had been the chief representative within the army, and its leaders were suspected of supporting Simbolon's coup. In 1960 Parkindo was a major factor in the nomination of an army officer for the office of Regional Head in Simalungun, and continued to work closely with him after his appointment. Despite this foot in the door, however, Parkindo's influence in the regency/municipality and provincial army hierarchies remained very limited.

28. PNI-PKI strength was 15 of a total of 29 seats actually occupied in 1963.

3. BASES OF PARTISAN SUPPORT: VOTERS, MEMBERS, AND LEADERS

In Chapter 1 of this book I argued that a half-century of colonialism, occupation, and revolution has brought about a profound transformation in conceptions of personal identity, patterns of social cleavage and consensus, and attitudes toward politics and government among the people of Simalungun/ Siantar. Following Clifford Geertz, I proposed that this transformation was in essence an "integrative revolution," in which formerly dominant ties to village, clan, and kingdom became subordinate to new loyalties based on common ethnicity, religious affiliation, socioeconomic status, and, at the most inclusive level, common Indonesian nationality. The task of the present chapter is to relate these developments to the efforts of national political parties to obtain support in the region.

In my discussion of party organization, objectives, and strategies I suggested that the secular parties attempted to build local support by appealing across ethnic and religious cleavages to the material interests of the relatively detraditionalized plantation workers and squatters, while the religious parties sought the politicization of religious communities. The effects of these strategies in terms of partisan support actually achieved may now be spelled out. What was the relationship that developed in the 1950s and early 1960s between, on the one hand, the national party system, and, on the other, the cleavages of the local environment?

The 1955 Parliamentary Elections

Examination of the 1955 election results indicates clear differences among the bases of support of the major parties in the regency. The most broadly integrative party was PNI, which obtained 27.4% of all votes cast in the regency, and whose supporters were drawn more evenly from all ethnic and religious groups than any other major party. While PNI strength was greatest in the ethnically mixed plantation subdistricts of Lower Simalungun, the party was also able to win 20 percent of the vote in both Upper Simalungun (largely Simalungun Batak) and along the Road to Parapat (North Tapanuli Batak). Support for PKI in the regency (17.9% of total vote) was not as broadly distributed as the PNI vote; while the Communists won 20 percent of the vote in Lower Simalungun and along the Road to Parapat, they were unable to gain a following in Upper Simalungun (see Fig. 3–1).

For both PNI and PKI, the six subdistricts of Lower Simalungun represented the core of party strength in the regency. These subdistricts, containing 72.6 percent of the regency electorate, accounted for 79.5 percent of the PNI vote and 80.8 percent of the PKI vote in Simalungun.[1] More specifically, the election results for PKI show a strong correlation between the size of party vote and the presence of plantations in a given subdistrict (see Fig. 3–2). When a product moment coefficient of correlation was computed for the degree of association between the PKI vote and the percentage of arable land under plantation concession, an r of .83 was found. From this it may reasonably be inferred that the great majority of the PKI electorate consisted of plantation workers (almost all of whom are Javanese) and squatters on plantation land (North Tapanuli Bataks and Javanese), the two dominant socioeconomic groups in the plantation subdistricts.

The size of the PNI subdistrict vote, on the other hand, was independent of the presence or absence of plantations. While PNI did well in the plantation subdistricts, with a mean percentage of 23.4, it did even better in the subdistricts without plantations, where it averaged 27.4 percent of the vote. The product moment correlation coefficient, computed for the degree of association between the PNI vote and the percentage of arable land under

1. The subdistricts along the Road to Parapat, with 13.7 percent of the electorate, accounted for 10.5 percent and 16.0 percent of the PNI and PKI vote respectively, while Upper Simalungun, with 13.8 percent of the electorate, was responsible for 9.0 percent of the PNI vote and 3.2 percent of the PKI vote.

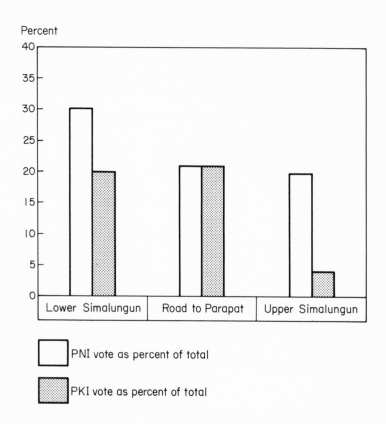

Figure 3.1   PNI and PKI Vote in the 1955 Parliamentary Elections (by region)

Source: Adapted from Pemerintahan Daerah Tkt. II Simalungun, *Daftar: Perhitungan hasil2 pemungutan suara dalam daerah Kabupaten Simalungun/Pemilihan Anggota Dewan Perwakilan Rakjat* (Government of the Second Level Region of Simalungun, A List of the election results in the Regency of Simalungun/Election of Members of the People's Representative Council), Sept. 29, 1955. (Subsequently referred to as *Simalungun election results.)*

concession, was only .18. The PNI electorate thus contained a mixture of individuals both inside and outside the plantation environment. Ethnically, at least three major groups contributed substantially to the PNI vote: Javanese (in Lower Simalungun), North Tapanuli Bataks (in Lower Simalungun

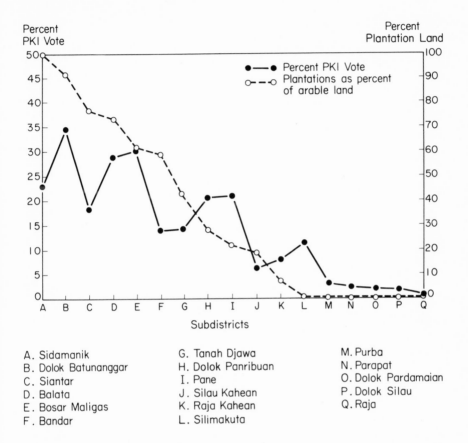

Figure 3.2   PKI Vote by Subdistrict, Compared with Plantation Hectarage as a Percentage of Total Arable Land

Sources: Electoral data from *Simalungun election results;* plantation hectarage as percent of arable land from *The General Agricultural Condition of Simeloengoen,* p. 17.

and the Road to Parapat), and Simalungun Bataks (in Upper Simalungun). The extent to which South Tapanuli Bataks also supported PNI is not possible to determine, as there are no subdistricts in which they are the predominant group.

In contrast to PNI and PKI, support for the two major religious parties,

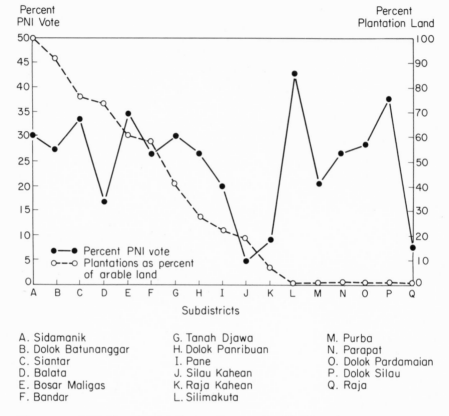

A. Sidamanik
B. Dolok Batunanggar
C. Siantar
D. Balata
E. Bosar Maligas
F. Bandar

G. Tanah Djawa
H. Dolok Panribuan
I. Pane
J. Silau Kahean
K. Raja Kahean
L. Silimakuta

M. Purba
N. Parapat
O. Dolok Pardamaian
P. Dolok Silau
Q. Raja

Figure 3.3   PNI Vote by Subdistrict, Compared with Plantation Hectarage as a
Percentage of Total Arable Land

Sources: Electoral data from *Simalungun election results;* plantation hectarage as
percent of arable land from *The General Agricultural Condition of Simeloengoen,*
p. 17.

Parkindo and Masjumi, tended to follow rather than cut across ethnic divisions in Simalungun. Parkindo's vote (16.2 percent of the regency total) came
largely from the North Tapanuli Bataks, concentrated in the subdistricts
along the Road to Parapat and in Lower Simalungun. Despite the fact that 51
percent of the largely Simalungun Batak population of Upper Simalungun is
Protestant, Parkindo's vote in the region was less than 10 percent. By sub-

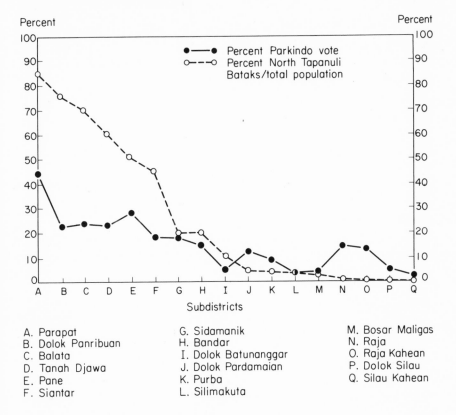

Figure 3.4   Parkindo Vote by Subdistrict, Compared with the Estimated Percentage
of North Tapanuli Bataks in the Subdistrict Population

Sources: Electoral data from *Simalungun election results;* North Tapanuli Bataks
as percent of subdistrict population estimated from interview data and a table on
religious affiliation in Pemerintahan Daerah Tkt. II Simalungun, *Lapuran Tahan
1963* (Government of the Second-Level Region of Simalungun, *Report for 1963),*
p. 115.

district the relationship becomes even clearer (see Fig. 3–4). The correlation
coefficient, measuring the degree of association between the Parkindo vote
and the percentage of North Tapanuli Bataks in the subdistrict population,
was a high .86.

Electoral and interview data also clearly reveal an inverse relationship between the size of the Parkindo vote and the extent to which a particular area with a sizable North Tapanuli Batak population was characterized by a plantation environment. In other words, in those villages in which many of the North Tapanuli Bataks were squatters, i.e. their legal claim to land was in dispute, the vote for Parkindo tended to be small; conversely, in regions where titles to land were not in question, the Parkindo vote was greater. In a North Tapanuli Batak village in subdistrict Siantar, for example, informants reported a considerable division in partisan support, the major parties being PNI, PKI, and Parkindo. The principal concern of the villagers, expressed repeatedly in interviews, was the expansion of village rice fields, hemmed in on all sides by the plantations. Many villagers, members of PNI and PKI farmers' organizations, criticized Parkindo for its lack of interest in the problems of the squatter population. In a small town in subdistrict Tanah Djawa, on the other hand, where land problems were much less pressing, informants reported a large Parkindo vote in 1955 and very little party or organizational activity of any kind in 1964. Interviews in other villages in Lower Simalungun and along the Road to Parapat confirmed this general impression.

Additional evidence supporting this hypothesis is provided by comparing "Parkindo support ratios" (percent Parkindo subdistrict vote divided by percent of North Tapanuli Bataks) in the six Simalungun subdistricts with a large North Tapanuli Batak population (see Fig. 3–5). For these six subdistricts the correlation coefficient measuring the degree of association between the Parkindo support ratios and the percentage of plantation land was −.54, indicating an inverse relationship between the two variables.

The vote for Masjumi (16.1 percent) was largely restricted to Lower Simalungun, the only part of the regency with a substantial santri Muslim population. Masjumi's vote was highest in subdistricts Bandar (29.4 percent) and Dolok Batunanggar (24.0 percent), whose towns of Perdagangan and Serbelawan have the highest concentration of South Tapanuli Bataks in the regency. In Sidamanik, where there are few South Tapanuli Bataks (but many Javanese and some Simalungun Batak Muslims), Masjumi's vote was only 7.9 percent of the subdistrict total. For Lower Simalungun as a whole, the Masjumi percentage of the vote was 19.3 percent.

In the "core area" of Upper Simalungun, inhabited largely by Christian

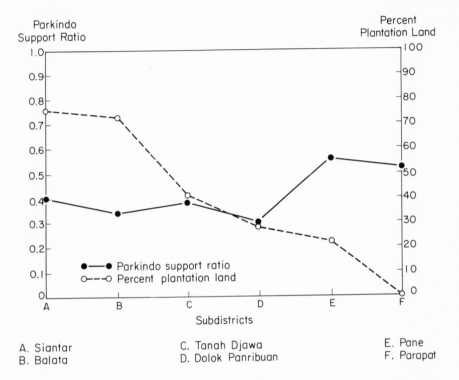

Parkindo
Support Ratio

Percent
Plantation Land

● ● Parkindo support ratio
○--○ Percent plantation land

Subdistricts

A. Siantar   C. Tanah Djawa   E. Pane
B. Balata   D. Dolok Panribuan   F. Parapat

Figure 3.5 Parkindo Support Ratios in Six Subdistricts with a Large North Tapanuli
Batak Population, Compared with Plantation Hectarage as a Percentage
of Total Arable Land

Sources: Electoral data from *Simalungun election results;* North Tapanuli Bataks
as percent of subdistrict population estimated from interview data and the table
on religious affiliation in Pemerintahan Daerah Tkt. II Simalungun, *Lapuran Tahun
1963,* p. 115. The Parkindo support ratio was determined by dividing the percent
Parkindo subdistrict vote by the percent of North Tapanuli Bataks in the subdistrict
population. For plantation hectarage as percent of arable land, see *The General
Agricultural Condition of Simeloengoen,* p. 17.

Simalungun Bataks, Masjumi's vote was small but corresponded roughly with the proportion of Muslims (mostly Simalungun Bataks) in the population. In Silau Kahean and Raja Kahean, two subdistricts on the northern fringe of Upper Simalungun where the Muslim population is larger and more ethnically diverse (South Tapanuli Bataks, Simalungun Bataks, Javanese, and Coastal Malays), Masjumi did well, with 23.0 percent and 20.6 percent of the vote. Along the Road to Parapat there are few South Tapanuli

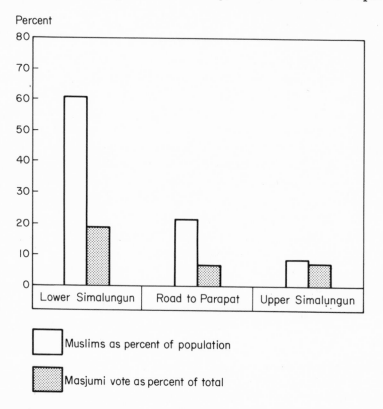

Figure 3.6   Masjumi Vote in the 1955 Parliamentary Elections (by region)

Sources: Muslims as percent of subdistrict population from Pemerintahan Daerah Tkt. II Simalungun, *Lapuran Tahun 1963*, p. 115; electoral data from *Simalungun election results.*

Bataks; the Muslim population in these subdistricts includes Javanese and smaller groups of Simalungun and North Tapanuli Batak Muslims. The Masjumi percentage of the vote in this region was only 6.7 percent.

Without precise data on the ethnicity of the Muslim voters of the various subdistricts of the regency (which is unobtainable), it is not possible to be sure how much of the Masjumi vote can be attributed to the South Tapanuli Bataks. Among the Muslims of Lower Simalungun, according to village informants, the Masjumi versus PNI-PKI division followed closely the cleavage between santri (South Tapanuli Bataks) and abangan (Javanese), although I found Javanese villages in which a Masjumi vote of as much as 20 percent was reported. At least part of this support may be attributed to the fact that the conflict between santri and abangan is rather less intense in Simalungun than in East and Central Java, despite the added complication of ethnic cleavage. In the predominantly Javanese villages of Lower Simalungun it is common to find a few South Tapanuli or Simalungun Batak Muslims who serve as the spiritual leaders of their communities. During and after the election campaign, these individuals provided a nucleus for Islamic political organizations (both Masjumi and NU) and were able to attract a minority of the Javanese in their villages to the religious parties.[2] In the less densely populated subdistricts of Upper Simalungun and along the Road to Parapat, most of Masjumi's support clearly came from non-South Tapanuli Batak Muslims. In the core area of Upper Simalungun in particular, almost all of the Masjumi vote was contributed by Simalungun Bataks. Despite these qualifications, it seems clear that on a regency-wide basis the large majority of Masjumi voters were South Tapanuli Bataks.

Among the remaining parties, Partai Buruh (Labor Party) received almost

2. A considerable proportion of Javanese support for Masjumi may be attributable to Javanese women, whose interest in Islam is much greater than that of their husbands. The tendency for women to support the religious parties and to urge their husbands to do so is common in the region. Parkindo's women's organization played an important role in the election campaign, as did the women's organizations of Masjumi and NU. PNI leaders in Siantar expressed much concern over the success of the NU women's group among the Javanese women of Bantan. The activities of their own women's affiliate, Wanita Demokrat, in Bantan were heavily religion oriented.

half of its votes (less than 3 percent of the total votes cast) in subdistrict Tanah Djawa, where it had some labor union support. The vote for the Indonesian Socialist Party (1.6 percent) was concentrated in Bandar and Bosar Maligas (together constituting half of the total PSI vote) and was based on the small PSI labor unions in those subdistricts. Partai Katholik, with a vote of less than 3,000 (1.5 percent), was strongest in subdistricts Purba (Simalungun Batak Catholics), Dolok Panribuan, Pane, and Tanah Djawa (North Tapanuli Batak Catholics); these four subdistricts accounted for two-thirds of the party's vote. Finally, almost all of NU's 1,673 votes (.6 percent) came from the four subdistricts of Bandar, Bosar Maligas, Tanah Djawa, and Sidamanik, all in Lower Simalungun. Interviews in these subdistricts indicated that the largest proportion of NU voters were Javanese and Simalungun Bataks.

In the city of Siantar voters seem to have been motivated in their choice of party primarily by ethnoreligious loyalties, with the South Tapanuli Bataks supporting Masjumi (38.3 percent of total votes cast), the North Tapanuli Bataks supporting Parkindo (29.3 percent), and the abangan Javanese favoring PNI (13.9 percent). Unfortunately, a breakdown of the vote by ward was not available (even from the ward heads, who keep few records) but it was clear from conversations with party leaders and others that the North Tapanuli Batak wards (Kristen Barat and Kristen Timur) were solidly Parkindo, while the South Tapanuli Bataks (in Timbang Galung Lama, Timbang Galung Baru, and Melaju) voted heavily Masjumi. NU's small vote in Siantar was cast largely by the Simalungun Batak Muslims in the old radja's village in the central city and by a tiny group of Coastal Malays in Melaju.

The only solidly PNI ward in Siantar was the Javanese-inhabited Bantan, with the Javanese in Melaju and Timbang Galung Baru also voting heavily PNI. By making some rather tenuous assumptions about the population of Siantar at the time of the elections and the likely percentage of PNI voters in the Javanese sections and extrapolating from the election figures available, it is possible to conclude that Javanese voters accounted for perhaps 1,000 of PNI's 2,310 votes, with the rest of the party's vote probably distributed roughly equally (relative to proportion of population) among all

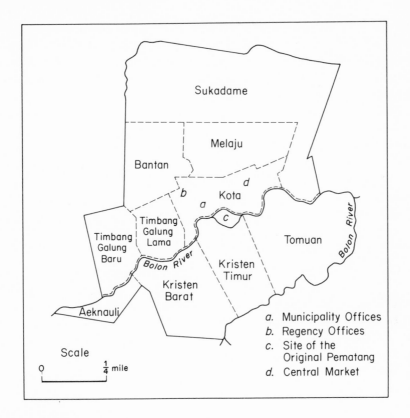

Map 6. Pematangsiantar

Source: Department of Public Works, Municipality of Pematangsiantar, 1957.

other ethnic groups.[3] In terms of electoral support, the Javanese seem to have been a more important element in the PNI city than in the PNI regency vote, constituting the largest single ethnic bloc in the party column.

PKI, which received only 445 votes (2.7 percent) in the city, was unable to break the PNI hold on the Javanese and was able to offer no competition

3. In the Siantar election 15,605 votes were cast, representing a third of the estimated 1955 population of 50,000. (The population of Siantar in 1950 was 48,427; by 1963 it had more than doubled, but most of this growth took place during the

to Parkindo and Masjumi for the support of the Batak Christians and Muslims. A majority of PKI's vote was probably cast by Javanese members of Communist-affiliated labor unions, with the remainder contributed by North Tapanuli Bataks who had been active in PKI-sponsored revolutionary groups in the late 1940s. The vote for the remaining parties (Partai Katholik, Partai Buruh, and PSI) was infinitesimally small.

Party Membership

Party membership figures, where available, show an ethnic distribution similar to the 1955 election results. Membership in PNI's regency branch was comparatively well distributed throughout the regency, with a sub-branch in each of the seventeen subdistricts and ranting in 113 villages or groupings of villages. PNI membership in Simalungun in 1963, according to the General Report issued by the Branch Leadership Council, was 7,935.

If the 1963 PNI report accurately reflected the distribution of party members in the regency, the subdistrict branches in Lower Simalungun contained 47.7 percent of the total number of members, while the branches in Upper Simalungun contained 41.8 percent (concentrated in Raja Kahean and Silau Kahean, plantation regions outside the "core area" of Upper Simalungun), and those along the Road to Parapat 10.4 percent.[4] Compared with the election results, the subbranches in Upper Simalungun were relatively larger

---

rebellion of 1957–60, when security was better in the city than in the countryside. A further 30,000 people were incorporated into the city when the city limits were extended some time after the election.) Assuming that the proportion of voters to population was reasonably consistent from ward to ward, there were roughly 1,000 to 1,500 voters in Bantan. If Bantan's vote was 60 percent PNI (many of the Javanese women probably voted for Masjumi, whose women's organization was strong there) something like 600–900 of the PNI's 2,310 votes came from Bantan alone. Add to that another 200 or so votes from Javanese in other wards and one arrives at the figure of 800 to 1,100, or one-third to one-half of the total PNI vote. Such an estimate is obviously not very reliable and is offered only to give an indication of the ethnicity of PNI voters in Siantar.

4. In terms of votes at the regency Party Conference held in 1964 (for which the report was prepared) subdistrict branches from Lower Simalungun were represented by a total of 19 voting delegates, while Upper Simalungun had 20 votes (7 of them in Raja Kahean and Silau Kahean), and the Road to Parapat subbranches had 8.

Table 3–1. Ethnicity and PNI Membership in Siantar

Ethnic Group	Number	Percent
Javanese*	376	48.2
North Tapanuli Batak	208	26.6
South Tapanuli Batak	59	7.7
Simalungun Batak	41	5.3
Karo Batak	17	2.2
Other and not clear†	79	10.1
Total	780	100.1

Source: This table was compiled from lists of names of party members compiled by the various PNI ranting from 1961 to 1963 and placed on file in the Political Affairs Office, Regency of Simalungun. (Different types of Bataks are for the most part easily recognizable by their clan names; abangan Javanese are also usually readily distinguishable.)

*For Bantan ranting only the total number of members (293) rather than a list of names was available. As Bantan is an almost exclusively Javanese ward, its total membership is entered in this row.

†The residual category in the table is almost wholly composed of individuals with purely Islamic names (e.g. Abdul Kohar, Mohammad Jusuf) who could be South Tapanuli Bataks, Javanese, or Muslims from other parts of Sumatra or other islands. According to party officials, most of these individuals are of South Tapanuli origin (52 of them lived in Timbang Galung Lama and Melaju, where the ranting party leaders were, with only one exception, South Tapanuli Bataks). South Tapanuli Bataks thus constituted perhaps 15 percent of the city party's membership.

in proportion to the electorate than those in Lower Simalungun. These membership figures should not be taken too literally, however, as lists of members were kept rather casually and numbers could be juggled for the benefit of one or another faction at a party conference.[5] Although no specific

5. At the 1964 conference some questions were raised about the validity of certain lists, particularly those in Upper Simalungun. Data obtained in interviews conducted on several occasions with PNI leaders and others in subdistrict Raja strongly suggested that PNI strength in the subdistrict was rather less than the number cited in the report.

data were available on the ethnicity of PNI regency branch members, this subdistrict distribution clearly indicated a mixture of Javanese, North Tapanuli Bataks, and Simalungun Bataks. PNI subbranches in Dolok Batunanggar and Bandar also contained a number of South Tapanuli Bataks.

The firmest figures available on PNI membership in Siantar city show a distribution comparable to my estimate of the distribution of party vote, with the largest ranting (there are no subdistricts in Siantar, and thus no party subbranches) in the Javanese ward of Bantan. The three major ethnic groups represented in the city PNI branch were the Javanese, North Tapanuli Bataks, and South Tapanuli Bataks, who together constituted about 90 percent of the membership. By ranting, the ethnic affiliations of party members were roughly comparable to the distribution of ethnic groups throughout the city. The North Tapanuli Bataks constituted the bulk of party membership in those wards in which their ethnic group is predominant, as did the South Tapanuli Bataks in their wards, and the Javanese in theirs. According to the government data, petty traders and small businessmen were the largest occupational group in PNI-Siantar, followed by white-collar employees (mostly government officials and teachers in government and private schools), and laborers.

Table 3–2. Occupation and PNI Membership in Siantar (excluding Bantan*)

Occupation	Number	Percent
Trade/small business	175	36
White collar	120	25
Laborers	93	19
Students	86	18
Farmers	8	2
Other	5	1
Total	487	101

Source: Data on file in Political Affairs Office, Regency of Simalungun, November 1963.

*PNI members in Bantan (for whom occupational data were not available) were mostly laborers and petty traders.

Membership in PKI's regency-level section was distributed among eleven party subsections, six of which were located in Lower Simalungun and four of the remaining five in the subdistricts of the Road to Parapat. As of 1961 (the only year for which data were available), PKI in Simalungun had 160 members. The government files containing data on PKI included a complete list of the names and occupations of party members, making it possible to determine the ethnic and occupational diversity of the party membership. (see tables 3–3 and 3–4). Most PKI subsections were dominated by the members of one ethnic group. What significance may be attributed to this fact is not clear, since the PKI seemed freer of ethnic tension than any other political organization in the region, and membership recruitment was controlled by the Party Section Committee, which had no conceivable interest in the ethnic purity of party subsections.

Table 3–3. Ethnicity and PKI Membership in Simalungun, 1961

Ethnic Group	Number	Percent
Javanese	80	50.0
North Tapanuli Batak	60	37.5
Simalungun Batak	18	11.25
Karo Batak	2	1.25
Total	160	100.0

Source: Data on file in Political Affairs Office, Regency of Simalungun, 1963.

Table 3–4. Occupation and PKI Membership in Simalungun, 1961

Occupation	Number	Percent
Farmer	99	62.4
Laborer	55	34.3
Trader	5	3.1
Other	1	.1
Total	160	100.0

Source: Data on file in Political Affairs Office, Regency of Simalungun, 1963.

In 1963 PKI-Siantar claimed a membership of 135, with an additional 270 candidate-members. According to government files (which were not broken down into subsections or groups) PKI membership in 1961 was 100. North Tapanuli Bataks and Javanese represented 94 percent of the membership, and laborers constituted the largest economic group.

The religious parties, as indicated in the previous chapter, were not, strictly speaking, membership parties. Rather, they corresponded more closely to Duverger's structural model of the cadre party, "a grouping of notabilities." For the purpose of reporting membership figures to the government or to higher party officials, the local leadership tended to assume that all members of the religious community, or at least all those who voted for the party in the 1955 elections, were also party members. Thus Partai Katholik, when required by presidential edict to submit membership totals in 1961, reported 5,700 members in its Simalungun and Siantar branches. This figure is almost twice as large as the party's vote in 1955 and constitutes one-third of the total Roman Catholic (adult and child) population of the region. Parkindo's reported total was 16,263 members in the regency and 6,123 in the city. The General Report issued by Parkindo-Simalungun in 1961, after listing the number of members by subdistrict, added this note: "Besides the results given above, there are still many members not yet listed, remembering the results of the 1955 elections in which Parkindo obtained 35,856 votes."[6] Nahdatul Ulama reported a membership of 1,972 in 1961, 300 more than its 1955 vote. For Masjumi no membership data were available.

Of the three religious parties that reported their membership to the government, only NU provided a list of the names of members that could be used to indicate ethnic affiliations. In the regency, Simalungun Bataks and Javanese each accounted for almost 50 percent of the NU membership, while in Siantar city 22 percent of NU members were in the "Other Muslim" category (mostly Coastal Malays and South Tapanuli Bataks). A high proportion of party members were women, in some subdistricts accounting for half the membership.

6. Partai Kristen Indonesia, Tjabang Simalungun, *Lapuran Umum* [Indonesian Christian Party, Simalungun Branch, *General Report*] (P. Siantar, 1961), p. 4; and Partai Kristen Indonesia, Tjabang Kotapradja Pematangsiantar, *Lapuran* [Indonesian Christian Party, Siantar Branch, *Report*] (P. Siantar, 1961), p. 3.

Parkindo's data were available only in the form of subdistrict totals. Apparently no real list of members was ever drawn up; rather, subdistrict Parkindo leaders were merely asked how many members they had, and they in turn asked village leaders to submit a figure. The results of this process were peculiar, as no Parkindo members were listed for Parapat, where the party was strongest in 1955, a figure of 1,371 was given for Raja, a Simalungun Batak subdistrict where the party had few supporters (Parkindo's total vote in Raja in 1955 was 901), and Sidamanik was said to have 1,464 Parkindo members, compared to an electoral total of 1,932. Despite these deficiencies, the data indicate that the main source of Parkindo's strength was in the North Tapanuli areas of Lower Simalungun, especially Tanah Djawa, and along the Road to Parapat.

Party Leadership

The clearest contrast between the secular and religious parties in terms of their relationship to the ethnic cleavages of Simalungun and Siantar may be found at the level of the party and organizational leadership. While representatives of nearly every major ethnic group in the region served as leaders of PNI and PKI, the religious parties' leadership tended to be dominated by the members of a single ethnic group.

The ethnicity of PNI leaders at the subdistrict level reflected in general the ethnic composition of the particular subdistrict (see Table 3–5). In Upper Simalungun two-thirds of the PNI leaders were Simalungun Bataks, with the principal exception of subdistricts Silimakuta and Dolok Silau, located on the border of Karo regency.[7] In the four subdistricts along the Road to Parapat, PNI leadership was primarily North Tapanuli Batak. In Lower Simalungun North Tapanuli Bataks also represented the largest group in the leadership, partly because they predominate in the towns (such as Perdagangan and Tanah Djawa) where the party offices are located, while it is more difficult for the Javanese who live on the plantations to come to town for party meetings. A more important reason, however, is that the Javanese tended to concentrate on the organization and activities of the

7. Here the leadership had been for many years in the hands of a Karo Batak secondary school principal who maintained connections with the large and well-financed PNI branch in Karo. Since the Revolution, PNI has been the strongest party in Karo; in 1955 it polled 59 percent of the vote there.

Table 3–5. Ethnicity of PNI Subdistrict Leaders in Simalungun and Ranting Leaders in Siantar

Region	Simalungun Batak	North Tapanuli Batak	Karo Batak	Javanese	South Tapanuli Batak	Coastal Malay
Upper Simalungun	20	3	5	1	1	—
Road to Parapat	4	17	—	—	—	—
Lower Simalungun	6	13	—	10	2	—
Siantar	1	31	1	12	10	1

Source: For Simalungun, data on file in office of PNI in Simalungun; for Siantar, data provided by PNI branch secretary.

party subsidiaries in and near the plantations and left the subdistrict party branches to the North Tapanuli Bataks.

At the regency level party leadership positions in PNI were held by members of all the large ethnic groups in the region. From 1961 to 1963 the membership of the Branch Leadership Council included two Javanese, a North Tapanuli Batak Muslim, a South Tapanuli Batak, and a Simalungun Batak. The leadership elected in 1964 for the term 1963–65 consisted of two Javanese, one North Tapanuli Batak Christian, two South Tapanuli Bataks and one Simalungun Batak.

* In Siantar city, the PNI ward leadership reflected the general patterns of ethnic distribution of the various wards and of the party membership in the wards. In ten out of twelve ranting (the exceptions were Kota and one of the two ranting in Tomuan, where no one ethnic group had a majority of the membership) all or all but one of the leaders were members of the same ethnic group as the majority of the party membership. From 1960 to 1962 the branch level (municipality-wide) PNI leadership included three North Tapanuli Bataks, one Javanese, and one South Tapanuli Batak. The party leadership council elected at the 1962 Party Conference (actually held in 1963) consisted of three North Tapanuli Bataks, one North Tapanuli Batak Muslim, and the Kalimantan-born chairman of ranting Kota.

In PKI, each party subsection was led by two officials, the first and second secretaries. In Lower Simalungun, two-thirds of the leaders were Javanese, while all but one of the eight subsection leaders in the subdistricts along the

Table 3–6. Ethnicity of PKI Subsection Leaders in Simalungun

Region	North Tapanuli Batak	Javanese	Simalungun Batak
Upper Simalungun	—	—	2
Road to Parapat	7	—	1
Lower Simalungun	2	8	2

Source: Data on file in the Political Affairs Office, Regency of Simalungun.

Road to Parapat were North Tapanuli Bataks. In Silimakuta, the only PKI subsection in Upper Simalungun, both of the officials were Simalungun

Bataks. PKI regency-level leadership consisted of a North Tapanuli Batak and a South Tapanuli Batak; the comparable officials in the Siantar section were both North Tapanuli Bataks.

Data on the ethnicity of PNI and PKI subsidiary organization leaders below the regency level were difficult to obtain, as in most cases these organizations did not maintain subdistrict branches and lists of village leaders were not available in party or government offices. In general, however, village-level labor leaders in both the PNI and PKI unions were Javanese (since nearly all plantation workers are Javanese), while the leadership of other organizations was divided roughly equally between Javanese and North Tapanuli Bataks. At the regency level, Javanese were dominant in the leadership councils of PNI's farmer and labor organizations, with North Tapanuli Bataks in control of the motor workers' union and neither group dominating the youth organization. In Siantar, North Tapanuli Bataks tended to dominate the PNI affiliates, although Javanese and South Tapanuli Bataks also held leadership positions. Offices in PKI's regency and city organization councils were more evenly distributed, with each organization containing some Javanese and North Tapanuli Batak leaders, and usually South Tapanuli and Simalungun Bataks as well.

Both secular parties also attempted to maintain an ethnic balance in their nominations for seats in the prestigious regency and city legislatures. PNI's delegation in the Simalungun legislature included two Javanese, two South Tapanuli Bataks, and one Karo Batak. Representatives from "functional groups" affiliated with PNI included three Javanese, three Simalungun Bataks, and one Karo Batak. In the Siantar legislature the PNI delegation consisted of one South Tapanuli Batak and one Coastal Malay born in Kalimantan; PNI functional group representation included two North Tapanuli Bataks and one South Tapanuli Batak. PKI's delegation in Simalungun included one Javanese, one North Tapanuli Batak, and one Simalungun Batak, while the party's single representative in the Siantar Regional Representative Council was a North Tapanuli Batak.

In contrast to PNI and PKI, Parkindo was dominated by North Tapanuli Bataks at both the subdistict and regency/municipality levels. According to the most recent General Report of the party (1961), all Parkindo subdistrict leaders in Lower Simalungun and all but two in the Road to Parapat subdistricts were North Tapanuli Bataks. In Upper Simalungun the leadership was almost entirely Simalungun Batak, but in four of the seven subdistricts of the region the party subbranch had only one official, while all other subbranch councils in the regency had four or more members. The clear inference, confirmed by interviews and observations, is that the majority of Parkindo subbranches in Upper Simalungun were one-man operations

Table 3–7. Ethnicity of Parkindo Subdistrict Leaders in Simalungun

Region	North Tapanuli Batak	Simalungun Batak	Karo Batak
Upper Simalungun	—	21	2
Road to Parapat	26	2	—
Lower Simalungun	42	—	—

Source: Parkindo, Tjabang Simalungun, *Lapuran Umum,* 1961, pp. 1–3.

and almost totally inactive. At the regency level, five of the seven members of the party's leadership council were North Tapanuli Bataks, one was a Simalungun Batak, and one a Karo Batak.

In the municipality of Siantar Parkindo had ten branches with a total ranting leadership of 77, of whom 66 were North Tapanuli Bataks. The remaining ward leaders included seven Karo Bataks (who together constituted the Parkindo leadership of a section of Kristen Timur ward called Kampung Karo), three Simalungun Bataks and one individual from the island of Nias. The city-wide leadership consisted of seven North Tapanuli Bataks. Parkindo's representatives in the regency legislature included two North Tapanuli Bataks and one Simalungun Batak; in the city legislature all four Parkindo members were North Tapanuli Bataks.

Partai Katholik, with subbranches in both North Tapanuli and Simalungun Batak areas, had a somewhat more diverse leadership. At the regency level four party officials were Simalungun Bataks, three were North Tapanuli Bataks, and one was a Karo Batak. In Siantar city, where there are few Simalungun Batak Roman Catholics, all four party leaders were North Tapanuli Bataks. Partai Katholik's two representatives in the regency legislature (the party had no representatives in the Siantar body) were Simalungun Bataks.

Nahdatul Ulama's leadership at the village level in the regency (NU had no subdistrict branches) was predominantly Simalungun Batak. Of 37 party ranting, Simalungun Bataks were a majority on the leadership council and held the chairmanship of 29, with Javanese dominant in seven, and one South Tapanuli Batak chairman in a village in Bandar. The regency-wide party leadership council included five Simalungun Bataks and one Javanese (the party treasurer). In Siantar city NU's seven ranting were each led by a chairman and a secretary. Of the fourteen leaders six were Simalungun Bataks, five were Coastal Malays, and three were South Tapanuli Bataks. The city-wide leadership included seven Coastal Malays (who held most of the important offices), two Simalungun Bataks, two Javanese, and one South Tapanuli Batak. NU's two legislative representatives in the regency were both Simalungun Bataks; the party's Siantar delegation included one Simalungun Batak and one South Tapanuli Batak (who did not use his clan name and preferred to be considered a Coastal Malay).

For Masjumi, firm data were available for only the regency/municipality level leadership. In Simalungun four of the five members of Masjumi's leadership council prior to 1960 were South Tapanuli Bataks, while one was a Coastal Malay. In Siantar all Masjumi leaders were South Tapanuli Bataks. According to information from party leaders, the great majority of sub-district and village level Masjumi leaders were also South Tapanuli Bataks. In the first Simalungun legislature, inaugurated in 1956, Masjumi's delegation consisted of three South Tapanuli Bataks, one Simalungun Batak and one Javanese; its six Siantar representatives were all South Tapanuli Bataks. As a banned party, Masjumi had no representation in the regional legislatures in 1964.

The Integrative Revolution in Patterns of Partisan Support

From the available data on the 1955 elections, and from lists of party members and leaders, a fairly clear picture of similarities and differences among the parties emerges. The most important distinction is between the secular parties—PNI and PKI—which did in fact obtain the support of individuals of a variety of ethnic and religious backgrounds, and the religious parties—Parkindo, Masjumi, and to a lesser degree Partai Katholik and NU—which were restricted not only to particular religious groups but also to particular ethnic communities. In these patterns of partisan support three factors, earlier identified as principal dimensions of the integrative revolution in the region, stand out as the most critical determinants of party choice: ethnicity, religious affiliation, and the impact of the plantation environment. A fourth factor, Indonesian nationalism, seems also to have played an independent role of some importance.

Among the South Tapanuli supporters of Masjumi and the North Tapanuli supporters of Parkindo the first two variables were so completely intertwined that it is impossible to assign them separate weights. For many South and North Tapanuli Bataks ethnicity, religion, and partisan affiliation were coterminous. Each party thus represented both an ethnic and a religious community.

In contrast to Masjumi and Parkindo, data on the two smaller religious parties indicate at least a partial separation of the religious and ethnic variables. Partai Katholik, the party of a small religious minority, included both North Tapanuli and Simalungun Bataks in its membership. Like Parkindo and Masjumi, however, it also became to a significant extent the representative of an ethnic segment (Simalungun Bataks in the regency, North Tapanuli Bataks in the city) within the larger religious community. For the dominant groups in the party branches, ethnic and religious interests were fused. NU, on the other hand, represented not a religious minority within Islam but rather two distinct ethnic minorities (Simalungun Batak Muslims, themselves a minority within their ethnic group, and Coastal Malays) who happen to be Muslim. In the distinction between Masjumi and NU the importance of the ethnic variable was considerable, although it tended to be sharper at the leadership level (where NU's leaders were nearly all Simalungun Bataks and Coastal Malays and Masjumi's leaders were nearly all South Tapanuli Bataks) than among the party members and supporters (both parties had Javanese electoral support and Javanese members, and Masjumi also obtained votes from Simalungun Batak Muslims).

The transformation of the religious parties into ethnoreligious parties was not the intention of the party leaders, especially at the national and provincial levels. Even within Simalungun/Siantar, prominent party leaders resisted the tendency toward ethnic exclusiveness. Parkindo, for example, attempted to encompass within itself all of the Protestants of the region, including North Tapanuli Bataks, Simalungun Bataks, and the small group of Karo Batak Christians in Siantar and subdistrict Silimakuta. The leadership councils of Parkindo included representatives of all three groups. It was evident, however, that the party in the region (and in North Sumatra as a whole) was largely controlled by North Tapanuli Bataks. The Karo Bataks in Siantar (but not in Silimakuta, where the pull of PNI has been greater) were willing to accept the political leadership of Parkindo, which appointed a leading member of their group to the regional legislature. The Simalungun Bataks, however, have continued to distrust the North Tapanuli Bataks who took over their rice fields in the early decades of the century and rose to positions of prominence under both Dutch and Republican rule. Simalungun Batak church leaders and ministers (who were until 1963 affiliated with the North Tapanuli-dominated HKBP church) admitted to having spoken a good word or two for Parkindo during the election campaign and still claimed to be sympathetic to the party. Their sympathy did not extend to a willingness to provide a nucleus for Parkindo organization in their districts, however, and was outweighed by their bitter criticism of North Tapanuli Batak control of the party. Lay leaders and ordinary members of the Simalungun church were even more outspoken in their opposition to Parkindo.

Like Parkindo and the Protestants, Masjumi hoped to appeal to all Muslims in Simalungun/Siantar. With few exceptions, however, its leaders were of South Tapanuli origin. When the national NU organization broke with Masjumi in 1952, a number of Simalungun Batak Muslims (several of whom had participated in the Dutch-sponsored State of East Sumatra in the late 1940s and had close ties with the radja of Lower Simalungun) and some Coastal Malays, politically ambitious but feeling themselves blocked by South Tapanuli dominance of Masjumi, turned to NU to provide them with positions of leadership. As a result, the difference between Masjumi and NU in the region was largely an ethnic one (with pro- versus anti-Revolution overtones) and bore little relation to the modern versus traditional-syncretist split, which provided the bases of support for the two parties in Java.

In contrast to the religious parties, PNI and PKI were heavily dependent on the support of plantation workers and squatters, who saw in the secular parties a concern for their interests and welfare. PNI's partisans, however, were more widely distributed throughout the regency and municipality and were more diverse in social origins, ethnic group affiliations, and educational and occupational backgrounds than were those of PKI. There are several reasons for the disparity between PNI and PKI support. Of central importance was the unique identification of PNI with the nationalist movement and the struggle against the Dutch. The party was able to gain many supporters, irrespective of direct material interests, among those sympathetic to the goals of the Revolution. Although PKI guerrilla units also fought in the Revolution, the party did not share the special position of vanguard of the nationalist movement generally accorded to PNI. Moreover, PKI's nationalist credentials were considerably discredited by its role in the Madiun Affair of 1948, an event widely known in Simalungun/ Siantar among those involved in the Revolution.

PNI's identification with nationalism and with the figure of Sukarno also gave it an air of legitimate authority, of being the inheritor of Dutch power, which attracted many members of the local Western-educated social and governmental elite—and those who looked to the elite for political leadership—particularly during the early postrevolutionary years. PKI, as the chief opponent of the newly established order, had no significant support among this elite.

PNI was also the beneficiary of a certain amount of support based primarily on ethnic loyalties. Because of the prominent position of locally influential Javanese in the party leadership, PNI became identified, especially in Siantar city but also in the regency, as the party of the abangan Javanese. Similarly, in Upper Simalungun PNI had the exclusive support of those Simalungun Bataks who opposed the traditional aristocracy on revolutionary grounds but were in favor of a more influential role for their ethnic group in regency political life. PKI had no comparable ethnic-related appeal in any part of Simalungun or Siantar.

Finally, the association of communism with atheism, a frequent theme in religious party (and PNI) propaganda, severely hampered PKI's electoral campaign in 1954–55, and its growth thereafter. Among those individuals who were neither plantation workers nor squatters, for whom the party's strategy had little appeal in any event, the stamp of atheism provided an additional deterrent to PKI support. Even among North Tapanuli Batak plantation squatters who were members of PKI's farmers' organization, there were reportedly many defections to Parkindo and even to PNI. Such defections were apparently less common among Christian PNI organization members, who were not as heavily cross-pressured by religious loyalties and economic interests. Neither inside nor outside the plantation regions was the tarbrush of atheism effectively applied to PNI.

The impact of ethnic and religious loyalties on patterns of partisan support was perhaps most marked in the municipality of Siantar. Thrown into close association with a wide variety of individuals of varying ethnic and religious groups, the resident of Siantar identified strongly with his own community. Politically, he supported the party that most closely represented communal interests—Parkindo for the North Tapanuli Protestants, Masjumi for the South Tapanuli santri, PNI for the abangan Javanese. Parties which had no ethnic or religious base and which attempted to cut across communal lines on the basis of socioeconomic interests, such as PKI, were notably unsuccessful in Siantar. The effect of urbanization has thus been a politicization of ethnic loyalties rather than, as in Lower Simalungun, a shift toward economic interests as the basis of partisan choice.

Beyond the specific findings concerning the relationship between the cleavages of the local environment and the development of patterns of partisan support, at least three other generalizations are suggested by the data presented above. First, I would suggest that the patterns of partisan support that emerged in the region were, given the nature of local loyalties and cleavages, an inevitable outcome of a situation of open partisan competition such as existed in Indonesia in the 1950s (and a restoration of which continued to be hoped for in the early 1960s). The successes of the four national parties in obtaining—and to a considerable extent maintaining—

local support meant that they had made themselves meaningful to substantial segments of the local population.

Second, it seems apparent that there has been a general shift in political orientation from an essentially passive to a more active conception of the proper role of the individual in political life. At the turn of the century and for some time thereafter partisan political activity as a means of influencing the decisions of those in authority or of determining the personnel of government was unknown to the people of Simalungun/Siantar, who viewed the roles of the traditional rulers and the Dutch as immutable and not amenable to popular influence. In the postrevolutionary period, particularly during the early 1950s, the popular response generated by the efforts of the political parties to obtain support in the region attests to the ubiquitousness of a new sense of political efficacy, a sense that men might, by their own actions and through organizations representative of their interests, affect the choice of their governors and the outcomes of governmental decision-making processes.

Finally, there has also been a shift in political orientations in recent decades from a highly parochial to a more national focus. Whereas fifty years ago the effective political community, as perceived by the ordinary villager, was the village or traditional kingdom, in the 1950s and early 1960s the sense of belonging to a much more inclusive political unit, the Republic of Indonesia, was widespread. This shift is reflected in the extensive support given to national political parties in the 1955 elections and in the continuing ability of the parties to retain the support of their followers in the postelection period.[8] The fact that the most successful parties in the region were nationally prominent parties implied a heightened sense of individual involvement in an Indonesian rather than a village or regional political process, albeit mediated through group affiliations of primarily local origin.

8. This is not to argue that there were no differences among the parties in terms of firmness of partisan support. For a discussion of this problem see Chapter 4.

4. PARTY LEADERSHIP: RECRUITMENT AND LINKAGE

The contributions that party systems in the new states can make to the closing of the elite–mass gap and to the bridging of primordial and other kinds of "horizontal" cleavages are dependent to a significant extent on the characteristics of party leadership. Parties in which the leaders are remote from their constituencies and in which internal party decision-making is exclusively a game of the elite can be of little assistance in overcoming the obstacles to effective integration. If, on the other hand, decision-making within the parties includes ordinary members as well as leaders and takes account of the interests of whatever social groups are present within the party, the party system is likely to play a more positive integrative role.

Within Simalungun/Siantar, the integrative potential of the individual parties was limited by the fact that several party branches were closely tied to the interests of a single ethnic group. Where only one ethnic group was represented in the party and affiliated organization leadership (as was the case for Parkindo, Masjumi, and Partai Katholik in Siantar and for NU in Simalungun), the party could not serve as a structure within which conflicts based on local ethnic cleavages might be resolved. At best, it might provide a means by which subethnic loyalties, in particular those to clan and region of origin, could be represented in the political arena. Where one ethnic group was numerically superior but not absolutely dominant in party leadership councils (as was the case for Parkindo, Masjumi, and Partai Katholik in Simalungun and for NU in Siantar), integrative potential was slightly higher; but only in PNI, with its broadly based multiethnic leadership and membership, might this potential have been fully realized. PKI, because of its almost total dependence on plantation workers and squatters, was more limited in its integrative potential than PNI. In general, given the relationship between the parties and the local environment, only at the level of interparty relationships within meaningful regional legislatures might it have been possible for the party system to ameliorate local ethnic-based differences and conflicts. And, as we have seen, the parties were never really given the opportunity to make the local legislatures effective structures of decision-making in the region.

Integration of horizontal groups in the political process of a new state is dependent, however, not only on the capacity of local party systems to bridge local cleavages but also on the capacity of the parties to bring local interests into the national political arena. All of the parties under discussion were, after all, multi-ethnic, multi-interest organizations at the national level. Even the Siantar branches of Masjumi and Parkindo, whose leaders were with almost no exceptions South and North Tapanuli Bataks respectively, provided structures through which the interests of these groups could be represented in multi-ethnic national party councils and in the decision-making processes of the central government. Whether or not these interests were in fact represented depended upon the extent of the elite–mass gap within the parties and the responsiveness of the various levels of leaders to the wishes and demands of their members (and also, of course, on whether or not the parties played an important role in the national political process).

Within the framework of this study it is not possible to describe leadership characteristics and to trace out leader–follower and leader–leader relationships in the various parties from the village to the national level. It is possible, however, to examine in some detail patterns of leadership recruitment, relationships between leaders and followers, and the nature of intraparty decision-making for each of the parties in the regency and municipality and to assess the strengths and weaknesses of each local party branch in terms of its contribution to an amelioration of horizontal cleavages (both locally and more broadly within the national party system and political process) and to the establishment of regular channels of communication between elite and mass.

The Secular Parties

Most of the leaders of PNI and PKI and their affiliates, especially at the regency/municipality but also at the subdistrict level, were professional politicians who owed their stature in the community and their level of income to the positions they had achieved in the party hierarchy. They came from humble backgrounds, the Javanese as sons of plantation workers or themselves former plantation workers, the North Tapanuli Bataks as migrant farmers or sons of migrants, the South Tapanuli Bataks from a petty trader or religious teacher origin, and the Simalungun Bataks from nonaristocratic peasant families. The level of formal education they had achieved was low, although higher than for the population as a whole. In the early 1950s men with higher education and independent standing in the community (doctors, teachers, civil servants) formed a higher percentage of PNI (but not PKI) leadership; by 1955 most of these individuals had left the party's leadership councils, as they were not willing to compete in the rough-and-tumble world of PNI politics and had little in common with the radical nationalistic spirit of the more militant revolutionaries.

The older generation of secular party leaders, age forty or over, were in fact almost all former revolutionaries, active participants in the struggle for independence against the Dutch. The Revolution was a critical turning point in their lives, for this was when they joined the party and became imbued with the nationalist idea or the vision of a communist society. Originally inspired by revolutionary zeal, they came to view partisan political activity in the postindependence period as a channel for personal advancement as well as a means of reaffirming their commitment to the values of their youth. Few of them were much concerned with questions of ideology; the older PNI leaders viewed their party much more in nationalist than in Marhaenist terms, and the PKI leaders' image of communism did not seem to extend beyond a vaguely defined utopia of prosperity, equality, and social harmony. Both groups were uncomfortable when discussing party ideology; their lives clearly revolved around the immediate concerns of the local organization and they were content to leave more fundamental problems to the higher leadership.

The youthful party and organization leaders were the major exception to this general pattern, as they were of the postrevolutionary generation.

These individuals were aspiring professional politicians who consciously chose political careers in preference to other possible channels of personal advancement. Particularly among those unable to continue their education beyond elementary or junior high school and thus enter the bureaucracy or officers' corps of the armed services, party politics was seen as an attractive career which offered an escape from the anonymity of the rural *desa* or urban *kampung*. Alternative careers, for example as private entrepreneurs, seemed to offer less hope of success and were somewhat tainted in an ideological environment which excoriated capitalism as *exploitation de l'homme par l'homme* (Sukarno's phrase).[1] Moveover, partisan political activity satisfied a desire to contribute to nation-building, to follow in the footsteps of the revolutionary generation that had preceded them.

For PNI it is possible to distinguish three main subtypes of leaders according to the personal styles they adopted in their quest for party office: organizational activists, administrators, and old revolutionaries. Particularly in the regency party, it was the organizational activist who was most successful. In the early 1950s a number of individuals, mostly Javanese, rose rapidly to positions of prominence within the party as a result of their organizational efforts among the plantation workers and squatters. Their strategy was to build what party leaders call a "basis," i.e. a substantial and loyal personal following, among lower-level leaders and rank-and-file members whom they had recruited primarily into the labor and farmer organizations but also into the party itself. These bases were mostly located in Lower Simalungun and were heavily Javanese in membership.

The chairman of PNI in Simalungun, Umbar Subroto, was representative of the organizational activists. Subroto, a Javanese, was born in 1917 into a peasant family. After receiving five years of elementary education and two

---

1. Alternatives have varied of course from group to group: for the Javanese, who have had little opportunity for education, little interest in religious careers, and few commercial or entrepreneurial connections, politics has been most attractive; among the North Tapanuli Bataks, education has been more widespread and entrepreneurship more highly valued, and fewer young men have sought political careers; among the Simalungun Bataks, the church and its school system have offered the most highly valued path to personal advancement, followed by careers in the civil service; and finally, careers in commerce or religious education have been attractive and generally available to South Tapanuli Bataks.

years of teacher training, Subroto left Java in 1942 and came to Simalungun, where he joined PNI in 1945 and became a well-known guerrilla leader in Lower Simalungun. In 1950 he was elected to the PNI Branch Leadership Council in Simalungun and in 1953 led the organizational efforts of the party's farmer and labor organizations in Lower Simalungun. In 1959 he became the third highest ranking official in the regency party and in 1961 was elected chairman.

Subroto was a Muslim, but of the abangan variety, and had little interest either in Islam or in traditional Javanese culture. As a party leader he was most at home in planning membership drives and cultivating the support of subdistrict and village leaders. Neither an ideologue nor a polished speaker, he was uneasy before large crowds and tended to leave detailed explanations of Marhaenism to others. His ambition was to follow in the footsteps of his predecessor and become the North Sumatran provincial chairman. To build and maintain support for his position as party and gerakan massa leader, Subroto leaned heavily on the Javanese subdistrict and village leaders in Lower Simalungun and on his personal following on the plantations. Other party leaders (both friends and opponents) greatly respected his influence among the Javanese population of the regency. A few other Javanese leaders in the regency party had similar bases of support, but these were much smaller numerically and territorially than Subroto's, usually restricted to a few villages, plantation workers' local unions, or at most a subdistrict. Their careers were closely tied to Subroto's.

In Siantar city the PNI organizational activists were North Tapanuli Bataks who began to exert influence in the youth organization Pemuda Marhaenis around 1960 and the PNI motor workers' union in 1963. The chairman of Pemuda Marhaenis and first vice-chairman of PNI in Siantar, H. W. D. Tampubolon, was representative of this group. In 1960, Tampubolon returned to Siantar after six years in Medan, Djambi, and Djakarta (where he had attended PNI cadre courses and become an official of the Djakarta branch of Pemuda Marhaenis). After securing his control over the organization in Siantar, Tampubolon gradually expanded his influence over the party ranting in the North Tapanuli Batak wards of the city, which he was instrumental in reorganizing. In 1961 he became a member of the municipal legislature, representing the youth functional group, and in 1963 he was elected first vice-chairman of the party.

In late 1962 another North Tapanuli Batak, Paul Siringo-ringo, emerged to prominence in the city party by spearheading the newly formed motor workers' union, KBKB. The son of a plantation foreman in Karo, he had attended elementary school in Karo and a Muhammadijah teachers' training school in South Tapanuli. During the 1930s Siringo-ringo lived in Karo, where he was most active in church affairs, and in 1945 he joined the Karo-based PNI guerrilla group called Napindo Halilintar. In 1951 he moved to Siantar where, with help from Karo Bataks prominent in the city's numerous bus companies, he acquired a few buses and became a moderately successful businessman. In 1961 he became a member of the regency legislature (representing PNI) and in the same year was elected treasurer of the Siantar PNI chapter (largely because of his financial contributions to the party). The growth of the PNI bus union in the city was due primarily to Siringo-ringo's efforts, and its leadership consisted mostly of individuals personally loyal to him. Siringo-ringo was also active in the party ranting in Sukadame and Tomuan, and in 1963 he was elected chairman of PNI in Siantar.

The second subtype of PNI leader, the administrator, had more limited but still substantial success in the party. The administrator's strategy was one of nonparticipation in factional conflicts and strict devotion to party duty, comparable perhaps to the role of the nonpolitical civil servant exemplified by the British bureaucrat. When combined with an aptitude for record-keeping, financial management, and general administrative work, this strategy produced second-rank leaders who rose in party office despite changes in the chairmanship and their lack of a basis. A few North Tapanuli Bataks in the regency and municipality parties and rather more South Tapanuli Bataks were representative of this type. (There were relatively few South Tapanuli Batak PNI members in the regency, and they were not as heavily concentrated in particular subbranches, so that an aspirant South Tapanuli Batak politician found it difficult to build a basis of his own in the PNI.)

The most successful of the administrators was Zainuddin Hasan, chairman of PNI in Siantar until 1963. The son of a moderately well-to-do South Tapanuli Batak trader, Hasan was educated in Siantar and Bandung (HIS and MULO).[2] In 1945 he joined PNI and during the Revolution he was a guerrilla leader in Simalungun and a party propagandist in Atjeh, Tapanuli, and West Sumatra. With only a small basis among the Muslim Bataks in Siantar, Hasan rose in the party hierarchy as a propagandist and administrator under the wing of Abdullah Jusuf (then regency PNI chairman, in 1964 North Sumatran chairman), who selected him to organize the Siantar branch when it was established in 1957. For the next five years Hasan led the party without substantial opposition, devoting most of his time to the affairs of city government.

The third subtype of party leader, the old revolutionary, was the least successful in winning high party office. The lack of success of the men in this group stemmed from their inability or unwillingness to expand the base of support they had acquired during the Revolution. Unlike the organizational activists or the administrators, the old revolutionaries were often part-time politicians, devoting most of their time to commercial activity or regular employment as schoolteachers or civil servants. Typical of the old revolutionaries were the North Tapanuli Batak subbranch chairmen in Lower Simalungun and the Road to Parapat who built the party organization in their subdistricts during and immediately after the Revolution. As indicated earlier, the development of party affiliates, carried out by cadres under the direction of the regency leadership, served to undermine the local authority of the old revolutionaries, who as a result commanded the direct allegiance of only a part of their membership. In some areas, in fact, their continuance in office rested on the sufferance of the regency party chairman, Subroto.

The most prominent Simalungun Batak PNI leader in the regency, Aloysius Djulan Purba, was in most respects an old revolutionary. Purba was born in Tapanuli around 1920 into a Simalungun Batak Christian, non-aristocratic family and was raised in Upper Simalungun and Siantar, where he received most of his formal education (five years of elementary school). After the Revolution he attended a MULO school in Djakarta and junior high school in Siantar, but did not graduate. At TALA PETA during the Japanese occupation, Purba subsequently joined PNI and was a leader of

2. HIS: Dutch-Native School, a seven-year elementary school; MULO: More Extended Lower Education, a continuation of the HIS.

Barisan Harimau Liar in Upper Simalungun during the Revolution. Although he had lived most of his adult life in Siantar, he considered Haranggaol in subdistrict Purba his home and had his base of support within the party in the subdistrict branches of Upper Simalungun. He had no ties with any of the party affiliates. In the late 1950s he was a member of BAPOST (Badan Penuntut Otonom Sumatera Timur, Body to Demand East Sumatran Autonomy), a nonparty organization of the indigenous peoples of East Sumatra (Simalungun Bataks, Karo Bataks, and Coastal Malays) which demanded the separation of East Sumatra from Tapanuli. From 1959 to 1961 Purba was second secretary of the PNI Branch Leadership Council and after 1961 was a member of the regency legislature, representing the Veterans' Legion, of which he was chairman for a time. Purba differed from the North Tapanuli Batak old revolutionaries in that he actively sought higher party office, challenging rather than accepting the dominant role of the organizational activists. His local prestige and chances for financial success were also more closely tied to the party, as he had no regular employment beyond his membership in the legislature.

Leadership styles in PKI are not strictly comparable to those of PNI, as advancement within the Communist Party was unrelated to periodic elections and the building of personal bases. Moreover, there was a fairly strict separation between party and subsidiary organization leadership; at least within Simalungun/Siantar, success in a party affiliate did not normally lead to a position in the party itself.

After the reorganization of the party in the early 1950s (there were at that time two groups calling themselves PKI) PKI leadership in Simalungun and Siantar was relatively stable. In the regency only two individuals had held the post of first secretary since 1952, and one man had led the party in Siantar since its separation from the regency branch in 1957. Like most of the PNI leaders, those individuals prominent in PKI in 1963–64 were of the revolutionary generation and were full-time politicians. They were not organizational activists, however, and seemed to have little connection with the leaders of the party affiliates, who were more closely directed from Medan and Djakarta. On the basis of interviews with PKI leaders and observation of their activities, it seems apparent that their selection as leaders was designed to provide a certain image of the party to non-Communists and potential PKI supporters—an image of devotion to the nationalist ideals of the Revolution and of moderation in politics, religion, and personal style of life. (Sumatrans were also given preference over Javanese, presumably because PKI was generally regarded by Sumatrans as Javanese dominated.) The party organization was thus primarily a façade intended to provide respectability; the real work of PKI in the region was performed by the affiliated organizations.

The first secretaries of PKI in Siantar and Simalungun, K. Sitanggang and Abel Tampubolon, both North Tapanuli Bataks, exemplified the spirit of moderation. Sitanggang was born in Tapanuli in 1916, the son of a teacher in a missionary school, and received his formal education (HIS, MULO) in Medan. In 1936 he moved to Siantar, where he worked as a teacher and became a member of Indonesia Muda, the nationalist youth organization. During the Revolution he was active in the Indonesian Socialist Party (PSI) and a variety of guerrilla groups, and he fled to Tapanuli when the Dutch occupied Simalungun. He claimed not to have joined PKI until 1951; in that year he was also selected as PKI first secretary for Simalungun/Siantar, giving up this post the following year. In 1957, with the formation of a PKI section in Siantar city, Sitanggang became its first secretary.

Tampubolon, the son of a lay leader in the Batak Protestant Church, was born in Tapanuli in 1905 and educated (five years elementary school) at a mission school in Siantar. In the 1930s he was employed as a chauffeur on a plantation in subdistrict Tanah Djawa and he was active in the nationalist movement there. In 1946 Tampubolon joined PKI because, he said, it was a "movement that would help the people." From 1950 to 1959 he was PKI first secretary in Tanah Djawa, and in the latter year he became first secretary of PKI in Simalungun.

Both Sitanggang and Tampubolon were Christians but by their own admission only infrequently attended church. Examination of their speeches in the regency and city legislatures, and conversations with them and with others about them, revealed little evidence of political fanaticism. Both men lived simply but comfortably (Sitanggang in a government-provided house) and were continually concerned to demonstrate that their leadership of the party did not make them different from other members of the community or the local political elite. Like other Communists, however, they were for the most part rejected by members of their ethnic group, who were suspicious of the hidden motives behind attendance at church services or even at adat functions. They were also kept at arm's length by non-Communist politicians and government officials, who saw them not so much as individuals and members of a common political elite, but as automatons who carried out to the letter instructions from their party superiors. At the same time they were not regarded as "true" Communists, i.e. committed ideologues, but rather as men who used the party for personal career reasons and were in turn used by the party to promote its current goals in the region. Several experienced non-Communist politicians were of the opinion that in the event of a Communist takeover in Indonesia, Sitanggang, Tampubolon, and other local PKI leaders would quickly be "retooled" (a euphemism for demotion or dismissal).

The labor, farmer, and youth organization leaders were the organizational activists of PKI in Simalungun/Siantar. In contrast to the moderation and *embourgeoisement* of the party leadership, the leaders of the affiliated organizations were more rigidly ideological and proletarian in their style of life. Like the party leaders they had often lived most of their lives in Simalungun, but many were cadres imported from Medan or other plantation areas in East Sumatra. Taat Pohan, until 1963 chairman of SOBSI, PKI's labor federation, in Simalungun, and K. Silitonga, chairman of BTI, the farmers' organization, in Simalungun, were representative of PKI's organizational activists.

Pohan, a South Tapanuli Batak born in 1923 in East Sumatra, was the son of a plantation clerk. After graduation from a trade school in Tebingtinggi in the late 1930s, he worked as a plantation clerk in the regency of Asahan, East Sumatra, and in 1945 joined the nonparty youth organization Pesindo and the SOBSI plantation affiliate. After the Revolution he was first a cadre and then chairman of SOBSI in Asahan. In 1956 he was sent by the SOBSI provincial leadership to Simalungun, where he was assigned the task of reactivating the local organization (during the election campaign, some leaders, mostly at the ranting level, had formed an alternative organization which offered candidates of its own rather than supporting the PKI). In 1961 Pohan led the SOBSI strike against government-owned plantations in Simalungun, for which he and other SOBSI leaders (over 200 in all) were briefly imprisoned by the military. In 1963 Pohan left Simalungun to become second vice chairman of the provincial SOBSI leadership council; during the period of this study he frequently returned to Siantar and apparently continued to be closely connected with the day-to-day conduct of the organization's affairs.

Silitonga, a North Tapanuli Batak, was born in Pane Tongah in 1920 and, like Pohan, had a trade school education. His exposure to PKI began in 1945 when he joined the Communist-led guerrilla organization Barisan Merah. In 1950 he became a BTI cadre in Tanah Djawa, then chairman of BTI in the subdistrict, and finally in 1958 chairman of BTI in Simalungun, replacing an open PKI member who had been transferred by the provincial BTI leadership to Tapanuli.

Like all other SOBSI and BTI leaders interviewed, Pohan and Silitonga denied affiliation with any political party. Their public statements, the resolutions they framed, and the vocabulary they used to describe Indonesia's and Simalungun's current problems, however, indicated a greater degree of facility with Marxist terminology and categories than that of the party leaders. In contrast to Sitanggang and Tampubolon, neither Pohan nor Silitonga was a "public man," appearing frequently before non-Communist audiences or spending time in idle conversation with other politicians in the offices of local government. When in Siantar, Pohan was most often in the SOBSI office, reading reports and discussing organizational affairs; Silitonga spent much of his time making the rounds of BTI ranting on the plantations. Like the leaders of the PNI affiliates, they were most at home in their role as activists and organizers.

In the final analysis, it is the similarities rather than the differences between the PNI and PKI leaders that are most striking. Despite differences in partisan affiliation and ideological orientation, their careers and even their political views were remarkably similar. Almost all of them had some formal education (though not enough to prepare them for careers as civil servants or licensed schoolteachers) and some exposure to various parts of Sumatra or beyond. Often in interviews they spontaneously referred to personal ignominies they had suffered at the hands of the Dutch (in contrast to the leaders of the religious parties—Parkindo, Partai Katholik, and NU in particular—who almost never mentioned such experiences). Although several of them had spent at least part of their student years in religious schools, none were religious leaders in their communities. Nearly all of them had eagerly joined revolutionary guerrilla organizations as soon as they were formed, and many had been guerrilla leaders.

The PNI and PKI leaders also shared a common attitude toward the role of political leadership and organization in revolutionary and postrevolutionary Indonesia. They strongly believed that ethnic and religious differences were irrelevant to the problems of a modern—or modernizing—society, and they had little use for the traditional and religious leadership of the region. This attitude was of course particularly strong among the abangan Javanese leaders, few of whom had any interest in Islam as a religion, let alone as a basis for political organization, but it was also characteristic of the North Tapanuli Bataks and members of other ethnic groups who became PNI and PKI leaders. If Indonesia were to be radically transformed, they argued, religious and traditional leaders and institutions would have to give way to a political organization that could win the support of all the Indonesian people, regardless of religion or ethnicity.

What they meant by a radical transformation they could define in terms of ultimate goals—general prosperity, social justice, an end to economic exploitation, the creation of a unified nation—but only vaguely in terms of specific means. During the Revolution the means had seemed clear enough—victory over the Dutch would more or less automatically usher in a new world. In the 1950s and 1960s the complexities of nation-building and their roles as activists and implementers rather than as policy-makers led them to accept the simple notion that party victory was the key means toward the realization of the new Indonesia. The specific content of party policy and ideology, which in any event they played no part in formulating, could thus be safely left to others.

Their memories of why they had joined one guerrilla group rather than another were often cloudy, but when probed the common responses were that "the group was the only one in my area," or " I followed the advice of a friend." Aside from their preference for secular as opposed to religious political organization, therefore, their initial choice seems to have been largely accidental, that is, unrelated to party ideologies.

Once having joined a guerrilla organization and having discovered the channels for upward mobility provided by its affiliation with a political party, the PNI and PKI leaders tended to stick with their original choice.

The longer they remained within the party and the more successful they were in achieving their personal political ambitions, the firmer their tie to the party became. Ideological commitment, the Marhaenization and communization of the leaders, came both chronologically and in order of importance after the establishment of their initial loyalty to the party as an organization which provided them with a channel of upward mobility. (Courses in ideology were a specific feature of leadership training in PKI; more diffuse indoctrination, including speeches by higher party leaders, reading of party pamphlets, and so forth, was more characteristic of PNI).

In sum, the leaders of PNI and PKI in Simalungun/Siantar in 1963–64 represented a single political elite. In their lack of higher education, their revolutionary militancy, their opposition to traditional and religious political leadership and organizations, and in their status as professional politicians they were a unique group. What distinguished the leaders of the one party from those of the other was not so much ideological commitment as it was organizational loyalty.

So far in this chapter I have been discussing the active, professional PNI and PKI politicians found primarily at the regency/municipality and to some extent at the subdistrict levels. There is another group of leaders, however, numerically far larger than the above. These are the village level leaders who provided the link between the membership and the professional politicians. PKI local leaders (actually at the subdistrict rather than the village level) shared with their superiors in Siantar a career orientation (although many of them had full-time employment outside the party) and a hope for future status through positions of party leadership. Because of the careful screening of potential party members and leaders and the intensive ideological indoctrination, they were consistently and unequivocally loyal to the party.

Many PNI village leaders were also thoroughly committed to their party, although they did not normally share the career orientation of the higher-level leaders. In Lower Simalungun this loyalty was based on the almost family-like relationship which had developed during the Revolution (particularly among the Javanese) between guerrilla leaders at the regency and subdistrict levels and those in the villages, and more broadly on the identification of the party with Indonesian nationalism. In the early 1960s personal ties continued to be assiduously cultivated, both among the older village leaders and the emerging postrevolutionary leadership generation, alongside the more publicly stressed appeals to the socioeconomic interests and nationalist commitments of the villagers. In Siantar city, the high status of a Javanese schoolteacher and prominent PNI leader was primarily responsible for the party's support in the Javanese wards, and a similar pattern of support explains the loyalty of the smaller group of South Tapanuli Bataks.

In Upper Simalungun and among the nonsquatter North Tapanuli Bataks in the small towns of Lower Simalungun and along the Road to Parapat, PNI support depended neither on personalities nor on appeals to material interests, but rather on disaffection from the locally dominant social and political elites. Those Simalungun Bataks, to some extent nationalistically inclined, who opposed both traditional authority and the dominance of the church in village life found a congenial home in PNI and saw their leaders rise to regency-level office in the party. Similarly, many North Tapanuli Bataks with a measure of secular Western education and occupational status not dependent on the HKBP church and church-school hierarchies (e.g. public school teachers, government officials, some private entrepreneurs) tended to resent the pervasive influence of the HKBP and Parkindo. These individuals and their almost entirely town-based followings chose to affiliate politically with PNI, a powerful alternative hierarchy which provided them with organizational backing in their opposition to the local religious leadership and at the same time did not involve a total rejection of community values. Neither of these leadership groups was attracted to the Communist Party in any significant numbers, since an acceptance of PKI ideology would have placed them, if not totally beyond the pale, at least in an extremely tenuous position within their respective communities.

At least some PNI village leaders, however, exhibited only weak commitments to the party. This was particularly apparent in Siantar city, where a number of North Tapanuli Batak ward heads joined the party and became its ranting leaders in the late 1950s and early 1960s as PNI gained ascendancy in municipal government. Local PNI leadership positions served to strengthen their hand in dealing with the PNI mayor and vice chairman of the municipal legislature. These leaders were quite capable of shifting with the political winds, as several of them did in 1964 when they wrote letters of support for a non-PNI mayoralty candidate actively and indeed passion‐ ately opposed by the branch party leadership.

In contrast to the party leadership, village-level subsidiary organization leaders were frequently only loosely connected with and intermittently loyal to the party. Their primary orientation was to their village, and they affili‐ ated with an organization in order to further specific village interests or to enhance their own political influence among their followers within the vil‐ lage. Thus a village irrigation committee might become affiliated with PNI or PKI because these parties had influence with the government or provided protection if the villagers decided to expand their rice fields illegally at the expense of the local plantation. Similarly, a plantation worker influential among his fellow workers might join the PNI or PKI union in order to gain the necessary political resources to make demands upon the plantation ad‐ ministration and simultaneously to solidify his own local power by meeting the expectations of his followers. If the party was unable to meet their de‐ mands these leaders were likely to seek support elsewhere. In the most extreme case related by informants, a local leader in Tanah Djawa who had a substantial following among bus company workers had been in and out of PSI, Masjumi, and PKI labor unions before he joined PNI in 1964. PNI and PKI were of course aware of the tenuous loyalties of village-level lead‐ ers and their followers and paid considerable attention to ideological indoc‐ trination and to the placing of regular party cadres in key positions on local leadership councils. These efforts met with such limited success, how‐ ever, that the fragility of loyalties among village level worker-squatter leaders continued throughout the early 1960s to be the major weakness of the secular parties in Lower Simalungun.[3]

3. Some important evidence for this assertion is provided by the emergence in late 1962 of a new labor organization, SOKSI (Sentral Organisasi Karyawan Sosialis Indonesia, Central Organization of Socialist Functionaries of Indonesia), established by the military (with support from plantation administrators) primarily for the purpose of reducing PKI influence. At least in part through a policy of providing gifts of clothing and other commodities to potential leaders and members combined with threats of transfer to less attractive employment, SOKSI succeeded in a very short time in becoming one of the largest labor organizations in Simalungun. Both PNI and PKI labor federations were substantially weakened by the develop‐ ment of SOKSI.

The Religious Parties

The leaders of the religious parties at the regency/municipality and sub-district levels were neither organizational activists nor administrators, nor even, in many cases, old revolutionaries. Since these parties were not oriented toward the development of a mass base tied to the organization by the services it performed, the skills of the activists were not in demand. Similarly, since party organization was minimal, with no party headquarters other than the home of the chairman, few formal meetings of either leaders or the general membership, and almost no activities for which funds had to be obtained or distributed, the religious parties required little in the way of administration.

The leaders of the religious parties in Simalungun/Siantar were essentially the political spokesmen of religious and ethnic communities. They were men of independent stature and modern education and employment who had been active in the affairs of the church or religious organizations before they became politically active. Their acceptance of positions of party leadership had the effect both of legitimizing the party as the principal articulator of community interests and of establishing their status more firmly within the larger intracommunity elite while requiring, in the absence of elections, only minimal levels of political activity.

One of the most striking differences between the secular and religious parties was the latter's almost complete lack of youthful leadership. While the secular parties had many cadres of the postrevolutionary generation, not only in the mass organizations but in the party organization as well, almost no religious party leaders were under the age of forty. Their youth organizations, even at the university level, were either largely inactive or led by the older generation of party leaders. This absence of youthful leadership was indicative not of a rejection of the religious parties by the younger generation, but rather of differences in the nature of leadership recruitment between the two types of parties. Instead of rising to positions of leadership after years of cadre activity (as in the case of the secular parties) the leaders of the religious parties were generally co-opted into leadership positions after having attained a measure of success in nonpolitical activities. Leadership recruitment thus tended to be lateral (from the community) rather than vertical (upward within the party). Since the religious parties did not provide channels of social and financial mobility, the ambitious young political careerist turned instead to PNI or PKI and their subsidiary organizations, where examples of the successful cadre were legion. The frustration of activist-minded youth was exemplified by the North Tapanuli PNI cadre in his twenties who, explaining why he had left Parkindo's youth organization for PNI, said, "All they ever do is pray and sing hymns. What we need is action!" The majority of santri Muslim and Christian youth, however, seemed as committed to the religious parties as their fathers. Efforts by PNI and PKI youth affiliates to organize at the HKBP church-owned Nommensen University, for example, were almost totally ineffective. Although Parkindo's youth organization rarely had meetings and many of the students could not name the organization's leaders, nearly all considered themselves members or supporters of it.

With these introductory remarks, let us turn more specifically to an examination of the leadership of the religious parties. Parkindo was established in Simalungun/Siantar in 1945 by North Tapanuli Batak Protestants, most of whom were members of the HKBP church. These early leaders were government officials, schoolteachers (predominantly in HKBP schools), and private entrepreneurs. As a group they were well educated by the standards of the time, spoke Dutch, and patterned their life-styles after those of the Dutch. In the radical atmosphere of the period, they appeared to many (particularly non-North Tapanuli Bataks) by virtue of their partial assimilation to Dutch culture as at best lukewarm to the goals of the Revolution. Caught up in the spirit of the Social Revolution, some of the more militant guerrillas (not to mention those individuals whose motivation was simple looting) had murdered or confiscated the belongings of anyone who looked prosperous, who seemed to have personally benefited from the colonial period. Moreover, several incidents occurred, in particular the assassination of the wife and child of a prominent Batak Christian doctor in Siantar, which were in some quarters attributed to Muslims bent on precipitating a holy war against the Christian community. As the Christian leaders viewed this situation and the vacuum of authority that permitted such threats to their personal and group security, the only solution was to create political and paramilitary organizations of their own.

With the return of the Dutch to Simalungun, Parkindo was temporarily disbanded. Some of its leaders, like those of the secular parties, fled to the Republic-controlled Tapanuli highlands, but most remained behind and continued in their former occupations. This latter group, despite the label of *co* (-operator) applied to them by the *non-co* secular party leadership, had no difficulty reestablishing themselves as Parkindo leaders after the Revolution. While revolutionary activity was a sine qua non for secular party leaders in the postindependence period, the issue never arose within Parkindo, where leadership capacity was measured in terms of (at least outward) commitment to Christian values and to the interests of the community rather than participation in the Revolution or devotion to revolutionary ideals.

Parkindo was reborn in the region in 1950 but did not become fully active again until 1954, when campaigning for the elections provided an incentive to establish a formal leadership structure at the regency and subdistrict levels and to develop links with the villages. The new leaders were of the same background (in many cases they were the same individuals) as those of 1945—civil servants, teachers, and entrepreneurs, most of whom were lay leaders in the HKBP church. Within the Batak community they represented the modernizing segment of the elite. Their claim to community leadership was based on the possession of a modern education and modern employment and their consequent ability to deal with the non-Batak world of Siantar, Medan, and Djakarta. Leadership in Parkindo, an organization whose principal responsibility was to deal with the outside world as the political representative of the ethnic and religious community, was attractive because it added legitimacy to their role as community spokesmen.

The assumption of political leadership by the modernizing elite found ready acceptance among the North Tapanuli Bataks of Simalungun/Siantar, who have for decades been oriented toward the kind of success the members of this elite had achieved. In Tapanuli, many Bataks reported to the author, there has long been a dual system of elites— the modernizers, well educated and close to the HKBP church, and the traditionalists, clan leaders and adat experts whose influence is greatest in the less accessible upland areas. In Simalungun, perhaps because of the pioneer mentality of the migrant North Tapanuli Bataks and the fact that it was the attractiveness of social and economic mobility that first brought many of them to the region, traditional leaders have had little political influence. Although still important in the settling of village disputes, the organization of adat rituals, and the operation of the supralineage organizations, few of them were active in Parkindo or any other political party. Nor did the Batak villager turn to the clan leader or adat expert for political advice or information about, for example, how to get along in the city; instead he consulted the educated elite, who were presumed to have experience with and wisdom in these matters. There are thus two spheres of influence in the Batak village: the sphere of family and intra-Batak affairs, in which the traditional leader is still influential; and the sphere of Batak relations with non-Bataks and the modern world, in which the modern elite and its political arm, the Parkindo leaders, have been granted full authority.

Not all of the occupational subgroups that make up the modern elite were represented in the leadership of Parkindo. Despite their active role as Parkindo propagandists during the election, few ministers became party officials, partly because of the general feeling that political activity was inappropriate to their position as spiritual leaders. Moreover, it was party policy to discourage ministers from seeking leadership positions because of a desire to keep Parkindo free of control by any particular church hierarchy.

Another segment of the modern elite, the most affluent Christian businessmen (North Tapanuli Bataks, after the Chinese, have been the most economically successful of the ethnic groups in the region), also declined to participate directly as Parkindo leaders although they made sizable contributions to the party's campaign chest in 1954–55. Perhaps because of their dependence on the good will of the central government (textile manufacturers, for example, have benefited handsomely from government subsidies) these individuals were wary of partisan commitments that might put them on the wrong side of the political fence in the highly unpredictable future. Moreover, because of their wealth, they were able to establish good relationships with city, regency, and provincial government officials independently of party mediation. Party support thus seemed irrelevant (and often contrary) to their personal and economic interests.

Most of the Parkindo leaders of 1963–64 were thus part-time politicians whose political activity was supplementary to their regular employment. Only a few, in fact, most of them regency/municipality-level leaders, were regularly engaged in political activity of any kind. These few included the party chairmen, one or two other members of the party leadership council, and the party's representatives in the regional legislature. At the subdistrict level, this group consisted primarily of the subbranch party chairmen (whose degree of activity varied from subdistrict to subdistrict but was generally low). Unlike the political efforts of the secular party leaders, those of Parkindo's leadership were oriented largely toward participation in the affairs of local government rather than the development of a base of support.

The chairman of Parkindo's regency branch, Dj. P. Nainggolan, was the most active party leader in Simalungun. Born in 1920 on the island of Samosir in Lake Toba, Nainggolan was educated in Simalungun (six years elementary school) and in Medan and Djakarta, where he received training as a hospital assistant and malaria specialist. During the Revolution he worked in a plantation hospital in subdistrict Tanah Djawa and was instrumental in establishing a Parkindo branch there in 1946–47. After the return of the Dutch in the latter year he remained in Tanah Djawa and did not resume political activity until 1950, when he became chairman of Parkindo in the subdistrict and a member of the party's regency-level Branch Leadership Council. When the regency legislature was established in 1956 Nainggolan was one of its three Parkindo representatives and in 1961 he was elected chairman of Parkindo in Simalungun. Throughout this period he continued to be employed as a malaria specialist in Tanah Djawa and, after 1961, in the General Hospital in Siantar city.

After 1956 most of Nainggolan's political activity revolved around the affairs of the legislature, where he was a skillful exponent of Parkindo policy and a superb tactician in interparty conflict. He met infrequently with his Branch Leadership Council, preferring informal discussions with its most prominent members concerning important decisions, and making occasional trips to the subdistricts to confer with subbranch leadership. Almost none of his time was spent on the expansion of party membership or the development of subsidiary organizations. In his view, it was preferable to deal directly with plantation administrators and regency government officials (many of whom were also North Tapanuli Batak Christians) when controversies arose over such matters as squatters' rights rather than to build a mass organization that would require skills and personal commitments generally unavailable within the party. Active in church affairs, he was a prominent figure in a conflict over control of the HKBP which occurred during the period of this study. His knowledge of Batak adat, however, was limited and he was impatient with the demands which attendance at adat ceremonies placed on his time. Like many educated Bataks, he favored a thoroughgoing reform of the adat in order to simplify and shorten the many complicated rituals, which he felt to be unnecessary and incompatible with an urban way of life.

Parkindo leaders below the subdistrict level were members of the same elite as the leaders in Siantar and the smaller towns of the regency. In most North Tapanuli Batak villages visited by the author, no formal Parkindo leadership structure existed, although one or more villagers were generally recognized as party spokesmen and as liaisons with higher party leadership. In almost all cases, these individuals stood out from the other villagers by virtue of their education, their position in the village as schoolteachers or civil servants in the subdistrict capital, and their membership on the governing board of the local church. Their supravillage contacts with members of the modern elite were nearly as extensive as their contacts with fellow villagers, and they often traveled to Siantar or even to Medan on personal or job- or church-related business.

Despite the frequency of their contacts with fellow elite members, there was little political content to the communication. The regency party chairman, as indicated above, made only occasional trips to the subdistricts and was in even less contact with the villages. Similarly, village Parkindo leaders rarely saw Nainggolan or other regency leaders in Siantar. Even in Parkindo's Siantar city branch, where communication between municipality and ward leaders was facilitated by geographical proximity, formal or informal meetings were extremely rare. Two of the most active members of the Siantar Branch Leadership Council were, in fact, unable to name half of the party's ten ward chairmen without consulting the records of the most recent Party Conference (1961).

The reasons for this apparent communications gap lie in the nature of Parkindo's relationship with its members and supporters. Without an interest in expanding membership or deepening the loyalties of those already affiliated with the party, there was little for subdistrict or village leaders to do and little reason for frequent communication between party leaders at the various levels. Instead, all that was required was the maintenance of a minimal organization so that the villagers continued to be aware of the party's existence. The regency chairman's visits to the subdistricts were thus designed largely to heighten the local leader's (and through him, all those who considered themselves Parkindo members') sense of participation in regency affairs (without, in fact, requiring much real participation) and to maintain the regency–subdistrict–village link for the purpose of future party conferences and, hopefully, general elections.

The leadership of Partai Katholik may be passed over briefly here as it did not differ significantly from that of Parkindo except in its somewhat greater ethnic diversity. Like Parkindo, Partai Katholik was essentially an electoral party. Its internal organization was minimal, with little activity below the regency level or in Siantar city (where it was too small to obtain a seat in the legislature), and heavily dependent on the organizational structure of the church. Partai Katholik's leaders were members of the educated elite, employed as teachers, civil servants, and entrepreneurs, and were active in the affairs of the church. Like the Parkindo leaders they tended to be recruited laterally and were almost all of the preindependence generation. They were generally accepted as the political spokesmen for the tightly knit Catholic community, and had little difficulty in winning a majority of the small Catholic vote in 1955.

Much of the analysis of the Christian parties applies also to the former leadership of Masjumi in Simalungun/Siantar. Masjumi's regency/municipality and subdistrict leaders, mostly South Tapanuli Bataks, were migrants or the sons of migrants who had come to Simalungun with the development of Siantar as a commercial and administrative center during the colonial period. In terms of education and occupation they were a fairly homogeneous group; the great majority had received a measure of modern education in schools established by the Islamic reformers, who placed great emphasis on the purification of Islam from traditional adat practices and on the development of technical and commercial skills. These ambitious young merchants and aspiring civil servants who came to Simalungun were accompanied by religious leaders and teachers (often the roles were combined in a single individual) motivated by a desire to minister to the spiritual needs of the growing South Tapanuli population in the region and attracted by the opportunity to bring Islam to the animistic Simalungun Bataks. Religious schools, at first independent and later under the aegis of social and educational associations such as Aldjam'ijatul Waslijah, Al-Ittihadijah, and Muhammadijah, were established in the late 1920s and 1930s. South Tapanuli Batak social organization, to a large extent liberated from the adat and traditional leadership, was centered around these associations and their schools in the small towns of the regency.

In the postindependence period Masjumi was dominated by the leadership of Aldjam'ijatul Waslijah, the largest Muslim association in the region. All five members of the executive board of the party's regency leadership council at the time of its dissolution were affiliated with Aldjam'ijatul Waslijah, either as association officials or as teachers and administrators in its schools. Besides these duties, all of them were also employed by the government in its Office of Religious Affairs.[4] In the subdistrict branches Aldjam'ijatul Waslijah also provided the majority of Masjumi's leadership, although Muhammadijah and Al-Ittihadijah were represented as well. In the Siantar branch the leadership was divided among members of Aldjam'-ijatul Waslijah and Muhammadijah, since the latter organization had its largest following in the city. As in the regency party, most of the Siantar leaders were employed by the government's Office of Religious Affairs.

As in the case of the Christian parties, and for essentially the same reasons, a close bond existed between the regency/municipality and village Masjumi leadership despite a weakly articulated party organizational structure. For the most part village leaders were of the same ethnic group as the regency/municipality leaders and were members of a common elite whose values were those of the Islamic-entrepreneurial political culture. Even before Masjumi existed in the region they had been closely associated in the Muslim educational and social organizations. The formation of the party had required only the establishment of a coalition of these organizations and the superimposition of a party structure and leadership hierarchy. Given the

4. The central ministry to which this office is subordinate was controlled by Masjumi until 1953, when the Religious Affairs portfolio was given to NU. See Feith, *The Decline of Constitutional Democracy in Indonesia,* pp. 338–39. At the local level Masjumi leaders remained predominant until the late 1950s.

goals of the party, the homogeneity of its leadership, the communications network available through the associations, and the widespread electoral support it received from the santri community, a highly articulated organizational structure along the lines of PNI and PKI was felt to be redundant and of little value. It was unnecessary, according to Masjumi leaders, to strengthen a link that was already firm.

Masjumi's position in Simalungun/Siantar as of 1963–64 would seem to confirm the leaders' estimate of the firmness of party support. In the aftermath of the party's dissolution, few leaders at any level defected to other parties. Instead they preferred to wait, maintaining their connections with each other through the still-active associations. Similarly, the former Masjumi membership simply withdrew from the political arena, remaining loyal to the party which they saw as the only true representative of their community's interests. In the event of a rebirth of Masjumi (or a meaningful successor party) the local organization will undoubtedly spring back into existence almost as though it had never been banned.[5]

Leadership recruitment and leader–member linkage in Nahdatul Ulama, to an even greater extent than in the other religious parties, was based on ethnicity. NU, it will be remembered, largely lacked the natural organizational and popular base enjoyed by the other religious parties in Simalungun/ Siantar. An educational and social organization founded in 1926, NU has at the national level represented the syncretistic traditions of Javanese Islam in opposition to the modernist reform movement led by Muhammadijah. Cooperation between the two variants of Islam, forged during the colonial period in opposition to the Dutch and maintained during the periods of occupation and revolution, broke down in 1952 with the establishment of NU as a separate political party. In Simalungun/Siantar, a branch of the organization as a political party was first founded in 1953. Prior to that time NU as an educational association had not existed in the region; the ten elementary schools run by NU in 1963–64 all postdated the formation of the party branch.

The driving spirit behind the creation of NU's Simalungun/Siantar

5. Brief discussions in late 1968 with former Masjumi leaders in Simalungun, at that time busily organizing a local branch of a new Muslim party, suggest that this is in fact what is happening.

branches in 1953 was Hadji Djamil Dahlan, an *alim* (Islamic scholar and teacher) of South Tapanuli Batak ancestry but born in East Sumatra and regarding himself as a Coastal Malay. Hadji Djamil came to Simalungun in 1927 and taught for a time in the schools of Islamijah and Aldjam'ijatul Waslijah, where most of his students were Simalungun Bataks. In the 1920s he became the official alim in the court of the radja of Siantar and was also active as a proselytizer and mosque-builder throughout Simalungun. During the Revolution, along with many Simalungun Batak Muslims and Coastal Malays (Islam in East Sumatra was closely tied to the traditional aristocracy, which stood to lose the most from the Revolution) he was an active supporter of the Dutch-created State of East Sumatra and an adviser to those radja who had escaped the Social Revolution.

With the formation of the unitary Republic, Hadji Djamil and other indigenous East Sumatran Muslim leaders were politically inactive for a time. Masjumi, they explained in interviews, was unattractive because of the dominant position of Muhammadijah (which, they argued, does not officially subscribe to any of the four schools of Islamic law) within the party at the national level. NU, on the other hand, appealed to them because they were in agreement with its strict adherence to the *sjafi'ie* interpretation of Islamic law. This argument, based on supposed doctrinal differences between the two parties, loses a great deal of its force when it is realized that the leaders of Masjumi in Simalungun were not for the most part from Muhammadijah but from Aldjam'ijatul Waslijah which, like NU, accepts the sjafi'ie interpretation.[6]

In reality, the differences between Masjumi and NU leaders were based not so much on the issue of religious interpretation as on revolutionary background and ethnicity. Where the leaders of Masjumi had been active in revolutionary groups, their counterparts in NU had been supporters of the Dutch or politically inactive during the Revolution. Where the leaders of Masjumi were for the most part South Tapanuli Bataks, the founders of NU

6. Strictly speaking there are no doctrinal differences among Indonesian Muslims, all of whom belong to the sjafi'ie school of interpretation. They do not argue that Muhammadijah or any other Islamic organization belongs to any other school. The conflict within Indonesian Islam is thus quite different from the situation in countries (such as Iraq) where there are Muslims adhering to different schools. (Personal communication to the author from Harry J. Benda.)

were mostly Simalungun Bataks (including Hadji Djamil, who had spent the greater part of his life among Simalungun Bataks and spoke their language) with a sprinkling of Coastal Malays. Shut out of Masjumi by revolutionary and ethnic barriers, they turned eagerly to NU because it provided them with an opportunity to participate in local politics and to wield a measure of influence within a nationally powerful organization.

Neither in the two years preceding the parliamentary elections nor in the succeeding decade was NU able to recruit many village-level leaders in Simalungun/Siantar. Parkindo and Masjumi, as we have seen, were successful because they were able to identify themselves with important ethnic and religious groups which had a sense of community, an established leadership, and an organizational network to which the party could relate itself, either explicitly as in the case of Masjumi (Aldjami'atul Waslijah, Muhammadijah, and Al-Ittihadijah were formally affiliated with the party) or implicitly as in the case of Parkindo (where the HKBP and its lay leadership provided the backbone of Parkindo organization without any formal relationship between party and church). NU's leaders, on the other hand, had to build their party without the support of any religious organization and with no possibility of obtaining the loyalties of that majority of the santri community composed of South Tapanuli Bataks. Their major hope of support lay in the Simalungun Batak Muslim community, which at most represents 15 percent of the Simalungun Bataks in the region, and whatever other non-South Tapanuli santri (principally Coastal Malays and Javanese) could be brought within their orbit.

The recruitment of NU village leaders was accordingly heavily based on ethnicity. Regency and municipality leaders, because of their previous contacts with the Simalungun Batak Muslim community as religious leaders and teachers, were able to establish village branches wherever members of this group could be found. The village leaders, in turn, brought into the party their personal followings, composed of Simalungun Bataks and those Javanese who looked for political as well as religious leadership to the Simalungun Batak *ulama* (plural of alim) in their villages.

Even within the small Simalungun Batak Muslim community, however, NU did not win the support of a majority of prominent village- and sub-district-level community leaders. The party's influence was greatest in Lower

Simalungun and Siantar, where the radja of Siantar and Tanah Djawa and several lesser aristocrats (who had been converted to Islam during the colonial period) provided a leadership nucleus. In Upper Simalungun, however, the traditional rulers had not become Muslims but rather supported or were at least tolerant of Christianity. NU's regency leadership thus had fewer contacts with the Upper Simalungun Muslim minority, whose leaders preferred to support Masjumi in 1955 and in 1963–64 still remained largely aloof from NU, despite sporadic organizational efforts.

Party Leadership and the Elite–Mass Cleavage

The kinds of leaders recruited and the general characteristics of leader–follower relationships within the parties of Simalungun/Siantar were in large part a consequence of factors described in the preceding chapters, i.e. partisan objectives, strategies, organizational requirements, and bases of support. For the secular parties the lack of a substantial "natural" base of support related to the ethnic and religious cleavages of the region, and the emphasis upon the goal of regional predominance and upon use of the worker-squatter strategy to achieve that goal were crucial variables in determining the characteristics of party and subsidiary organization leadership: diverse ethnic and religious backgrounds, the dominant role of professional politicians (particularly organizational activists at the regency and subdistrict levels), and the prevalence of village level leaders with weak partisan commitments, especially in the subsidiary organizations.

The religious parties, with the partial exception of NU, faced an entirely different local environment. By the end of the colonial period cohesive ethnoreligious communities were well established in Simalungun/Siantar, with their own organizations and leadership, lacking only political spokesmen. The objective of the religious parties was simply to provide political leadership to these communities, and for this purpose they required neither an extensive new organization nor the kind of total commitment so necessary for the success of the secular parties. For these reasons few religious party leaders were professional politicians; most had full-time (and relatively high status) employment outside of politics and engaged in partisan activities in their spare time. Communication between the regency/municipality, subdistrict, and village leadership was much less frequent than in the case of the secular parties. At the same time, because of the shared ethnoreligious bond, the general acceptance of the party leaders as community spokesmen, and the already established nework of religious organizations on which these parties were built, there was considerable commonality of interests between the regency/municipality leadership and the village membership.

The significance of these findings is that, contrary to the views of some Indonesian specialists (discussed from a methodological perspective in the Introduction), and despite the differences found in recruitment and linkage, the leaders of the various parties in Simalungun/Siantar were not self-contained elites, divorced from or unresponsive to the interests of their members and supporters. The political parties and their leaders were, in fact, a bridge between elite and mass in the regency and municipality. The reasons for this are not difficult to grasp, although they differ for the two types of parties. In the case of the religious parties, it was due to the fact that leaders and led shared common goals and values and were committed together to the interests of the ethnic and religious group. In the case of the secular parties, it was because party and organization leaders, continually concerned to maintain and strengthen the mass base of the party and their personal bases as well, could not afford to neglect the interests of their members and those whose allegiance they sought. At least in the case of PNI (and to some extent in PKI as well) the demands of partisan competition and weak partisan loyalty also operated to recruit a type of leader—the organizational activist ambitious to rise within the party (and, especially in PNI, not very ideologically minded)—rather well suited in terms of the integrative consequences of efficient role performance to maintain the link between party elite and mass. In other words, in order to achieve his ambition the organizational activist was required to engage in continual fence-mending with both higher- and lower-level leaders.[7]

There were also, of course, deficiencies in these patterns of elite–mass

7. Some interesting evidence for this point was provided by a PNI leader asked to comment on the relationship between participation in ethnic group activities and success in partisan politics. He replied that in Indonesia a successful party career was dependent both on local support and on connections beyond the local area. To illustrate, he discussed the political careers of two prominent Simalungun Bataks. "X" (a member of the provincial PNI leadership council), he said, had no chance of

relationships. In the case of the religious parties, the regency/municipality leadership had considerable freedom to determine policies (or to use the party for personal gain) without consultation with lower-level leaders or members, for they knew that most members of the ethnoreligious group were solidly committed to the party for primordial reasons and were thus highly unlikely to change their partisan affiliation. For the most part, it must also be stated, ordinary party members did not demand a greater voice in party affairs, both because they trusted the party leadership where basic principles were concerned and also because they did not see any substantial gains to be achieved through active partisanship under the Guided Democracy conditions of weak party influence and nearly powerless regional legislatures.

In the case of the secular parties, elite–mass relationships were weakened to some extent by the fact that PNI and PKI leaders at the regency/muni-

---

becoming provincial PNI chairman or even regency chairman because he failed to attend to his basis, performed no services for Simalungun, was devoted 100 percent to the party and not at all to his (extended) family and ethnic group. "Y" (a judge in Medan and a PNI member without office in the party), on the other hand, had strong ethnic connections but few ties outside the group. Moreover he had been deeply involved in the movement for East Sumatran autonomy and afterward continued to be too openly "ethnic-minded" in an assimilationist ideological environment, thus reducing considerably whatever influence he might have had in PNI or in the wider North Sumatran and all-Indonesian society. A judicious combination of relationships within and outside the ethnic group, combined with the proper political viewpoint—which the respondent defined as pro-*kemerdekaan* (independence) with a tinge of revolutionary spirit—was the key to success in PNI and in Indonesian politics in general in the mid-1960s.

Recounting his own career, the PNI leader said that the secret of his limited success was constant attention to his adat obligations. Influence within the ethnic group depends largely, he said, on *pergaulan* (association). A man who has achieved some success outside the group in the larger, secondarily connected Indonesian society can easily be influential among his own people if he is diligent in attending adat functions, helps relatives and village mates when they come to the city, contributes to local projects, and so on. If he had not fulfilled these obligations, it would be thought that he had ignored his family and his ethnic group and he would lose considerable standing in the community. Without this standing and the connections it brings, he could have persuaded few people indeed to join PNI.

cipality level defined their roles principally in organizational or mobilizational rather than in policy-making or demand-channeling terms. By making a sharp distinction between policy-making (the role of the national leadership) and policy-implementing (their own role), they saw themselves as persuaders and mobilizers rather than as articulators, and thus tended to be less concerned about and responsive to local demands than they might have been. The point here is not to reverse the previous argument that the organizational activist was well suited to play an integrative role between elite and mass, but rather to suggest that there were forces pulling in both integrative and disintegrative directions.

For both types of parties, the extent to which effective elite–mass relationships could be created and maintained clearly depended on developments in the political system itself, in particular on the open or closed quality of partisan competition, the presence or absence of elections, and the extent to which the parties were permitted to participate in the governmental process. In the period of parliamentary democracy, freedom of partisan competition and the expectation of elections provided the people of Simalungun/Siantar with the opportunity to choose the party that most closely represented their interests as they defined them. The result was that the only successful parties and leaders were those whose objectives and appeals coincided with the demands and interests of a significant portion of the local populace. Under Guided Democracy the religious party leaders could afford to be more casual in attending to their bases, with the result that the general tendency toward poor elite–mass communications was intensified. In addition the banning of Masjumi meant that a large number of people in Simalungun/Siantar, almost a whole ethnoreligious group in fact, had no means of communication with the governing elite. PNI and PKI, on the other hand, continued to be motivated to build mass bases during the period of Guided Democracy partly because of an orientation toward the future and partly because of a sense of competition with each other for the critically important support of the plantation workers and squatters.

Still another requirement for effective elite–mass relationships, particularly in the case of the secular parties, was the ability to deliver the goods. The very tenuousness of the link between mass organization members and party leaders meant that, if the national parties or their regency/

municipality branches were denied influence in the governmental process, erosion of support was a highly probable consequence. This did in fact begin to happen to both PNI and PKI labor unions in Simalungun/Siantar in the early 1960s. Because of the different nature of their support, the religious parties were not as severely affected by this aspect of Guided Democracy.

5. PARTY LEADERSHIP: PATTERNS OF CONFLICT

In this chapter we turn from a general consideration of leadership recruitment and relationships between party leaders and followers in Simalungun/Siantar to an examination of actual processes of decision-making within each party. What were the sources of conflict within each regency/municipality party branch? On what basis did opposing factions form among the party elites, and to what extent did these factions involve lower-level leaders and ordinary members? Where conflicts existed, how was party cohesion maintained? In sum, did the parties and their leaders articulate the interests of the membership, playing a "middleman role" among various local groups and between these groups and the national political system, or did they operate autonomously of the demands and interests of the regency/municipality population?

The Secular Parties

In PNI, factionalism was primarily a function of the conflicting personal ambitions of various leaders and potential leaders who drew their support from ethnic constituencies. Issues (whether related to the implementation of party policy or to decisions to be taken by the local legislatures) played only a minor role in party factionalism except when they were closely tied to the personal aspirations of particular party leaders. Ideological differences, in terms of the interpretation of Marhaenism, do not seem to have been present at all.

For those who came out on top of the struggle for positions of leadership within PNI, the rewards were great. The status of a politician in the highly politici:ed Indonesian society of 1964 was high, particularly if he combined his party position with a government post (such as regional legislator or Daily Government Board member), as was commonly the case. Moreover, high party and government posts brought to their holders a considerable degree of financial security, a result both of "favor trading" between politicians and individuals who needed special dispensations or assistance from government agencies and used the politicians as go-betweens, and of the peculiar arrangements by which party activities were financed. In theory (according to the party constitution) the party's treasury was to be filled by "(a) subscriptions, contributions and dues of the members, (b) legal income, and (c) nonbinding contributions."[1] In practice, at least in Simalungun/ Siantar, no dues were collected and funds came entirely from individual contributions. From 1961 to 1963, according to the General Report issued at the 1963 Regency PNI Conference, personal contributions of the regency chairman accounted for two-thirds of total party income.[2] The chairman

1. Kongres Ke-IX Partai Nasional Indonesia, *Anggaran Dasar Partai Nasional Indonesia* [Ninth Congress of PNI, *Constitution of PNI*] (Solo, July 1960), ch. 6, art. 11.

2. PNI-Simalungun Statement of Income, 1961–63.

Contributor	Amount (rupiahs)
First Chairman (Subroto)	158,554
Second Chairman	860
Third Chairman	—
Secretary	2,013
Treasurer	3,000
Contribution from R. M. Hutabarat	44,000
Contribution from D. Rangkuty	18,000
Contribution from J. W. Saragih	750
Contribution from Jahja Hasibuan	500
Monthly contributions from PNI members of the DPRD-GR	3,675
Total	231,352

Source: Adapted from Dewan Pimpinan Tjabang Partai Nasional Indonesia, *Lapuran Umum* [Branch Leadership Council, PNI, *General Report*] (P. Siantar, July 1963), p. 18. These figures undoubtedly grossly underestimate true party income, but they are substantially accurate in terms of the proportion contributed by the chairman.
Note: At the 1963 conference R. M. Hutabarat became the new treasurer of the party.

in turn apparently (there is no clear evidence on this point) obtained most of his funds either directly from the provincial party chairman, with whom he was allied, or from sources jointly available to both, and from private individuals who supported the work of the regency party (and the leadership of the chairman). There was thus no system of accounting for party funds and no way of knowing what percentage of contributions given directly to the chairman actually reached the party coffers, a condition that clearly worked to the personal advantage of the leadership.

In the first postrevolutionary decade, 1950–60, there was little overtly expressed factionalism within PNI in Simalungun. The regency leadership during most of this period was in the hands of Abdullah Jusuf. Jusuf's leadership in the local party was based on his unique position as a man of high revolutionary status and on his ability to command the allegiance of men of diverse ethnic backgrounds. In part this was because he was both a North Tapanuli Batak and a Muslim by birth, and thus personally spanned the gulf between North Tapanuli Christians and South Tapanuli Muslims. His revolutionary experience (not only in Simalungun, but throughout East Sumatra) had also provided him with close ties with the Javanese PNI leaders who had been guerrilla leaders. Because of this diverse background, Jusuf was seemingly above ethnic conflicts—a "pure," unhyphenated Indonesian. Jusuf also understood the importance of patronage in maintaining intraparty harmony and saw to it that all ethnic groups were represented on the Branch Leadership Council and in the party's legislative delegations.

After Abdullah Jusuf's elevation to the provincial chairmanship, fissiparous tendencies emerged within the regency leadership. In part this may be attributed to the fact that his successor, Subroto, as a Javanese, lacked Jusuf's pan-Indonesian aura, and to Subroto's continuing reliance on Javanese associates, whom he placed in key posts. More serious, however, was the problem of restive Simalungun Batak PNI leaders, who felt that their group had gotten short shrift from both Jusuf and Subroto (who was allied with Jusuf in provincial party politics), and that their ambitions for higher party and government office had been thwarted.

Resentment on the part of the Simalungun Bataks began to build up over the nomination of a candidate for Regional Head in 1960. Under Presidential Edict No. 6 of 1959 the Regional Representative Council was to nominate candidates for the position of Regional Head; the Minister for General Administration and Regional Autonomy could then accept one of these candidates or he could reject them all. If the latter occurred, the Council would submit a second group of candidates to the Minister, who again could accept or reject. If all were rejected, the new Regional Head would be selected by the Minister (with the approval of the President) from outside the list of candidates. In 1960 PNI, after much discussion, nominated its incumbent chairman, Jusuf. In the first round all candidates were rejected, and the Simalungun Batak group then attempted to promote the candidacy of an army officer of Simalungun Batak descent, who had already obtained the support of Parkindo. The combination of forces within the PNI leadership was too strong, however, and Jusuf was renominated despite the certainty that he would fail to gain the Minister's approval. Embittered by this action, the single Simalungun Batak PNI representative in the council voted for the army officer and was subsequently suspended from the party for indiscipline.

By January 1964, when the 1963 regency Party Conference was held (it had been postponed from the previous July), the lines of cleavage within the party were clear. An incident in March 1963, involving a letter of support for the candidacy of the Regional Head of Simalungun (the above-mentioned Simalungun Batak army officer) as governor of North Sumatra, had resulted in the suspension of two Simalungun Bataks and the explusion of a third from party membership, thus further sharpening the conflict. At the conference, the delegates were divided into two blocs, those who favored the reelection of Subroto as party chairman and an opposition group led by one of the suspended leaders, Aloysius Djulan Purba.

The core of the Purba faction at the conference consisted of the delegations from Raja, Purba, Raja Kahean, Silimakuta, and Dolok Silau, with a total of seventeen votes. The first three of these subdistrict branches were largely Simalungun Batak in membership, and their leaders were personally loyal to A. D. Purba. The support of Silimakuta and Dolok Silau was obtained through an alliance with the Karo Batak leader in the area, who had long been an opponent of the Jusuf group in the party and a supporter of the provincial-level faction led by the former provincial chairman, Selamat Ginting, also a Karo Batak.

The Purba faction had also hoped to win support from some delegations in Lower Simalungun and along the Road to Parapat but was unsuccessful. In large part this was due to skillful maneuvering by Subroto. In Dolok Batunanggar, for example, the chairman of the subdistrict party, a South Tapanuli Batak named Nasution, had early announced his support for the Purba group. With the suspension of Purba from party membership, Nasution became the faction's candidate for party chairman. Just prior to the conference a subdistrict conference was held in Dolok Batunanggar, where a pro-Subroto group ousted Nasution from the chairmanship, thereby depriving the Purba faction of three additional votes at the regency conference.

In those subdistricts of Lower Simalungun (such as Tanah Djawa and Bandar) where the party leadership was North Tapanuli Batak but a substantial proportion of the membership was Javanese, the penalty for opposing Subroto did not need to be spelled out. It is worth noting also that there was, to some subdistrict leaders (particularly along the Road to Parapat), an air of illegitimacy about the Purba faction, since its leader had been suspended from the party. The argument that Purba was somehow not a true Marhaenist because of his suspension (despite the rather obvious fact that the suspension was a political maneuver) carried some weight, particularly among the older generation of party leaders.

The intraparty cleavage at the 1963 conference thus consisted essentially of a group of Simalungun Bataks allied with Karo Bataks in opposition to the dominant group of Javanese, who were allied primarily with North Tapanuli Bataks. At first glance this alliance pattern appears to contain strange bedfellows (particularly the latter group of Javanese abangan Muslims and North Tapanuli Batak Christians); in fact it is a reflection of a common pattern of cleavage in the wider arena of Simalungun and of East Sumatran politics, the cleavage between indigenous people (Simalungun Bataks, Karo Bataks, Coastal Malays) and migrant groups (North Tapanuli Bataks, South Tapanuli Bataks, Javanese). The antagonism between the indigenous groups and the migrants in the early decades of this century was described in Chapter 1; more recently it has erupted over a proposal to divide North Sumatra into two first-level, self-governing regions (provinces), Tapanuli and East Sumatra. The migrant groups (particularly the North

Tapanuli Bataks) feared that such a development would result in a monopolization of the East Sumatran government by the indigenous peoples and the introduction of discriminatory practices, perhaps to the extent of restricting further migration. Within PNI in Simalungun, the emergence of a group of assertive Simalungun Bataks created the fear that Simalungun control would mean the exclusion of migrant groups from party councils. It was also darkly rumored (not completely without foundation, but much exaggerated) that there was a secret Simalungun Batak organization, composed of representatives of the political parties and some government officials and church leaders who were conspiring to infiltrate and take over all parties and their affiliated organizations.

Between the two groups there seemed to be no major differences of opinion on issues related to party ideology. The key issue at the conference concerned the suspension of the two Simalungun Batak party leaders, with the Purba faction naturally opposing the suspension and the Subroto group supporting it. Some informants argued that the cleavage was in reality a left-right division, with the leftists (Subroto and at the provincial level Abdullah Jusuf) more Marxist in their ideological orientation than the rightists (Purba, presumably allied with Selamat Ginting). In fact there seemed to be no difference between the two factions on this issue, which was in any event a minor one at the regency level because such matters were decided in Djakarta. Both groups were anti-Communist (in actions, if not in public statements) because of their belief that a national victory for PKI would mean their organizational obliteration and because PKI was PNI's chief competitor for the political loyalties of the worker-squatter population. On matters of legislative policy, however, the two factions did differ in their attitude toward cooperation with PKI. While the Subroto group was willing to cooperate with the Communists in matters of government personnel (such as the selection of a Regional Secretary in 1964), the Purba faction would have preferred an alliance with non-PNI Simalungun Bataks in the legislature. Where the Subroto group, with PKI, consistently opposed the policies and programs of the (Simalungun Batak) Regional Head, the Purba faction would have preferred close cooperation. The division here was not ideological, but rather rooted in the desire of the Simalungun Batak PNI leaders to promote the appointment of members of their own ethnic group. On this issue they were consistently opposed by PKI.

It would be a mistake, however, to characterize PNI in Simalungun as a collection of ethnic blocs using a national party affiliation for their own purposes. The reality was rather more complex than such a simple analysis suggests. Reduction of the patterns of cleavage to ethnicity fails to explain, for example, the roles of Nasution, the South Tapanuli Batak who was the titular leader of the Purba faction at the conference; the other South Tapanuli Bataks in the party who supported Subroto or remained neutral; the position of a Javanese youth leader in subdistrict Silimakuta who aligned himself with the Purba faction; or the small group of Simalungun Bataks who supported Subroto.

A more fundamental explanation of intraparty factionalism lies in the career orientation of most PNI politicians, the nature of competition for party office, and the importance of the ethnic tie in Simalungun society. The organizational activist, like Subroto, or the old revolutionary, like Purba, depended initially for support on the basis he had been able to create. To some extent the loyalty of the basis was related to the leader's devotion to party duty, his responsiveness to the interests of his followers, and his general organizational ability, but the fundamental cement was common ethnicity.

Having established a firm basis among members of his own ethnic group (and in the process perhaps becoming a subdistrict party or organizational leader), the aspiring leader then attempted to negotiate alliances with similar leaders, either of his own or of other ethnic groups. At the same time he established connections with party leaders at the next highest level (to whom he could give support in party conferences in return for his own elevation to higher party office). These vertical alliances were of major importance as they provided a prime source of financial support for local party activities, there being no regularized, factionally neutral procedure for distribution of funds within the party. The wealth or poverty of local party organizations and their leaders, particularly at the village, subdistrict, and regency/municipality levels (where locally obtainable funds were somewhat limited), was thus directly related to the system of factional alignments that extended from Djakarta to the villages.

The above analysis is clearly applicable to Subroto, who built a support base among the plantation Javanese during the Revolution, expanded it in his years as farmer and labor organization leader, and formed an alliance with the North Tapanuli Bataks in order to retain his party chairmanship in 1963. His relationship with Abdullah Jusuf and with Javanese PNI leaders in Djakarta was also of considerable importance, particularly in terms of his plans for the future.

North Tapanuli Batak leaders, whose support was limited to particular subdistricts, also depended on an ethnic basis, though less heavily in the 1960s (when so many of their members were Javanese) than formerly. This group of leaders was on the whole less motivated to rise in the party hierarchy, partially because their nonparty income (from entrepreneurial activities, wet-rice farming, or teaching) was fairly high and might have declined if they had devoted much time to party affairs or moved to the city. They were thus content with the Subroto leadership which permitted them to retain control of the subdistrict branches. These comments do not apply, of course, to the younger North Tapanuli Batak cadres mentioned in the previous chapter.

A. D. Purba's rise in the party followed a course similar to Subroto's. With the transfer of sovereignty Purba returned to his village of Harang-gaol where he became subdistrict PNI chairman, a post he held for eleven years. He never succeeded in building a large party following, however, either in Purba or in Upper Simalungun as a whole. In 1952, A. D. Purba moved to Siantar, retaining his subdistrict chairmanship and his close ties with the subdistrict party by frequent visits home, and simultaneously expanding his relationships within the party and with other prominent Simalungun Bataks. For a variety of reasons, perhaps the most important of which were his small support base, the distrust generated among potential allies by his primarily Simalungun Batak associations, and the general fear of Simalungun assertiveness, Purba was not as successful as Subroto.

Factionalism in the Siantar branch of PNI was similar to that in the regency party, with ethnic support groups providing the power bases of the various leaders and ties with the provincial party leadership contributing important resources to the struggle for control of the party. Until 1963 the chairman of PNI in Siantar was Zainuddin Hasan, the South Tapanuli

Batak administrator described in the preceding chapter. From 1957 until about 1962 Hasan led the party without opposition by forming an alliance with the Javanese leader of Bantan, who became second vice-chairman of the party branch; he was supported for a seat in the city legislature and later nominated as a member of the mayor's advisory council, the Daily Government Board. Until 1960 the North Tapanuli Batak element in the party was weak and there were few leaders in the Christian wards. The most prominent North Tapanuli Batak in the party at the time, a school-teacher and labor leader, became branch secretary and was a close ally of Hasan. Financial assistance came primarily from Abdullah Jusuf and a few wealthy South Tapanuli Bataks in Siantar and was filtered through Hasan. No statement of income or expenditures was available from party leaders or presented at the city PNI conference in 1963. When asked about finances, party officials responded that they had "very little money," probably an accurate statement in view of the fact that the party had no paid activists and did not even maintain an office in the city until 1964.

With the emergence of the organizational activists H. W. D. Tampubolon and Paul Siringo-ringo, opposition to the leadership of Hasan began to grow. By the time of the city Party Conference in 1963, Siringo-ringo (reported to be allied with Selamat Ginting, with whom he had been associated in Karo during the Revolution) and Tampubolon (who had quarreled with Hasan over a seat on the Daily Government Board) had formed an alliance to challenge the incumbent leadership. The justification they offered for their opposition was that Hasan had neglected the primary task of party-building and that the party needed dynamic new leadership. (Hasan had in fact devoted most of his energies to the problems of city government, in which he was vice-chairman of the legislature, and he had been instrumental in increasing the party's influence in local government.)

Because the national PNI regulations governing party conferences made no provision for a situation in which there were no subdistrict branches, the city PNI had adopted a one-ranting, one-vote rule (regardless of the number of members per ranting) as a convention in 1958. This rule gave the opposi-tion faction (whose strength was broadly distributed among several ranting with few members) an advantage over the incumbent (whose support was limited to a few ranting with many members). The delegate strength of the

Siringo-ringo-Tampubolon group was entirely in the seven North Tapanuli Batak-led ranting, all of which voted for Siringo-ringo for chairman. Hasan's North Tapanuli Batak ally was unable to influence even the leadership in his own ward to vote for Hasan. Timbang Galung Lama and Melaju ranting (led by South Tapanuli Batak protégés of Hasan) voted for the incumbent, as did the Javanese-led ranting in Bantan and Timbang Galung Baru. Kota, whose Kalimantan-born Muslim chairman had shared with Hasan one of the two PNI seats in the first city legislature established in 1956, also remained loyal.

Hasan thus lost his position as chairman of PNI in Siantar primarily because the Siringo-ringo-Tampubolon faction was able to call upon the ethnic loyalties of the North Tapanuli Batak leaders who constituted a majority of the delegates to the conference. The change in leadership also led, apparently, to a realignment of the Siantar party in provincial PNI politics (from Abdullah Jusuf to Selamat Ginting) and a shift in the source of party finances (from Jusuf and wealthy South Tapanuli Bataks in Siantar to the friends of Siringo-ringo in the transportation industry and whatever support Ginting could provide).

In PNI, then, factionalism among the regency/municipality leadership was rooted in the competition for power among various leaders and aspirants whose local support rested primarily on an ethnic base; all intraparty conflict had a pronounced ethnic overtone. With such a powerfully divisive force at work within the party (ethnic affiliations are by their very nature mutually exclusive, except in rare cases such as that of Abdullah Jusuf, and in Simalungun/Siantar religious differences served in the main to reinforce ethnic cleavages), how was cohesion maintained?

In part, of course, I have already answered this question by describing the nature of factionalism within the party as a competition among individuals (whose support groups were based primarily on ethnic ties) rather than as a confrontation of ethnic blocs. Alliances among leaders of differing ethnic origins, the lack of solidarity among party leaders from one ethnic group (a majority but not all of whom were usually agreed on specific matters), and the existence of "neutral" party leaders of all ethnic groups all served to mute ethnic hostilities.

Another factor that contributed to the maintenance of party cohesion was the rather abstract but deeply felt sense of commitment to PNI. Most of the older leaders had been associated with the party at least since the Revolution and had built up an emotional attachment to it which made it difficult indeed for them to sever their affiliation. Moreover, as has been stated previously, the party was for most leaders the only vehicle that provided them with an opportunity to enhance their personal wealth, status, and power. There were many obstacles hindering the acquisition of a position of leadership in another party, although a few attempts had been successful. The potential rewards for compliance with the rules of party discipline were great, and the penalties for disobedience severe.

The effectiveness of these mechanisms of party discipline was clearly evident at the time of the selection by the regency legislature in 1964 of a Regional Secretary, the top-ranking administrative assistant for local affairs of the Regional Head. For the Simalungun Batak PNI legislators, at that time in disfavor in party councils, ethnic pressures against the party's choice of the incumbent North Tapanuli Batak were intense. General acceptance of the values of party discipline and the primacy of the branch party over the legislative representatives (including those who were technically functional group representatives) combined with the threat of suspension or expulsion from the party were sufficient in this important election to prevent defection. Similarly, PNI legislators in Siantar city in 1964 were called upon to nominate a Regional Head. The branch party leadership's candidate, who was not personally favored by at least two PNI legislators (including the former party chairman, Hasan, the single most influential individual in the municipal legislature), nonetheless received the full support of all PNI party and functional group representatives. Asked why he did not oppose his party's candidate, Hasan replied with a long and obviously deeply felt statement on the importance of discipline for ultimate party success, a goal to which he was strongly committed.

To conclude this discussion, it must be stated that, in terms of the developments of the early 1960s, continued cohesion within the PNI leadership in Simalungun/Siantar was by no means certain. Although the older leaders who shared a common revolutionary experience were beginning to give way to the new who shared a common (though only vaguely defined) ideological orientation, there was every sign that the ethnic support group would continue to be of central importance to the aspiring politician. Moreover, the older generation of North Tapanuli Bataks, in both the city and the regency, who made few demands on the party leadership was being replaced by an aggressive group of cadres who had to be assimilated into the leadership structure. In Siantar city there was a strong possibility that the new leadership in consolidating its control would eventually alienate important elements of the Javanese and South Tapanuli Batak membership despite Hasan's commitment to party discipline. In the regency there was the possibility that an intensified but unsuccessful campaign by the Purba faction might result in embitterment (and expulsion of the faction's leaders) and the withdrawal of the bulk of Simalungun Batak members from the party. Finally, a renewed and prolonged battle over East Sumatran autonomy (see Chapter 6) might well prove to be the straw that breaks the camel's back.

The PKI in Simalungun and Siantar was apparently free of internal conflict during the period of this study.[3] In the confusion immediately following the Revolution, there had been two groups of leaders in the region calling themselves PKI, one representing the remnants of the guerrilla band Tjap Rantai and the other consisting of former members of the PSI's Sjarifuddin faction.[4] This struggle was resolved, presumably in favor of the Sjarifuddin group, with the selection in 1951 of K. Sitanggang as party chairman. (Sitanggang had been a member of the Sjarifuddin faction of PSI during the Revolution; no PKI leader interviewed in 1963–64 had had any connection with Tjap Rantai.) From 1951 on, only one publicly known incident marred the internal unity of PKI—the defection of some labor leaders (who were not actually PKI members) during the election campaign of 1954–55, which precipitated the dispatch of Taat Pohan by the provincial union leadership to reorganize the local branch.

The striking contrast between PNI and PKI patterns of factionalism is related to a number of factors: (1) the lack of factionalism in PKI's Central

3. The qualifying adjective is used because it was impossible to get detailed information about internal party affairs from PKI comparable to that obtained for other parties. Nonetheless, I feel reasonably certain that the analysis of PKI, based on interviews with PKI party and subsidiary organization leaders and non-Communist politicians, is substantially accurate.

4. On the PSI's Sjarifuddin faction, see Kahin, *Nationalism and Revolution in Indonesia*, pp. 258–76 and passim. Tjap Rantai was one of the most radical guerrilla organizations in Siantar during the early Revolution.

Committee, (compared to the intense factionalism among PNI's national and provincial leaders); (2) the very limited autonomy of local PKI party and subsidiary organizations and the high degree of discipline demanded by the party (in PNI discipline was also required of all party leaders, but the scope for local decision-making and opportunities for the expression of divergent opinions were much greater); and (3) the purely formalistic nature of PKI internal elections (compared to the open competition for delegate support in PNI party conferences). Shifts in PKI leadership in Simalungun/Siantar were thus a result of decisions made by higher party committees. These decisions seem to have been based primarily on evaluations of performance (especially for subsidiary organization leaders) or considerations of image (in the case of the party itself).

In PKI's subsidiary organizations a regular pattern of leadership succession was apparent. If an organization chairman was removed from his post either to become an official at the provincial level (as in the case of Pohan) or because he failed to carry out satisfactorily the tasks assigned to him (as apparently occurred in the Siantar labor and youth organizations in 1964), he was succeeded by the first vice-chairman. All other members of the organization's leadership council were moved up accordingly, and one or more lower-level leaders were then brought in to fill the vacancies at the bottom. In most cases these latter individuals were young cadres who had been sent to Simalungun from other parts of East Sumatra and were being groomed for future positions of greater responsibility.

Because of the stability of PKI party leadership in the years following the Revolution, no clear pattern of succession emerged. Sitanggang had been second secretary of the regency party section when he was selected for the post of first secretary in Siantar in 1958; his second secretary in Siantar had been first secretary of the Siantar subsection before 1958. In Simalungun, Tampubolon rose in 1960 from first secretary in Tanah Djawa to first secretary of the regency section. His second secretary had previously been active as a legal adviser to PKI unions and had been the party's star campaigner in 1954–55 among the Muslim Bataks in the regency (he had once been a member of Muhammadijah and was generally conceded to be a devout Muslim). From 1957 on, he had been a representative of PKI in the regency legislature, but had held no party leadership post before 1960.

The Religious Parties

Conflict within Parkindo's Siantar branch was almost continual after its separation from the regency Parkindo organization in 1956. The patterns of factional alignment were not comparable to those in PNI, however, for Parkindo's Siantar leaders neither formed stable factions among themselves nor established bases of support among the ward leaders and members upon whom they were dependent for election to party office. Moreover, since the overwhelming majority of Parkindo leaders and members were North Tapanuli Bataks, ethnicity did not play a prominent role in intraparty factionalism.[5] The pattern was rather one of shifting alliances, only partially related to primordial cleavages within the North Tapanuli Batak community, among municipality-level leaders whose primary purpose was to obtain influence within city government.

In this competition for local influence there was no connection between factional alignments in the municipality and those in the provincial and national party organizations. On only two occasions did provincial party leaders participate in local conflicts, both times in an advisory capacity at the request of the municipality branch leadership. Party leaders at the various levels—municipality, provincial, and national—generally held the view that conflicts at each level should be worked out among the individuals concerned. Thus the major issue dividing Parkindo's national leaders in the late 1950s and early 1960s—whether and to what extent the party should participate in the institutions of Guided Democracy (North Tapanuli Bataks in Parkindo's central leadership could be found on both sides of the issue)—had no impact on factional alignments in Parkindo's Siantar (or Simalungun) branch.

The first major conflict within the Parkindo leadership in Siantar involved the selection of a Municipal Secretary by the Siantar Regional Representative Council in 1957. Parkindo's candidate, a party leader and civil servant named Herman Hutagalung, was also supported by PNI and PKI

5. The Karo Batak community had one representative on the Branch Leadership Council, who also served as a member of the regional legislature from 1956 to 1961. Neither he nor his constituency made claims on the party leadership or participated in party conflicts.

and he narrowly defeated the candidate of the Muslim parties.[6] Shortly after the election two Parkindo legislators decided that they had made a mistake and requested that the election be reviewed. Their opposition to Hutagalung was based on their support for another Parkindo candidate, a civil servant of higher rank than Hutagalung who was a brother of one of them. Apparently a bargain had been struck within Parkindo prior to the election by which Hutagalung would receive the nomination and the other candidate would be supported by Hutagalung for a promotion within the city bureaucracy. When the promised promotion was not given, the two legislators asked for the review, receiving the support of part of the Masjumi delegation.

The controversy continued off and on for over a year, with assertions of Hutagalung's misconduct in office being brought up on several occasions, but the opposition was never able to muster enough votes to force a review. A series of meetings in 1958 between the Parkindo Branch Leadership Council and the party's legislative representatives finally brought a decision to support Hutagalung and the issue was not raised again.[7] Opposition continued, however, on a variety of lesser matters and the dissidents continued to support the promotion of their candidate within the bureaucracy. This lack of unity seriously weakened Parkindo's influence in local government since the opposition faction (whose votes were crucial in a closely divided legislature) was often absent or simply refused to accept instructions from the branch leadership. Since the party did not have the legal right to recall its legislators, only one alternative remained to the branch leaders—expulsion from the party—and they hesitated to take this step for it would only make the break permanent and would have no effect on the legislative status of those expelled.

The second controversy arose in 1959 over the sudden withdrawal of Gustav Pakpahan, Parkindo's representative in the Regional Executive Coun-

6. The various parties in the newly created legislature had divided themselves into two blocs, a Muslim group with 7 votes (6 Masjumi, 1 NU) and a "Pantja Sila bloc" with a total of 8 votes (5 Parkindo, 2 PNI, 1 PKI). Pantja Sila in the 1950s reflected opposition to the Indonesian Islamic state proposed by Masjumi. Later, with the banning of Masjumi, it was used to imply anti-Communism.

7. *Lapuran2 sidang Dewan Pimpinan Tjabang Parkindo Kotapradja Pematangsiantar, pada tgl. 15 September dan 6 Oktober 1958* [Reports of the meetings of the Branch Leadership Council, Parkindo-Siantar, September 15 and October 6, 1958].

cil, the executive body of the city government. The Executive Council had been chosen in 1957 by the legislature from among its own membership on the basis of proportional representation of the parties (1 Parkindo, 1 Masjumi, 1 PNI delegate). By 1959, with frequent criticism of the Executive Council and rumors of corruption circulating throughout the city, all three Executive Council members resigned. The Parkindo chairman quickly called a meeting of the party's Branch Leadership Council, at which Pakpahan was reprimanded for failing to consult the party leadership.[8] No decision could be reached on a successor to Pakpahan, however, and an emergency session of the Party Council, consisting of the Branch Leadership Council, the party's legislative representatives, and delegates from the ten party ranting, was called to discuss the problem. Advice was also solicited from the provincial Parkindo leadership. The ranting leaders at this meeting voted overwhelmingly to support the chairman's position, requesting that all Parkindo legislators submit their resignations to enable the branch leadership to select a new, more unified and disciplined group. When the vote was taken Pakpahan and P. H. Marpaung (chairman of the municipal legislature) left the meeting, signifying their refusal to resign.[9] The branch leadership was thus frustrated in its attempt to enforce its will over its own legislators. When the Regional Executive Council was reconstituted a short time later, Parkindo's representatives were unable to reach agreement. The party's seat remained empty for the last year of the Executive Council's life and Parkindo's influence in city government declined still further.

In the reorganized municipal legislature, established in 1961, the three Parkindo representatives were L. Napitupulu (a wealthy Siantar business-man and party treasurer since 1957), Dr. Sutan M. Hutagalung (a member of the Faculty of Theology and Assistant to the President of Nommensen University), and P. H. Marpaung.[10] Conflict within this group soon flared over the selection of a Parkindo candidate for the Daily Government Board.

8. *Lapuran sidang Dewan Pimpinan Tjabang Parkindo Kotapradja Siantar pada tanggal 3 Mei 1959* [Report of the meeting of the Branch Leadership Council, Parkindo-Siantar, May 3, 1959].

9. *Lapuran ringkas sidang Dewan Partai Parkindo pada tanggal 8 Mei 1959* [Brief report of the meeting of the Parkindo Party Council, May 8, 1959].

10. The representative of the Protestant religious leadership functional group was also a Parkindo supporter, but he took no part in internal party conflicts.

Marpaung (who was then branch party chairman) wanted the post for himself but was opposed by Napitupulu and Hutagalung, whose candidate was a civil servant and member of Parkindo's Branch Leadership Council. After a clash in the legislature, Napitupulu and Hutagalung succeeded in persuading Marpaung to drop his candidacy.

The seeming unity following this affair was short-lived, for the legislature soon turned to Siantar's most pressing problem, the administration of the Office of Public Works. The city's water and electricity had been declining in quantity and quality for several years—in 1959 the Regional Head had issued a general order prohibiting new installations—and the legislature conducted several investigations to determine the causes of the problem and to try to work out solutions. Criticism was increasingly directed toward the head of the Public Works Office, a North Tapanuli Batak Parkindo sympathizer named T. H. Hutabarat, who was accused, among other things, of political expediency and technical incompetence, and of deliberately disobeying the 1959 standfast order. Hutabarat's severest critics were Hutagalung and Napitupulu (who had acquired an encyclopedic knowledge of the city's water and electrical systems); his only consistent defender was Marpaung, who appealed to party unity and the necessity of having a Parkindo man in such an important post.

As in the case of the earlier controversy over the Regional Executive Council, the party leadership (Marpaung in this case) was unable to enforce its will over its legislative representatives. The right of recall had not yet been given to the parties and for Parkindo no other effective sanctions existed. In the secular parties, as we have seen, control was firmly in the hands of the party leadership. In PKI, discipline was total and unquestioned, with the local leaders and legislative representatives always following instructions from the higher party leadership. In the PNI regency branch, despite restiveness on the part of the Simalungun Bataks, the party leadership under Subroto was able to enforce disclipline by threatening suspension or expulsion from the party, a severe blow to the career aspirations of a PNI leader. And in the PNI city branch, after the change in party leadership, loyalty on the part of the PNI legislators (two of whom were members of the faction defeated at the Party Conference) remained firm, despite differences over the candidate for Regional Head.

Parkindo's control over its legislative representatives was much weaker because party discipline was not a strongly held value of the party leadership or its legislative representatives and because expulsion from the party was an ineffective sanction. Marpaung, the champion of party discipline in the legislature during his tenure as party chairman, had with Pakpahan been its leading opponent when he was opposed to the policy of the branch leadership. For Marpaung, as for other Parkindo leaders, the value of party discipline depended on his own position within the branch leadership.

The threat of expulsion from the party held few terrors for Napitupulu and Sutan Hutagalung, who were prominent members of the local elite both within and beyond the North Tapanuli community. Napitupulu's wealth and Hutagalung's educational attainments and position within the university and church hierarchies assured them of influential roles in Siantar politics with or without party support. Moreover, both had personal contacts with Bataks and other Christians influential in Djakarta politics. Their attitude toward the Branch Leadership Council was one of detachment, for they realized that their position, barring unforeseen events in national politics, was secure. To follow the lead of Marpaung, they felt, would deprive them of their influence in city government and of their opportunity to bring about necessary administrative reforms. They were both to a considerable extent antiparty, in fact, holding the view that "petty partisan politics," in particular the competition among parties for control of personnel, was destructive of good government. They attempted, in the case of Hutabarat, to wield influence on a nonpartisan basis in the interests of improved water and electricity distribution. If at some later time they were to be removed from the legislature on grounds of indiscipline or in a general reorganization such as took place in 1961, so be it. They would still be able to influence government and party policy from the outside.

By 1963–64 at least three factions were identifiable among Parkindo's municipality leaders: (1) a group led by Napitupulu and Sutan Hutagalung, dominating the Parkindo legislative group and unconcerned with control of the party; (2) a faction led by Marpaung, who apparently had little support from other municipality-level party officials but many ties in the ranting and (3) one led by Pakpahan (by then out of party and legislative office and estranged from Marpaung) and Herman Hutagalung who were attempting to regain influence in Parkindo through the party's new labor affiliate.

It is difficult to relate these patterns of factional alignment to the various cleavages within Siantar's North Tapanuli Batak community. The distinction between adat leaders and the church-oriented elite, for example, does not seem to have provided a basis for party factionalism, since the adat leaders played no role in Parkindo politics at the ward or municipality level. The *dongan sahuta* (nonkinship neighborhood organization) played no role in ward or city-wide politics in Siantar, since it had not become a focus of political loyalties and was viewed by its members purely in terms of the services it provided within the neighborhood.

Clan and regional affiliations were of greater importance, however, as determinants of political behavior both among North Tapanuli Bataks in general and within Parkindo. Identification with clan and regional groups provided a means by which the individual, either as voter or party member, could discriminate among various candidates. Thus, candidates for ward head in the Siantar ward elections in 1952 were reported to have conducted their campaigns almost entirely on the basis of clan and regional loyalties, and voters were said to have made their choices primarily in terms of these factors. In Parkindo politics, while party leaders were willing to use regional and clan loyalties to strengthen their own position, none saw themselves as representatives of a particular group and none were prepared to support a clan- or region-mate at the expense of their own influence within the party or city government. In only the first of the three examples of intraparty conflict discussed above did loyalties related to clan or region seem to play a crucial role. Herman Hutagalung (from Silindung) was supported for Municipal Secretary by party leaders from various regions and clans but opposed by two Tobanese Parkindo legislators (who supported the candidacy of a fellow Tobanese). In the second conflict, the allies Marpaung and Pakpahan were from Toba and Samosir Island respectively and had no family connection; their alliance was based on years of friendship and a common interest in maintaining their influence vis-à-vis the party leadership (whose chairman was from Toba). At the Party Council meeting called to discuss Pakpahan's withdrawal from the municipal Executive Council, eight out of nine ranting leaders present, regardless of clan and region, were united in support of the branch chairman because they felt that Pakpahan and the Parkindo legislative representatives should follow party instructions rather than operate independently. In this case, their loyalties as party leaders to the interests of the party organization versus those of the legislative representatives superseded primordial affiliations. The three factions observed in 1963–64 were characterized by mixed clan and regional affiliations: Silindung (Sutan Hutagalung) and Toba (L. Napitupulu); Silindung (Herman Hutagalung) and Samosir (Gustav Pakpahan); and Toba (P. H. Marpaung) supported by Silindung (T. H. Hutabarat) and ranting leaders from various clans and regions.

It is probable that the lack of regular interaction between membership and leadership in the Siantar branch of Parkindo obscured to some extent the very real, if largely potential, importance of clan and regional loyalties in internal party politics. Throughout the seven years of the party's existence in Siantar the Branch Leadership Council and the Parkindo legislative representatives acted for most purposes as if the ranting leadership and membership did not exist. Formal meetings or informal communications between ranting and branch were extremely rare, and only two party conferences (in 1958 and 1961) were called. In 1963–64, in fact, no municipality-level leader was sure just who the ranting leaders were, since the ranting organizations were needed only for the purpose of electing the branch leadership, a function they had not performed since 1961. It is at the ranting- and municipality-level party conferences that clan and regional loyalties are most likely to assert themselves.

Unfortunately, there is little concrete evidence to support this assertion since the conferences of 1958 and 1961 were largely free of conflict. In 1958 a high-ranking civil servant (of Tobanese origin) won the general support of the ranting delegates and was elected chairman without opposition, while in 1961 only P. H. Marpaung actively sought the office and he was supported by Pakpahan (who did not push his own candidacy because of the opposition to him over the Executive Council affair). After the split between Marpaung and Pakpahan, a future conflict over the chairmanship became likely, and it is possible to speculate on the nature of a party conference in which these men would be the principal opponents.[11]

11. The following paragraphs are based on discussions with Parkindo city and regency leaders who were themselves attempting to estimate the likely outcome of a party conference, which they expected to take place in the near future.

If such a conference had been held in 1964, it would have been preceded by ranting-level conferences to elect new leadership and delegates to the municipality conference. Marpaung and Pakpahan would have been very active in the ranting, courting influential clansmen and members of affinally related clans and individuals from their respective regions. The outcome of the conference would not have been simply a matter of clan and regional arithmetic, however, since such loyalties are very complex and do not carry the same weight for all North Tapanuli Bataks.

Regional loyalties have been complicated by frequent intermarriage among migrants from different regions, vague regional boundaries, and the fact that many clans have branches in more than one region, so that various ties may conflict in a single individual. A Parkindo member of clan Sitindjak (from Samosir, and distantly related to clan Pakpahan, according to Batak genealogies[12]) married to a Marpaung, for example, might well yield to Marpaung family pressure in preference to the regional tie. Or, alternatively, nonprimordial factors such as a close personal or business relationship with Pakpahan or a supporter of Pakpahan might play the deciding role.

Within the clan, politically transferable loyalties tend to vary directly in relation to the genealogical distance between individuals. The more distant the family relationship the less likely that support will be forthcoming. At greater genealogical distances nonprimordial factors often outweigh the clan tie. Moreover, lineage and clan groups are not normally large enough in Siantar (even when affinally related clans are included) to form a substantial voting bloc at municipality or even in some cases ranting conferences.[13]

12. See for example Wasinton Hutagalung, *Tarombo-Marga ni Suku Batak* [*Marga Genealogy of the Batak People*] (Medan, 1961), p. 59.

13. Edward Bruner writes that in North Tapanuli "the members of the lineage usually do not band together for political purposes, since the major lines of tension in the social system are not one lineage versus another but rather brother against brother. If one man from a localized lineage were running for office against another Batak from a distant area, he would undoubtedly receive the support of the vast majority of those in his own kinship group, irrespective of his party affiliation. But in any election on the local level the candidates are almost always members of the same lineage as well as the same village, and, in the Batak system of reckoning relationships, are often brothers. The choice which must then be made tends to segment the descent group. Frequently brothers align themselves with different political

Despite these limitations, it is clear that clan and regional loyalties were a prominent feature of North Tapanuli Batak social relationships in Simalungun/Siantar, and that their effects spilled over into party politics and government. The marked predominance of Tobanese in key positions in the city government bureaucracy, for example, was attributed (by government officials from both Toba and Silindung) to a preferential policy on the part of Herman Hutagalung's predecessor as Municipal Secretary. The opposition to Hutagalung was thus based in part on the desire to maintain Toba hegemony over bureaucratic promotions.

The struggle for control of the HKBP church, which reached a peak in 1964 when a dissident group left the HKBP to form a new church, also had strong clan and regional overtones. In this conflict the dissidents, mostly from Silindung and including the majority of the educated elite (and most of the faculty at Nommensen University's Siantar and Medan branches), were opposed to the incumbent church leaders, largely from the Toba area, whose patron was an extremely wealthy Medan businessman and PNI member, a self-made man with an apparent contempt for formal education. Parkindo leaders all claimed that the church controversy, in which some of them actively participated, was not carried over into party politics, but the evidence suggests otherwise. For example, the conflict in the municipal legislature between Marpaung (who supported the church leadership) and Sutan Hutagalung (a leading member of the dissident group, who stood to lose his university professorship if defeated) was certainly exacerbated by the struggle for control of the church.

Clan- and region-based loyalties, then, were an important ingredient in Parkindo's internal politics but were not sufficient to assure success in an attempt to capture the party chairmanship or to wield great influence in party or legislative councils. Primordial loyalties had to be strengthened and expanded by alliances based on other kinds of relationships. In the case of a contest for the party chairmanship, each candidate would have attempted to win the support of other municipality and ranting leaders by promising them

---

parties." "The Toba Batak Village," p. 62. In Simalungun, where there is a plethora of clans in the North Tapanuli Batak village, rivalry among real or classificatory brothers in local politics is less prevalent than lineage and clan solidarity.

a seat on the Branch Leadership Council or governmentally dispensed favors (such as construction contracts or government employment or promotion) in return for the clan, regional, and other support they could deliver. It is clear that both Marpaung (most noticeably in his relationship with Huta-barat) and Pakpahan (with Herman Hatagalung and through Parkindo's new labor union) were attempting to develop such support in 1964.

In contrast to their Siantar counterparts, the leaders of Parkindo in Sima-lungun were relatively unencumbered by factional conflicts. In large part the absence of competition was a result of the lesser desirability of the prize: influence in local government. During the colonial period Siantar had al-ready become a municipality and was largely autonomous of higher admin-istrative levels. In the postindependence period, Siantar retained its auton-omy to a considerable degree, including control over the all-important Public Works Office. The government of Simalungun, on the other hand, while several of its bureaus and offices were eventually given legal auton-omy and placed directly under the authority of the Regional Head, de-pended to a much greater extent for its income on provincial and national assistance. And, despite legal autonomy, many regional officials were actually appointed from Medan and/or Dajakarta. Beyond a few key offices, of which the most prominent were the Regional Head (whose appointment, after local nomination, was actually made by Djakarta) and the Regional Secre-tary, there was little worth fighting for in the regency government. Most decisions of importance for Simalungun were made at higher levels or by officials (such as the police chief and regional military commander) not responsible to the regency government.

Among the dominant North Tapanuli Bataks in Parkindo's Simalungun branch there were no major conflicts in the 1950s or '60s. From 1955 to 1961 the party was led by Amos Silitonga, a longtime teacher and church lay leader in Simalungun. After the regional rebellions, which began in North Sumatra in late 1956, Parkindo lapsed into almost total inactivity. Distrusted by the military because the rebellion had been led by North Tapanuli Batak army officers, Parkindo's leaders (none of whom actually defected to the rebels, although many were apparently sympathetic to their cause) were for a time forbidden to travel outside Siantar except under military escort. At the most recent Party Conference, held in 1961, the aging

Silitonga was replaced by the younger, more aggressive Dj. P. Nainggolan who, as a medical worker, was permitted to travel freely and was thus able to restore at least minimal contact among the regency, subdistrict, and village leaders. Nainggolan's strongest backing at the conference came from the leadership of the Tanah Djawa subbranch, largely his personal creation, but there was little opposition to his candidacy from other subdistricts. As a reward for his long service to the party, Silitonga was nominated to Parkindo's seat on the regency Daily Government Board.

Like Silitonga and other party leaders, Nainggolan accepted the view that party-building in the subdistricts and villages was unnecessary, given the firmly established link between community and party. Most of his political activity thus centered around the regency legislature. Although this body was largely engrossed in trivia and enveloped in an atmosphere of futility, two matters of some importance required its attention: the nomination of a Regional Head in 1961 and the election of a Regional Secretary in 1964. In both of these decisions Nainggolan played an influential role. The party's original nominee for Regional Head, a North Tapanuli Batak provincial civil servant, proved unacceptable to the central government and was rejected in the first round of nominations. Aware that the constellation of forces in Djakarta and Medan looked most favorably on *anak daerah* (literally children of the region) and military officers for the post, Nainggolan consulted his Branch Leadership Council, whose Simalungun Batak member suggested a Simalungun Batak army officer (and a relative by marriage of the Minister for General Administration and Regional Autonomy), then stationed in Djakarta. The officer was contacted; he indicated his willingness to accept the position and was subsequently nominated by Parkindo (with the support of Partai Katholik, KRSST,[14] and PSI, all of whose representatives were Simalungun Bataks, and one PNI defector, also a Simalungun Batak) and approved by Djakarta.

In the election of a Regional Secretary in 1964 Parkindo's candidate was the incumbent, a North Tapanuli Batak Parkindo sympathizer. Although acceptable to the other major parties represented in the legislature (PNI and PKI) because of his reputation for impartiality, Parkindo's candidate was

14. Kebangunan Rakjat Simalungun Sumatera Timur. For a full discussion, see Chapter 6.

apparently initially rejected by the Regional Head (reported to be under pressure from prominent members of his ethnic group to support a Simalungun Batak), who was responsible for the nominations to the legislature. In the end, Nainggolan's influence and persuasive power with the Regional Head, whom Parkindo had staunchly and consistently supported through three years of PNI and PKI criticism, was a major factor in the nomination and reelection of the incumbent.

In both of these examples Nainggolan played a key role not only within the legislature but also within his party. For the most part members of Parkindo's Branch Leadership Council were willing to accept his advice on policy and personnel and he in turn was careful to consult with them, usually on an individual basis, on important matters. Neither during his tenure as party chairman nor during Silitonga's was the party rent by the kind of disputes characteristic of Parkindo's Siantar branch. Regional loyalties were deliberately integrated into the party's leadership structures in the selection of the Branch Leadership Council (two members from Silindung, one each from Samosir, Toba, and Humbang, plus one Simalungun Batak and one Karo Batak), the first regency legislature (two members from Silindung, one each from Toba and Samosir, and one Simalungun Batak), and the reorganized "Mutual Help" legislature (one member each from Samosir and Silindung and one Simalungun Batak). In this division of seats no significant regional group among the North Tapanuli Bataks was excluded, and no party leader interviewed suggested dissatisfaction with his group's representation or influence within the party. Even the schism within the HKBP church had no observable impact on the regency leadership despite the fact that Nainggolan was a prominent member of the dissident group.

Only one cloud marred the horizon of Parkindo unity in Simalungun in 1964: the tension between North Tapanuli and Simalungun Bataks. For several years only one Simalungun Batak, a civil servant named Lodewijk Purba, had played a role of any prominence in the party. Generally regarded by members of his ethnic group as a stooge of the North Tapanuli Bataks, Purba had no personal base of support in his subdistrict of birth or in Upper Simalungun as a whole and only limited connections with the Simalungun Batak church hierarchy. By 1964, having been promoted to a high-ranking post in the government bureaucracy, he was no longer a member of

Parkindo but continued to hold his seat in the legislature, and he had also become chairman of the party's labor union (whose principal targets in the regency were government-employed day laborers, clerks, and lower-echelon civil servants, many of whom were Simalungun Bataks). Increasingly close to the Regional Head (whose name he had originally suggested to the party leadership), Purba was suspected of plotting the eventual takeover of Parkindo with the support and connivance of the Regional Head and Simalungun Batak church leaders (who were known to be antipathetic to North Tapanuli dominance of the party).

The relationship between Purba and Nainggolan was particularly tense during the election of the Regional Secretary, as it was feared that a last minute attempt might be made by the Regional Head, with Purba acting as his legislative deputy, to exclude the incumbent from the list of nominees and force a Simalungun Batak candidate on the legislature. Although this maneuver did not in fact take place, perhaps because it had little chance of success and would have had severe repercussions, the suspicion that it had been planned remained.[15]

Factionalism within the remaining three religious parties need not be discussed in detail, as conflicts, where they existed, followed patterns generally similar to those described for Parkindo: minimal involvement of higher party leaders in local affairs, weak articulation between regency/municipality leaders on the one hand and subdistrict and village leaders on the other, an emphasis on influence in the institutions of local government and a subordination of the role of the branch leadership, and factional alignments related to ethnic and, rather less prominently, regional differences. Partai Katholik's city branch, with too few supporters to win a seat in the legislature, was in cold storage in 1964 while awaiting new national elections; the party's regency branch, its legislative representation and to a lesser extent its Branch Leadership Council dominated by Simalungun Bataks, was also free of observable conflicts, although some tension between Simalungun and North Tapanuli Bataks was reported by leaders of other parties.

As in the case of Parkindo, factionalism in Nahdatul Ulama was marked

15. For a discussion of this election from the Simalungun Batak viewpoint, see Chapter 6.

in the city branch and largely absent in the regency. The basis of conflict in the Siantar branch of NU was a competition for influence in city government between two ethnically distinct groups of leaders: Simalungun Bataks and Coastal Malays. When the municipal legislature was first organized in 1956, the Coastal Malays were in control of the branch leadership and selected their chairman as the party's legislative representative. By 1960, when nominations for the reorganized legislature were submitted to the government, the Simalungun Batak faction was dominant and nominated one of its members, I. B. Saragih. In 1961 the Malay group again gained control of the party and nominated its former legislative representative to the Daily Government Board. Saragih refused to accept his party's instructions, however, and nominated a member of his own faction to the position.[16] In 1964 Saragih (along with five other members of the legislature, mostly from PNI) was accused of accepting a bribe from a candidate for the post of municipal Regional Secretary and was expelled from the party, an action that had no effect on his position in the legislature.

In Simalungun, NU's Branch Leadership Council and legislative delegation were firmly controlled by Simalungun Bataks among whom there was agreement on all important matters. Despite the fact that a considerable proportion of the NU membership was Javanese, this group held few leadership positions at either the regency or ranting level and exercised no observable influence on party decisions.

The former leaders of Masjumi, continually under attack in 1963–64 by the spokesmen of Guided Democracy and by much of the government-supervised Indonesian press as counterrevolutionaries, were reluctant to discuss party affairs. Like the leaders of other parties, they tended to discount intraparty factionalism in an attempt to present a picture of unanimity behind the banner of Islam. Without the opportunity directly to observe internal party conflict as was possible with PNI, Parkindo, and NU, evidence of factionalism must be pieced together from the official transcripts of legislative sessions. These documents indicate a familiar pattern: conflict in the

16. According to Presidential Edict No. 6 of 1959 (as perfected in November 1959), article 10, paragraph 2, the regional legislature, and not the party branch leadership councils, has the right to nominate to the Daily Government Board. See Legge, *Central Authority and Regional Autonomy in Indonesia*, p. 272.

city branch and its absence in the regency. From the party's founding in
1957 until its dissolution in 1961, Masjumi leaders in Siantar could not
agree on the membership of the Branch Leadership Council, an issue on
which the legislative delegation was similarly split. In 1959 Masjumi's representative in the Municipal Executive Council, like Parkindo's Pakpahan,
resigned without consulting the party leadership and was replaced by a member of the opposing party group.

Two principal lines of cleavage, organizational/doctrinal (Aldjam'ijatul
Waslijah versus Muhammadijah) and regional (South Tapanuli is divided,
in terms of adat and dialect differences, into three regions: Mandailing,
Angkola, and Sipirok) are reported to have existed among the Masjumi
leadership in Siantar.[17] Neither of these patterns could be established on
the basis of the available documents, although they were reported by both
non-Masjumi and a few Masjumi politicians to play a role in determining
factional alignments.[18] It is probable, as in the case of Parkindo's Siantar
branch, that these loyalties were most useful during party conferences in
the competition for the party chairmanship and lesser offices, and tended to
give way to ad hoc alignments in the interconference periods.

In the regency branch of Masjumi, organizational/doctrinal differences
were overshadowed by Aldjam'ijatul Waslijah's domination of the party.
Regional differences among the South Tapanuli Batak regency party members existed, however, as did ethnic cleavages among South Tapanuli Bataks,
Simalungun Bataks, and Javanese. Since, as in the case of Parkindo and NU,
few Simalungun Bataks and Javanese were represented in the party leadership at the regency, subdistrict, or ranting levels, ethnic differences had
little effect on internal party decision-making. Moreover, few decisions of

17. The impact of Islam has rather successfully undermined the importance of
the extended family among South Tapanuli Bataks, and clan- and lineage-based support groups were absent from internal Masjumi politics in Simalungun/Siantar.

18. In the selection of a Masjumi Municipal Executive Council representative in
1957, the party's legislative representatives divided into two factions with mixed
regional and organizational affiliation. In 1959, when the party again selected an
Executive Council representative, the factions had shifted slightly. Supporting a
candidate from Mandailing without any organizational affiliation were three Masjumi
legislators from Mandailing, two of whom were leaders of Aldjamijatul Waslijah
and one of whom was a member of Muhammadijah. Supporting a second Masjumi

importance were taken by the legislature during the short life of the party in the region, so that ethnic-based differences had little opportunity to emerge.

Comparative Patterns of Cleavage

Three patterns of intra-party competition and conflict may be discovered in the data presented above. In PNI competition was directed toward winning positions of leadership within the party, with ethnic ties providing the main basis of factional alignment. At party conferences the aspiring leader depended primarily on a personal support group composed of members of his own ethnic group in the subdistrict and village branches, and secondarily on alliances he was able to forge with other party leaders possessing similar bases of support. Conflict at the regency/municipality level was further intensified by the involvement of local party leaders in provincial and national party decision-making and by the system of personal and financial alliances extending from Djakarta through the regency/municipality branches and down to the village ranting. The result was a pattern of decision-making in which participation by subdistrict and village leaders was relatively high and factions linking village members to regency/municipality and higher-level leaders were fairly rigid and stable over time. Because of the importance to the leaders of obtaining party positions, and in view of the close relationship between ethnic loyalties and the formation of opposing factions, conflict within PNI was intense and the maintenance of party unity was a continuing problem.

Like PNI, PKI was a multiethnic party led by professional politicians whose main ambition was advancement within the party or its subsidiary organizations. Unlike PNI, however, conflict was not characteristic of PKI's regency and municipality branches since absolute discipline was required of all party leaders and members and since decisions as to personal advancement were not made within the local party and were not dependent on personal bases of support. Moreover, for over a decade the Aidit leadership held a monopoly on authority within the national party and had total con-

candidate, a man from Sipirok who was chairman of Muhammadijah (and who won the seat with the vote of non-Masjumi legislators) was an Ittihadijah leader from Sunda (West Java).

trol over the distribution of funds for local party and organizational activities. Within this monolithic structure important resources for intraparty competition at the local level were simply not available.

In the religious parties, specific locally implemented programs designed to build mass support and requiring the participation and financial assistance of provincial and national party organizations were largely absent. At the regency/municipality level the most jealously guarded value was local autonomy, the right of the local branch, within broad national policy guidelines but without interference from above, to select its own leaders, make its own decision regarding local affairs, and settle its own internal disputes. Because of the lack of emphasis on party-building (especially in the post-election period) and the weakly articulated party organizations at the sub-district and village levels, the branch leadership was relatively autonomous of lower party units as well. Important party decisions were thus made for the most part by small groups of regency/municipality leaders with little participation from below.

The principal goal of the religious party leadership—both as individuals and as party leaders—was to obtain influence within the institutions of local government rather than to rise within the party. The presence or absence of conflicting factions was directly related to the importance in the eyes of the party leaders of the regional legislature and of the regional government as a whole. Intraparty competition was thus more marked in Siantar, where regional government had broader authority, than in Simalungun. As in PNI, ethnic cleavages provided the principal bases of factional alignment in the religious parties. Where these cleavages were largely absent, as in the Siantar branches of Parkindo and Masjumi, factions tended to be based at least in part on somewhat weaker subethnic loyalties (e.g. to region or clan) and were thus temporary and shifting rather than permanent and stable.

These findings add further weight and a few new dimensions to the conclusions reached in the discussions of the characteristics of partisan affiliation and of party recruitment and linkage patterns. Perhaps the most striking findings are the overriding importance of ethnicity as a basis for factional competition (attesting to the strength of ethnic loyalties in the region) and the contribution made by ethnic loyalties to the encouragement of lower-level participation in regency/municipality party decision-making.

Of the two secular parties, PNI did indeed provide a forum in which the interests of various groups were presented and adjusted. This very comprehensiveness, however, particularly in view of the rather rigid and unyielding qualities of factions rooted in ethnic loyalties, represented a continuing threat to PNI's ability to maintain itself as a multiethnic party. In the case of PKI, the suppression of factions and conflict had the effect of diminishing the potential of the party as a "middleman," for there were no regular, legitimate channels for the expression of divergent opinions and interests. PKI leaders, in their designated roles as organizers and mobilizers, were freer than their PNI counterparts of the fetters of local demands. To the extent that PKI did in fact represent the interests of a segment of the local population, then, it did so almost purely through assessments of those interests made by higher-level party leaders attempting to choose among alternative mobilization strategies.

In terms of the extent of participation in party decision-making, the religious parties fit perhaps somewhere in between the PNI and PKI extremes, closer to the PKI than to the PNI model, but for different reasons. Whereas in PKI opportunities for factional conflict were not available, unanimity of views on basic issues in the religious parties, combined with the dominance of a single ethnic group and poor organizational articulation, made the lines of factional competition difficult for the ordinary party member or the village leader to understand. This was most clearly the case in the Siantar branches of Parkindo and Masjumi, but was also true in their Simalungun branches. Only in the Siantar branch of NU and perhaps in Partai Katholik in Simalungun was there a clear line of division (in both cases based on ethnic differences) that made struggles for power readily comprehensible to the ordinary party member. For most of the religious parties, the widely accepted value of the autonomy of each level in the party hierarchy tended also to obstruct the development of a tradition of subdistrict and village participation in decision-making at the regency/municipality (and higher) levels.

Finally, one of the most interesting findings of this chapter is the direct correlation between the existence of intraparty conflict and the extent of the authoritative decision-making capability of the local government; that is, the more powerful the local government, the more conflict within the

parties. The implication here is that, in the event of a greater decentralization of authority from Djakarta to the regions, intraparty conflict is likely
to increase. For PNI, it is likely in such a situation that the observed pattern
of conflict and the fairly extensive participation of lower-level leaders would
continue, but in a more intense (since meaningful governmental decisions
are at stake) and thus dangerous (to party unity) fashion. For the religious
parties there is the possibility, particularly if decentralization were combined
with the restoration of the electoral process, of heightened participation of
subdistrict and village leaders and members, again because decisions affecting their interests were being made by government. It must be pointed out,
however, that a comparison of levels of participation in the religious party
branches in the municipality and regency for the parliamentary and Guided
Democracy periods does not reveal a substantial difference. In both Simalungun and Siantar, religious party leaders were convinced that their supporters had nowhere else to turn and thus need not be brought too directly
into party decision-making councils. Given the demonstrated willingness of
village partisans to tolerate this situation, it is perhaps arguable whether
future decentralization and regular elections would produce a meaningful
change in the level of participation.

6. POLITICAL ORGANIZATION AND LEADERSHIP AMONG THE SIMALUNGUN BATAKS

The core of this book has been designed to provide a picture of the patterns of interaction between the national political parties and the local social and cultural environment in Simalungun/Siantar as they related to the problems of national integration confronting the Indonesian political system in the 1950s and early 1960s. These patterns of interaction have been extremely complex, as is clear from the preceding chapters, and it is an oversimplification to view party politics in the region as merely an extension of ethnic loyalties and conflicts. It is also true, however, that there was during the period of this study a considerable measure of ethnic group identification with particular parties: North Tapanuli Bataks with Parkindo, South Tapanuli Bataks with Masjumi, and the Javanese, although more divided in their partisan loyalties, with PNI. Of the four major ethnic communities only one, the Simalungun Bataks, failed to support a national party, giving the bulk of their votes in 1955 to a political organization that explicitly restricted its appeal to members of the ethnic group. In the postelection period the Simalungun Bataks have been for the most part without political organization, relying instead for the resolution of their grievances and the communication of their demands on the personal influence of individual Simalungun Bataks prominent in the civilian and military bureaucracies and in the regional legislature. The reasons for this distinctive pattern, and its consequences for the integration of the group into the political system of independent Indonesia, are the subject of this chapter.

An earlier version of this chapter, entitled "Suku Simalungun: An Ethnic Group in Search of Representation," was published in *Indonesia 3* (April 1967).

The 1950s: The Rise and Fall of Ethnic Political Organizations

As the indigenous ethnic group in the region, the Simalungun Bataks have been both more "ethnic-minded" in a political sense and more traditional in their social structure and patterns of elite formation than the migrant groups, who were forced by the circumstances of their migration to develop new elites and novel means of coping with the changed conditions of social life. The greater ethnic consciousness of the Simalungun Bataks stemmed from the feeling that their homeland was being taken over by the migrants, that rice land, commercial opportunities, government employment, and political influence were more and more coming under the control of others. As ethnic awareness developed among the Simalungun people, it had a marked political cast, emphasizing the necessity for the group to be politically united against the interlopers if Simalungun Batak hegemony was to be restored. The existence of a traditional elite group—the old aristocracy —provided the drive for Simalungun unity and for a place in the political sun in the early 1950s with a leadership respected by a majority of the Simalungun Batak population but without links to any national political party. Thus the idea of ethnic political organization under traditional leadership was born.

The first organization of this type in Upper Simalungun—KRSST (Kebangunan Rakjat Simalungun Sumatera Timur, The Awakening of the Simalungun People of East Sumatra)—was established during the period of political activity preceding the 1955 elections.[1] KRSST's primary objective was to obtain a seat in the national parliament or, failing that, representation in the proposed North Sumatran provincial legislature on behalf of the entire Simalungun Batak community. Financed by a wealthy Simalungun Batak businessman in Djakarta, the organization was led in the region by the former *tungkat* of Dolok Batunanggar. Its leadership at the regency and sub-district levels, while dominated by former aristocrats and other individuals closely associated with them, cut across most of the cleavages in the Simalungun Batak community, including aristocrats and nonaristocrats of all clans

---

1. Another ethnic organization, AKRAP ST (Aksi Rakjat Pemilih Sumatera Timur, Action of the Voting People of East Sumatra), designed to appeal to all the indigenous peoples of East Sumatra, also contested the elections. In Simalungun it won only 1,776 votes, one-third of which were in Dolok Pardamaian, the home subdistrict of AKRAP's Simalungun chairman.

as well as Christians, Muslims, and the followers of traditional religious practices. Only the militant revolutionaries and their supporters remained entirely aloof.

While the Simalungun Batak traditional elite was united behind KRSST, other leadership groups were more divided in their partisan loyalties. The Protestant leadership was heavily cross-pressured, torn between a desire to support the party of Protestantism (Parkindo) and yet deeply sympathetic to the objectives of KRSST. For many years Protestant leaders had opposed North Tapanuli influence in their church. By 1952 they had succeeded in gaining autonomy within the Batak church, but their final goal—total separation—was not to be achieved for another decade. To many of them Parkindo was not much more than the political extension of the HKBP church and was similarly dominated by North Tapanuli Bataks. They saw little possibility of an influential role for Simalungun Bataks in Parkindo. Many ministers and teachers resolved their internal conflict by limiting their political propaganda to anti-Communist and, less frequently, anti-PNI sermons and speeches. A smaller number came out boldly for Parkindo or for KRSST. Since Simalungun Batak Catholic lay leaders in subdistrict Purba played a prominent role in the regency leadership of Partai Katholik, the Catholic leadership found it less difficult to resolve the conflict between church and ethnic group. By supporting Partai Katholik one could be pro-Simalungun Batak and prochurch at the same time.

The Muslim elite was also divided. Nahdatul Ulama was established by Simalungun Bataks who had been closely associated with the traditional aristocracy and had participated in NST. With the support of the Simalungun Muslim community and whatever other ethnic groups (such as Coastal Malays and Javanese) could be attracted to the party, and with the financial assistance of NU's national leadership, they hoped to carve an independent role for themselves in local politics. Other Muslims, similar in background to the NU leaders, felt that a party based largely on an appeal to perhaps 15 percent of the ethnic group would be too small to play an effective role either in Simalungun or in the national NU organization, and gave their support instead to KRSST. Finally, Simalungun Muslim leaders who had fought against the Dutch found both KRSST and NU unattractive and turned to Masjumi.

The secular revolutionary leadership was less divided in its partisan affiliation than the religious elite. Most Simalungun Bataks who had participated in the Revolution were members of Barisan Harimau Liar. In the early 1950s the former leaders of BHL who continued to be politically active were, with few exceptions, PNI supporters and leaders.

The results of the 1955 elections showed that the Simalungun Batak community, and particularly its Protestant and animistic subgroups, was highly receptive to the idea of direct political representation of the ethnic group. KRSST's leaders had framed their appeal not in terms of a restoration of traditional rule (which they knew to be impossible) but rather on the basis of ethnic solidarity under traditional leadership in opposition to the migrant groups. Its popularity in Upper Simalungun was comparable to the support the ostensibly nonethnic parties Parkindo, Masjumi, and PNI received from the North Tapanuli, South Tapanuli, and Javanese communities respectively. In the seven subdistricts of Upper Simalungun, KRSST's mean percentage of the vote was 43.7 percent, and the party won a clear majority in Raja and Silau Kahean. In the regency as a whole, with 8.3 percent of the vote, it was the fifth largest party.

Table 6–1. KRSST Vote in Simalungun and Siantar in the 1955
Parliamentary Elections

Area	*KRRST Vote (by percent)*
Upper Simalungun	43.7
Subdistricts:	
Raja	61.8
Silau Kahean	51.3
Purba	43.8
Dolok Silau	43.7
Raja Kahean	37.6
Silimakuta	29.1
Dolok Pardamaian	22.9
Lower Simalungun and the Road to Parapat (mean)	3.2
Siantar City	2.0

Source: Adapted from *Simalungun election results.*

The second most popular party in Upper Simalungun was PNI, with a mean of 19.8 percent of the vote. PNI's support was concentrated in subdistricts Silimakuta and Dolok Silau (where many of the voters were Karo Bataks) and subdistricts Dolok Pardamaian and Purba, both of which were former Barisan Harimau Liar strongholds. Of the remaining parties, Parkindo won a mean 9.3 percent of the vote in Upper Simalungun and Masjumi obtained 7.2 percent, which included most of the Simalungun Batak Muslim voters in the region and a substantial proportion of non-Simalungun Bataks in Silau Kahean and Raja Kahean. Partai Katholik's vote was less than 4 percent of the regional total and NU received negligible support.

Table 6–2. PNI, Parkindo, and Masjumi Vote in Upper Simalungun, by Subdistrict

Subdistrict	PNI Vote (percent)	Parkindo Vote (percent)	Masjumi Vote (percent)
Raja	7.8	14.5	6.0
Dolok Pardamaian	28.7	12.4	2.4
Purba	20.6	8.9	.4
Silimakuta	42.9	3.9	1.9
Dolok Silau	37.8	4.8	.2
Silau Kahean	4.9	2.9	23.0
Raja Kahean	9.0	13.5	20.6
Total	19.8	9.3	7.2

Source: Adapted from *Simalungun election results.*

Despite its sizable vote in Upper Simalungun, KRSST failed to achieve its objectives of national and/or provincial representation. By 1957, when the first regency legislature was inaugurated, its most prominent leadership had turned to other activities and organizations, allowing second-rank leaders to fill its three seats. Until formally dissolved in 1961,[2] KRSST existed in name only, with no leadership other than its representatives in the legislature and no organization in the subdistricts.

2. Under Presidential Edict No. 7/1959 on the simplification of the party system.

During the unsettled period following the 1956 North Sumatran rebellion, a new organization called Rondahaim (after a former radja of Raja) was created in Upper Simalungun by former KRSST activists. Rondahaim's goals were twofold: (1) to provide protection to the Simalungun Batak community through its own paramilitary force and by establishing liaison with both rebel and government troops; and (2) to promote economic development in Upper Simalungun by organizing such projects as road-building and school and market construction. Because of its sometimes heavy-handed attitude toward the local population, its tendency to dragoon villagers into its work gangs, and the fact that nearly all of its leaders were from Raja,[3] Rondahaim was never widely supported. With the gradual return of security and the government presence in Upper Simalungun Rondahaim soon disappeared.

A second organization spawned during this period was BAPOST (Badan Penuntut Otonom Sumatera Timur, Body to Demand East Sumatran Autonomy); although established some months prior to the army rebellion it was not really active until 1957. In Simalungun, where it had branches at the regency/municipality and subdistrict levels, BAPOST's leadership was more inclusive than that of previous ethnic-based organizations. Beyond including members of the small Karo Batak and Coastal Malay communities, BAPOST was widely supported by the Simalungun Batak political elite irrespective of religious, regional, and even traditional-revolutionary cleavages. Only the few Simalungun Bataks in PKI, under party instructions, refused to support the movement. Within PNI the emergence of BAPOST provided the first sign of dissension. Most Simalungun Bataks in the regency and subdistrict PNI leadership became active BAPOST leaders, while the

3. Subethnic regional identification among the Simalungun Bataks, to date a minor theme in the ethnic group's politics, is a development of the postwar period. Its principal feature is hostility between the inhabitants of subdistrict Raja (whose version of the Simalungun Batak language is considered to be purest and whose nineteenth century Radja Rondahaim is celebrated as an anticolonial hero) and those of subdistrict Purba, once the target of Rondahaim's expansionism. The division of the Simalungun Protestant Christian Church into three districts (one centered in Raja, one in Purba, and the third encompassing the rest of Simalungun and East Sumatra) reflects the cleavage between the two areas and the church's concern to maintain a regional balance in its central leadership.

North and South Tapanuli Bataks and Javanese in the party lent their support to GAS (Gerakan Anti-Separatis, Anti-Separatist Movement), an organization created to oppose BAPOST. Simalungun Bataks affiliated with Parkindo also supported the movement for autonomy, increasing their alienation from the dominant North Tapanuli leadership (who, under suspicion as possible rebels, abstained from all political activity in this period). Despite apparent high-level support (particularly within the military), mass meetings, demonstrations, and implied threats of violence, the demand for a separate East Sumatra was in the end unacceptable to the central government and BAPOST went the way of KRSST and Rondahaim.[4] In its wake it left an intensified sense of ethnic identity both among the Simalungun Bataks and among their opponents. As the last of the ethnic organizations, it also left an organizational vacuum in Upper Simalungun.

The 1960s: An Organizational Vacuum

The fall of BAPOST signified the beginning of a new era in the political life of the Simalungun Bataks. In the 1950s ethnic organizations had proved singularly ineffective as means for gaining influence in government. The experience of KRSST had shown that, while an ethnic political party could win the support of a considerable segment of the Simalungun people, there were simply too few Simalungun Bataks to enable such an organization to dominate regency politics, let alone play a role on the provincial or national stage. Equally important, the dissolution of KRSST and the failure of BAPOST made it abundantly clear that overt "sukuism" (ethnic favoritism) and regionalism were unacceptable in an era dominated by the symbolism of Guided Democracy. By the end of the decade Simalungun Batak politicians had lost their taste for ethnic organizations.

The organizational vacuum left by the decline and subsequent dissolution of KRSST was not filled by any of the remaining parties. Regency-level party leaders, in fact, paid less attention to Upper Simalungun than to any other part of the regency. While minimal organizational structures were

4. A discussion of the autonomy movement at the East Sumatran level may be found in John R. W. Smail, "The Military Politics of North Sumatra, December 1956–October 1957," unpublished paper, Cornell University, n.d., pp. 36–37.

maintained, no attempts were made to create mass membership parties or subsidiary organizations with regular programs of activity reaching into the daily lives of the population. Nor was there a continuous link between the urban party leaders and the village population whom they claimed to represent in party and government councils. Parkindo's regency leadership, including its Simalungun Batak member, almost totally ignored the subdistrict party leaders in Upper Simalungun. NU, Partai Katholik, and PKI were also largely inactive in the region. Simalungun Bataks in the branch PNI organization communicated more frequently with the subdistrict and village leadership, whose support they needed at party conferences, but they devoted little time to problems of party- and organization-building. In the late 1950s and early 1960s, some Simalungun Bataks in Siantar became active in IPKI (these were former KRSST supporters and descendants of the aristocracy), Partai Murba, and to a lesser extent Partindo (former revolutionaries), but they made no substantial effort to organize in the villages.

The failure of the national political parties to develop a mass base in Upper Simalungun was not entirely the fault of the regency party leadership, for each of the national parties was limited in terms of its potential support. Roman Catholics and Muslims are too few to enable Partai Katholik and NU to play a prominent role in the region, and Parkindo was handicapped by its identification with the North Tapanuli Batak community. Among the large percentage of the village population that had supported KRSST and felt little enmity toward the traditional aristocracy, there was active hostility toward the revolutionary leaders of PNI, PKI, Partai Murba, and Partindo. PKI was further burdened by its identification with atheism and by its unwillingness to represent such ethnic interests as the demand for East Sumatran autonomy. IPKI's leaders, while of aristocratic blood and formerly supporters of KRSST, were either civil servants or youths without substantial political experience or contacts in the villages. The first-rank leaders of KRSST had by this time turned away from politics altogether.

In the absence of partisan links, upward communication between the Upper Simalungun villager and the regency government was severely hampered. Official government channels, in the persons of the subdistrict officer (appointed by the Regional Head in his capacity as regent) and the village head (according to law, popularly elected), did not provide an effective alternative to the party organizations. The relationship between the subdistrict officer and the village head was largely formal and paternalistic. For some time after the Revolution most subdistrict officers in Upper Simalungun were outsiders who did not speak the Simalungun language. In more recent years these posts were given primarily to Simalungun Bataks, but their function—to represent the central government to the people rather than the people to the government—remained, in the eyes of the villagers, unchanged. Communication between the subdistrict officer and the people within his jurisdiction was largely limited to meetings with the village heads called to convey instructions emanating from the Regional Head or his superiors. The village head tended to be somewhat awed in the presence of higher authority, and his sense of subordination was increased by the formality of the setting, his imperfect understanding of the Indonesian language (used as the official language at such meetings), and the fact that the subdistrict officer was normally flanked by the subdistrict representatives of the police and army.

The village head also knew from personal experience that attempts to soften the impact of government instructions (e.g. a reduction in the quantity of rice his village was required to supply to the government at a fixed price below the market value) or to make other requests of the subdistrict officer would mostly be unavailing. In one case a village in subdistrict Raja had been trying to obtain government assistance in the building of a road for seven years without success. In this instance the main channel used by the villagers was the official village head–subdistrict officer link, although direct representation to regency and even provincial administrators had also been made. The local military and police representatives, most of whom were not Simalungun Bataks and did not live in the subdistrict to which they were posted, were even less useful as channels for the expression of village demands than the subdistrict officer.

Even the village head was often regarded in Upper Simalungun as the last link in the downward chain of command rather than the first link in an upward chain of representation. Although he was popularly elected or, as was the case when vacancies occurred in the 1960s, chosen by the subdistrict officer after consultation with prominent villagers, the consolidation of small villages or hamlets into village complexes for purposes of administrative efficiency meant that to many of his constituents the village head was an outsider.

The village complex of Baringin Raja in subdistrict Raja, for example, consisted of five separate hamlets. In the last village election, held in 1953, three candidates, one from each of the three largest hamlets, were nominated for the post of village head. The vote was divided along hamlet lines, with the candidate from the largest hamlet emerging victorious. In 1964, when I visited Baringin Raja, the village head was held in low esteem, particularly outside his own hamlet. Considered primarily a tax and rice collector and bearer of instructions, he rarely visited the other hamlets under his authority and played no role in their internal affairs. Hamlet disputes were taken to him as a last resort and only after all attempts at mediation by family members and village elders learned in the adat had failed. According to the villagers, who jealously guarded their traditions of hamlet autonomy, such failures were extremely rare.

Without effective political organizations or official governmental channels of communication, contact between the village and the regency government tended to be based on personal relationships. The link between the villager who went to Siantar to make a request on behalf of his village and the government official or other member of the political elite who received him was most often the tie of family, village, region, past association, or merely common membership in the ethnic group. After the appointment of a Simalungun Batak as Regional Head (see below) the range of officials amenable to such contacts was fairly broad. Although not a party leader or member, the villager might also have stated his case to a Simalungun Batak party politician or legislator, or to an official of the church who would relay it to the appropriate government official. These channels were employed much more commonly in the 1960s than they had been in the 1950s but with only limited success. A principal obstacle to the success of this informal and personal kind of representation, as to that of party-related representation, was the relative powerlessness of regency government and the lack of resources with which it could meet local demands.

During the period of martial law (1957–63) the regional military commanders were of somewhat greater importance to the Simalungun Batak community as a source of social and political action. In Siantar city the army's regional commander from 1955 to 1958 was a Simalungun Batak. In the period of greatest insecurity in the countryside, he became the critical link between the municipality government and the many villagers who fled Upper Simalungun for the safety of the city. As the possessor of ultimate authority under the state of war and siege, he was able to secure land and building permits and day laborer jobs in the city government for the refugees. The combined regency/municipality army commander from 1961 to 1963 was also a Simalungun Batak and a grandson of the former radja of Raja; several local development projects, particularly the building of village schools, were carried out with his assistance. Plans for the construction of a commercially valuable road in subdistrict Raja Kahean under the army's civic mission program were also initiated by the army commander in this period. With the return to full civilian authority in 1963 the power and freedom of action permitted to the army leadership in Simalungun/Siantar diminished considerably. When a Karo Batak was subsequently appointed regional military commander, the link this office had provided between the villagers of Upper Simalungun and the regency political process was broken.

Regency-Level Leadership: The Search for Unity Continues

Although the Simalungun Batak political elite in Siantar failed to develop an organizational base in the villages in the 1960s, its influence in regency-wide politics increased considerably. The turning point in the group's fortunes came in 1960 with the appointment, after nomination by the regency legislature, of a Simalungun Batak army officer as Regional Head. A Protestant (but married to a Muslim) born in the former kingdom of Purba and somewhat distantly related to the radja, the new Regional Head was a professional soldier who had spent most of his adult life in Java. Already well connected nationally and with the provincial military leadership in Medan, his most critical problem was to build support in Simalungun. Like the party leaders whose careers we have described in previous chapters, his first concern was to establish himself as a leader of his own ethnic community without, insofar as possible, alienating non-Simalungun Batak members of the regency political elite or jeopardizing his support in Medan and Djakarta. He adopted a strategy of cultivating both the Simalungun Batak urban elite (of all parties and organizations) and simultaneously developing personal support in the villages independent of the party politicians.

The Regional Head's first major project after his inauguration, important for its symbolic as well as its practical value, was the asphalting of the

Haranggaol–Tiga Runggu road in Upper Simalungun. This project produced the first clash with PKI and (non-Simalungun Batak) PNI leaders in the legislature, who were already opposed to him because of his provincial and national allies. In the ensuing years he continued his activities in Upper Simalungun, assisting in economic development projects such as the planting of orange groves, arranging periodically for the supply of agricultural implements, seeds, and fertilizers to the village population at fixed government prices, and so on. Where possible, he appointed Simalungun Batak subdistrict officers and other officials, such as the head of the Department of General Administration (the immediate superior of the subdistrict officers), and he lobbied successfully in Medan for the appointment of Simalungun Bataks to the posts of head of Cultural Inspection and head of the Agrarian Service. He was also active in adat affairs and in 1964 organized and financed an impressive and well-attended ceremony in which the remains of a prominent aristocrat ancestor were moved to an elaborate new resting place.

The 1964 Seminar on Simalungun Culture, of which the Regional Head and other Simalungun Batak politicians were the chief organizers, provides an excellent illustration of the care taken to balance the need for ethnic support with the requirements of the national polity. The motto of the seminar, hung over the main street of Siantar, was: "Berantas Kebudajaan Asing, Bina Kebudajaan Nasional Bersumber Kebudajaan Daerah" (Combat Foreign Culture, Build National Culture Based on Regional Culture). The first part of the motto reflected a campaign, instigated by PKI and supported by President Sukarno and several political parties, to prohibit the importation of Western films and other paraphernalia of popular Western culture into Indonesia; the second part paid homage to Indonesian nationalism, and the third part was intended to win the support of the Simalungun Batak community.

In the selection of seminar participants, the organizers were careful to exclude or to give only subordinate roles to individuals linked with the traditional aristocracy and former KRSST activists, as well as some leaders of BAPOST who were thought to be too openly "suku-minded." The result was to diminish the value of the seminar as a scholarly conference designed to explore Simalungun culture (since the most prominent adat specialists were former aristocrats and KRSST supporters) but to enhance its value as a demonstration to Djakarta of the ethnic group's contributions to the Revolution and its loyalty to the regime. Despite the exclusion of "nonrevolutionary" political leaders, the seminar was well attended by delegates from all subdistricts with a substantial Simalungun Batak population and contributed handsomely to the organizers' reputations in the villages.

The Regional Head's greatest opportunity to increase Simalungun Batak political influence, and thus enhance his own position, occurred shortly after his inauguration in 1960, when the old regency legislature was abolished and machinery for the establishment of the new one set in motion. Two nominees for each seat in the new body (to be divided among party and functional group representatives) were requested from all legal parties and organizations, with the final choices to be made by the governor of North Sumatra on the recommendations of the Regional Head of Simalungun and the provincial military commander (who was in turn to receive recommendations from the regency/municipality military commander). From each party and organization the Regional Head requested, and in most cases received, at least one Simalungun Batak nominee. For unorganized functional groups such as adat, national entrepreneurs, cooperatives (of which there were many different kinds with no central leadership), and for the Protestant and Catholic religious leadership positions he played a leading role in the actual selection of nominees. His support for NU and IPKI representation (neither party had members in the old legislature) was also crucial. In the end, after months of complicated bargaining within the regency (mostly with the parties) and at the provincial level (mostly within the military), Simalungun Batak representation was increased from eight to fourteen, including two NU members, one member each from Parkindo, PKI, IPKI, and Partai Katholik, and the representatives of the police, veterans (also a PNI leader), Protestant and Catholic religious leadership, women (the chairman of PNI's women's organization), national entrepreneurs (a PNI leader), cooperatives, and adat (a KRSST representative in the old legislature).[5] The army's seat in the new body, however, went to a Karo Batak.

5. In the old legislature there were 3 Simalungun Batak members from KRSST and 1 each from PNI, Parkindo, Masjumi, Partai Katholik, and PSI.

After the inauguration of the new legislature cooperation between the "Simalungun bloc"[6] and the Regional Head became close, and, on matters of secondary concern to the party leadership, fairly effective. The bloc obtained informal representation on every legislative committee, enabling its members to keep the Regional Head informed of all committee activities designed to undermine his position or oppose his policies. It also lent support in committee and in the full council to the Regional Head's annual budget recommendations and backed various projects, such as the acquisition of plantation concessions (as a means of increasing regency government revenues) and the production of a film on the Revolution in Simalungun, which he proposed.

Despite common ethnicity and the personal obligations of the Simalungun Batak members to the Regional Head, without whose support they would not have been appointed, the bloc was not able to unite on important issues, particularly with regard to the selection of government personnel. As ethnic differences constituted the chief source of factionalism within the parties, so the principal obstacle to ethnic group unity in the legislature was loyalty to party. In the most extreme case, PKI's Simalungun Batak legislator refused to attend the occasional meetings of the bloc or to cooperate with it in any way. PNI's Simalungun Bataks were more willing to promote bloc activities and even assumed informal positions of leadership within it. In 1963, however, they overstepped the boundaries of party discipline by signing a letter supporting the candidacy of the Regional Head for the provincial governorship, for which two of them were suspended and a third expelled from party membership.[7]

The limitations of the Simalungun bloc were clearly in evidence during the selection by the legislature of a Regional Secretary in 1964. Many Simalungun Bataks, within and outside the legislature, took the position that such an important office, second only in responsibility to the Regional Head, ought to be given to a member of the indigenous ethnic group of the regency. Informal meetings, attended by some members of the bloc and by a

6. The designation given to the group by non-Simalungun Bataks. Simalungun Bataks in the legislature denied that such a bloc existed.

7. See the earlier discussion of this affair in the account of PNI factionalism in Chapter 5.

number of civil servants and other interested individuals, were held to discuss the problem, and pressure was applied on the Regional Head.

In the final analysis, however, nonethnic factors played the deciding role. The Regional Head, perhaps afraid of losing Parkindo's support and concerned that an attempt to push a fellow Simalungun Batak might make him appear too suku-conscious, provided only hesitant leadership.[8] Within the legislature, Simalungun Batak PNI members, under suspension because of their previous letter of support for the Regional Head, chose to adhere to the party line rather than support a Simalungun Batak candidate. NU's leaders insisted on a Muslim Simalungun Batak, Partai Katholik's representative wanted the secretaryship for himself, and even Parkindo's one Simalungun Batak leader (although no longer permitted by law to be a party member) was apparently wary of future reprisals from his party. When the final selection took place the candidate of PNI, PKI, and Parkindo, a North Tapanuli Batak, won a two-thirds majority. The nominee generally assumed to be the candidate of the Simalungun bloc won only two votes, both from nonparty functional group representatives. Rather than vote for a non-Muslim, NU walked out of the meeting. On this important issue Simalungun unity—and thus an influential role for the Simalungun Batak political elite—was unattainable.

Implications for Integration

This unique pattern of high ethnic political consciousness and the establishment of an ethnic political party, followed by the almost total absence of organization and the concomitant dependence upon prominent individuals, was not conducive to the effective integration of the Simalungun Batak community into postindependence Indonesian politics. The initial pattern, because of the uncompromising ethnic hostility, the dependence on traditional elites, and the lack of linkage beyond the region, was a blueprint for isolation, not integration. The developments of the 1960s did not represent

8. A few months earlier the Karo Batak Regional Head of the nearby town of Tebingtinggi, who had apparently engineered the selection of a Karo Batak Regional Secretary, was attacked by PKI, PNI, and several other parties and subsequently "retooled."

a real improvement, for the Simalungun Batak regency elite (with the partial exception of the Regional Head) was not dependent in any significant sense on the support of the ethnic community and thus was not influenced in any consistent or pronounced fashion by that community. Instead, their constituencies were in the civil and military bureaucracies, and they reacted primarily to stimuli from those structures. At best, the representation of group interests through the civil-military elite provided only a short-run, partial, and tenuous substitute for participation in effective national political organizations operating within a framework of authoritative legislative structures at both the local and national levels.

The transition from traditional to colonial to postindependence politics has been a difficult one for the Simalungun Batak community. Small in numbers, internally diverse, tradition oriented, and inward looking, the ethnic group and its leadership have been unable to play a significant role in the determination of their own destiny. The only kind of organization that has been able to win significant Simalungun Batak support has been based on ethnic exclusiveness, a principle that is unacceptable to the dominant national political elite and dysfunctional for the achievement of the ethnic group's individual and collective goals. Conversely, those few Simalungun Batak politicians, most of them residents of Siantar, who have associated themselves with national political parties have been unable to build support among their potential constituencies in the villages. Thus the Simalungun people and their leadership have not been able to develop the kind of political organization, rooted in the villages and linked with the national political system, that might enable them over time to achieve effective representation and a measure of integration into the national political process. Moreover, with continued army dominance of Indonesian political life, the prospects for organizational development do not seem bright. The case of the Simalungun Bataks, in sum, is an object lesson in how not to promote integration.

7. NATIONAL INTEGRATION IN A NEW STATE: IMPLICATIONS OF THE SIMALUNGUN/SIANTAR DATA

The problem of national integration in a new state (or in any political system) is fundamentally a problem of loyalties. Specifically, a modern polity may be said to be integrated (1) when most people accept the territorial boundaries of the nation-state as a given of political life and do not attempt to make them either more or less inclusive, and (2) when most people accept the structures of government and the rules of the political process as legitimate and authoritative for the whole society. National integration thus involves consensus on the limits of the political community and on the nature of the political regime.[1]

The achievement of national integration in Indonesia, and by extension in other new states, is the central question to which this book is addressed. In this chapter I want to indicate, on the basis of the Simalungun/Siantar data, what I believe to be the major obstacles to national integration and to suggest how these obstacles can be overcome. I do not claim universal validity for the viewpoint expressed here, although I would argue that its modification or refutation requires much more thoroughgoing empirical analysis in many new states and at the local level than has heretofore been attempted.

1. The terms regime and community are used as defined by David Easton in "An Approach to the Analysis of Political Systems," *World Politics,* 9 (1957), and in "Political Anthropology," in B. Siegel, ed., *Biennial Review of Anthropology* (Stanford, Stanford University Press, 1959).

In the Introduction I identified two major obstacles, widely discussed in the literature, to the creation of integrated political systems in the new states.[2] First, integration is hampered by the existence of a series of horizontal cleavages based on ethnic, racial, religious, regional, and other differences which compete with the nation-state as the ultimate focus of political loyalties. To the degree that individuals identify with a subnational grouping as the terminal political unit, disintegration of the nation is a constant threat.

A second obstacle to the achievement of integrated polities is the existence of a national elite in many respects culturally distinct from the majority of the population. While still sharing some of the values of the predominantly rural population, the elite "is more oriented to the international patterns of intelligentsia culture common to ruling groups in all the new Bandung countries."[3] Elite members tend to look outward for their behavioral models and their guiding values. In their personal life they desire a high standard of living, a chance to acquire the products of industrial society, an opportunity to conform to what they take to be a modern way of life. For their societies, they desire a modernized, industrial economy, a government with extensive and effective authority based on popular sovereignty, prestige and power in international affairs, and so on.[4]

The diffusion of the world culture,[5] like cultural diffusion in other times and places, has had an uneven impact on the peoples of Asia and Africa. Its effects have been most marked on the elite and have only lightly brushed the ordinary villager or town-dweller, who remains deeply embedded in his traditional culture and patterns of social interaction. Many of his daily needs are filled through the networks of traditional and semi-traditional social structures upon which he is likely to be more dependent than he is upon the government. His view of the world is defined and

2. See the literature cited in the Introduction.

3. Clifford Geertz, "The Javanese Kijaji: The Changing Role of a Cultural Broker," *Comparative Studies in Society and History, 2,* 228.

4. The model of modernity, as perceived by elites in the new states, is presented most eloquently in Edward Shils, "Political Development in the New States," *Comparative Studies in Society and History,* vol. 2 (1960).

5. This phrase is adopted from the writing of Lucian Pye. See, e.g., his *Politics, Personality and Nation-Building.*

limited by the various subnational groupings—from the nuclear family to the village, lineage, clan, ethnic, religious, or regional group—of which he is a member by birth. Because, unlike the educated urbanite, he is extremely dependent on these groups it is difficult for him to rise above the loyalties and commitments they demand. Because he has been less exposed to the world culture, he does not share, or feels much less intensely, the drive for modernity so characteristic of the elite. His goals in life tend to be limited, heavily influenced by the traditional culture, and oriented toward those local groups with which he most closely identifies. The goals of the elite, by contrast, are on a much grander scale, are heavily influenced by the world culture, and are oriented toward the development and progress of the nation (as these concepts are defined by the elite). Elite and mass in the new states thus suffer from a communication and comprehension gap of major proportions.

The Simalungun/Siantar data, as presented in the preceding chapters, suggest several modifications of this analysis. First, with regard to the problem of horizontal cleavages, my findings indicate the existence of complex patterns of local and supralocal loyalties in the Indonesian setting. Less than a century ago, at the time of the first sustained Dutch incursions in the region, the most inclusive governmental units with a claim on individual loyalties were the traditional kingdoms of the Simalungun Bataks. Among the neighboring North and South Tapanuli Bataks loyalties were directed primarily toward the localized lineage group, and there is some evidence to suggest that it was really the village group that made the strongest claim on the Simalungun Bataks.

The impact of more than half a century of social change altered these patterns in significant ways, producing what I have called, following Clifford Geertz, an integrative revolution. For at least the last few decades the inhabitant of Simalungun/Siantar has identified most strongly with his ethnic or ethnoreligious group, and local loyalties and hostilities have been heavily colored by this ethnic self-identification. Practically all aspects of social life—residence, educational and occupational opportunities, religious belief and practice, friendship, political organization—are today affected by the perception of ethnic differences.

However, ethnic group loyalty in Simalungun/Siantar is not seen as an alternative to membership in the Indonesian nation. No group in the region is totally isolated from supralocal affiliations. The North Tapanuli and Simalungun Bataks share Christian and other values with groups scattered throughout the archipelago; the South Tapanuli Bataks are adherents of a Muslim-entrepreneurial culture common to much of Indonesia; and the Javanese visit their kin in Java and share many common problems with their North Tapanuli neighbors in the plantation villages. The region-based antagonisms over the rights of indigenous versus immigrant peoples have also contributed to a measure of cooperation among, on one side, the Coastal Malays and Simalungun and Karo Bataks, and on the other, the Javanese and Tapanuli Bataks. The party system, by providing national structures within which most local groups have participated, has done much to develop these affiliations with supralocal groups. Finally, there is the critically important sense of belonging to the nation, irrespective of local differences and supralocal affiliations. Difficult to measure, this commitment to the idea of an Indonesian nation is deeply rooted in the colonial and revolutionary past and exists at present independent of and higher than the various subnational loyalties. While national commitment varies in degree and is more intensely felt by the local political and governmental elite and by the more urbanized and educated elements, it is clearly present in the minds and behavior of a large and diverse segment of the Simalungun/Siantar population. Moreover, there is no longer any significant segment of local society actively opposed to the nationalist ideal.

Thus the original formulation of the problem of horizontal cleavages has been modified to some extent; but it has not been analyzed out of existence. At both the local and national levels in Indonesia there remain extremely serious obstacles to national integration, particularly with regard to the nature of the regime. In Simalungun/Siantar, ethnic or ethnoreligious loyalties, based as they are on the ineluctable primordial givens of social life, produce deeply rooted hostilities which make compromise on local political issues difficult to achieve. A party system structured in large part in terms of ethnoreligious cleavages compounds the difficulty, for it throws the burden of decision-making on the governmental structures and on inter- rather than intraparty negotiations. At the national level some of these problems are mitigated by the multiethnic character of the national parties, but the fundamental cleavage in Indonesian politics, that between the Islamic-entrepreneurial and Javanese-aristocratic political cultures, remains. Between these two blocs there have been major and nearly unreconcilable differences with regard to the nature of the regime—Muslim versus secular state—and even within the blocs there have been profound differences. All of these conceptions have been opposed by such parties as Parkindo and Partai Katholik.

With regard to the elite–mass gap in the Indonesian setting, some modifications are also in order. First, a simple dichotomy between elite and nonelite is inappropriate to the Simalungun/Siantar data and should be replaced by a concept of intermediate elites at the village, subdistrict, regency/municipality, and provincial levels. Although there is not a simple one-to-one relationship, I would suggest that conformity to the norms of the national elite varies directly with position in the various hierarchies of political leadership, i.e. elite members at the provincial and regency/municipality levels are in general more oriented toward the national elite culture than are those at the subdistrict and village levels. Similarly, as one descends the elite hierarchy, regional and local leaders are likely to share to a greater extent the values and aspirations of the nonelite.[6] In Simalungun/Siantar it is not the cleavage between a coherent regency/municipality elite and an undifferentiated rural or urban mass that is critical, but rather the cleavages among ethnoreligious groups. While the type and the strength of links binding elite to nonelite vary, each ethnoreligious group in the region has (or has had) political party leadership which its members have recognized as more or less representative and working for the interests of the community. The major nonprimordial social groups in the region, the plantation workers and squatters, have also had party support for their interests. In fact, of all the major interests and combinations of interests in Simalungun/Siantar, only the pressures for and against a separate province of East Sumatra were not articulated through the party system. Moreover, the desire for regency/ municipality autonomy, for an increase in the authority of the local gov-

6. Hildred Geertz ("Indonesian Cultures and Communities," in Ruth McVey, *Indonesia,* pp. 39–40) makes a further distinction along the same continuum between "metropolitan" and "local" elites in Indonesia's small towns.

ernment and in the role of the parties in that government, has been shared
by nearly all of the local elite and nonelite, irrespective of ethnic and other
differences.

A second modification of the elite–mass dichotomy is the observation that
even in terms of the extremes the gap in values and aspirations is not complete. Both national elite and village nonelite share, to varying degrees, values associated with modernization.[7] In those countries, like Indonesia, in
which the nationalist revolution was long and violent (or in which, like
India, there was prolonged nationalist agitation), a large segment of the
society has been exposed to the national idea. With increasing urbanization,
education, and exposure to the mass media, ordinary citizens also come to
desire a standard of living, if not commensurate with that of the most advanced Western countries, at least better than that which they have known
previously. With increased demands comes, moreover, an increased desire
to participate in the making of political decisions, for it is fundamentally the
political system in the new states that is believed to govern the distribution
of valued goods and services.

Most frequently, however, (and it is here that the national-elite–village-
mass gap begins to assume critical proportions) rising demands are articulated through political organizations heavily dependent upon primordial
loyalties. The reason for this is apparent. Unlike the national elite member,
the villager is deeply enmeshed in traditional social structures and culture
despite his revolutionary experience and/or partial exposure to the modern
world. When he acts politically, he is likely to do so in ways and through
organizations that are at least in part familiar to him. He wants a recognizable relationship between the new and the old, he tends to define new demands and problems in terms of old loyalties, and he seeks assistance from
those individuals whom he feels he can trust, i.e. individuals with whom he
shares a traditional relationship.

It is this need for familiarity on the part of the nonelite member and the
concomitant identification of his present aspirations and their fulfillment
with traditional patterns of behavior, attitudes, and loyalties that goes a
long way toward explaining the success or failure of party organizational

7. And, it should be noted, both groups also share some traditional values and
attitudes.

efforts in Simalungun/Siantar. KRSST was, in its limited way, successful because most Simalungun Bataks put community interests first and see solutions to all other problems in terms of increased power for their ethnic group. Any demand a Simalungun Batak might make on the government—for schools and teachers, for roads, fertilizers, a job in the city—will, he believes, get a positive response only if members of his ethnic group are in positions of political influence. Parkindo and Masjumi were successful because the North and South Tapanuli Bataks viewed these organizations as representative of their interests not only as religious groups but as ethnic groups as well. These parties provided, moreover, structures within which the somewhat weaker but still relevant subethnic loyalties to clan and region of origin could have a voice. PNI's success was due in part to the ability of the leadership to capitalize on the disaffection of segments of various ethnic groups from the dominant values of their communities, especially among the North Tapanuli and Simalungun Bataks. While the party was multi-ethnic at the regency/municipality level, most of its subdistrict and nearly all of its village branches were dominated by members of a single ethnic group. These very local leaders in turn supported the aspirations of their ethnic-mates at the regency/municipality and higher levels. For the Javanese members of the party and its subsidiary organizations, attracted initially by the appeal to workers and squatters as a social class, ethnic loyalty to subdistrict leaders and to Subroto and the view that PNI is *the* party of the ethnic Javanese have been important ingredients in the maintenance of support. Even PKI, at the very lowest levels in its mass organizations, traded on ethnic-related support although to a much lesser extent than PNI. Its success was due in considerable measure to the unique plantation situation and could not be duplicated in the very different circumstances of Upper Simalungun and Siantar precisely because the party refused to associate itself with primordial loyalties.

From the viewpoint of the national elite, two problems emerge from this tendency to act politically in familiar ways and to shape political organizations in terms of traditional attitudes and loyalties. First, the natural response of the elite member to demands articulated through semitraditional structures or structures heavily rooted in subnational primordial support is

Table 7–1. Major Political Parties in Simalungun/Siantar: A Comparison

Party	National Significance	Ethnicity of Membership	Organizational Type	Dominant Leadership Type	Leadership–Membership Bond	Bases of Intraparty Factionalism
PNI	national	Javanese, North Tapanuli Batak, Simalungun Batak	mass	professional politicians	weak despite much communication	ethnic ties, alliances among leaders with ethnic support groups; factions stable
PKI	national	Javanese, North Tapanuli Batak	mass	professional politicians	weak for subsidiary organizations, strong for party	apparently absent
Parkindo	national	North Tapanuli Batak	cadre	civil servants, entrepreneurs, traders	strong despite intermittent communication and minimal organization	ethnic, subethnic, friendship; factions unstable
Masjumi	national	mainly South Tapanuli Batak; some Javanese, other devout Muslim groups	cadre	religious leaders and teachers, civil servants, traders	strong despite minimal organization and (since 1961) illegal status	ethnic, subethnic; factions unstable
KRSST	local	Simalungun Batak	cadre	traditional leaders, civil servants	strong while party existed	unknown

fear, for he sees in such demands and organizations a threat to the very foundations of the national state, the limits of the political community. At the same time, the elite member is often committed to democratic values, to ideals of popular sovereignty and popular participation, which he sees as components of modernity. His ultimate response, however, is likely to be repression rather than accommodation, for his fear of national disintegration is greater than his democratic commitment. In the Indonesian case, all but ten political parties were banned during the Guided Democracy period on grounds of behavior disruptive of national unity, and those that remained were peripheral to the decision-making process. In place of the party system as articulator and aggregator of demands stood President Sukarno who, as "extension of the people's tongue," would personally serve as the channel for all demands not dysfunctional for the unity of the nation. Since he represented the nation as a whole, there could not possibly be a proliferation of disruptive primordial-influenced organizations.

A second problem brought about by the relationship between political organization and primordial loyalties relates to the effectiveness of the political system as chief agent of social and economic development for the society. There is ample evidence in the recent political history of both new and old states that, in a culturally fragmented society, a party system based on cultural differences will have enormous difficulties in arriving at solutions to great questions of national policy.[8] The resultant immobilism may, moreover, carry over to the organization of the state, producing regime dissensus; if unresolved over a considerable period of time the acceptability of the political community itself may be called into question. In a situation of governmental immobilism, then, a process of deterioration of loyalties is begun which, if unchecked, may eventually result in national disintegration. In the Indonesian case, it was just such a process that was believed to have been set in motion by the inability of the party-dominated parliament and con-

8. There is, of course, a large literature on fragmented party systems. For recent treatments, see Giovanni Sartori, "European Political Parties: The Case of Polarized Pluralism," in Joseph LaPalombara and Myron Weiner, eds., *Political Parties and Political Development;* (Princeton, N.J., Princeton University Press, 1966); Robert A. Dahl, ed., *Political Oppositions in Western Democracies* (New Haven, Conn., Yale University Press, 1966); Gabriel Almond and G. Bingham Powell, Jr., *Comparative Politics: A Developmental Approach* (Boston, Little, Brown, 1966).

stituent assembly to resolve the social, economic, foreign policy, and constitutional issues of the day. Guided Democracy was thus a response not only to the direct challenge to national unity of subnational loyalties as reflected in the cultural pluralism of the party system, but also to the immobilism resulting from party rigidity on policy.

We come, then, to an evaluation of Guided Democracy as a solution to the integrative problems of the Indonesian political system. In opposing the parliamentary system of the 1950s, President Sukarno and his supporters argued that culturally fragmented political organizations and governmental immobilism were weaknesses inherent in the "liberal" party system and in the parliamentary form. The new order would promote national unity by relying on the integrative abilities of the President himself, by incorporating the major (acceptable) strands of Indonesian political thought—nationalism, religion, and communism—in all governmental bodies, and by creating a Parliament and People's Consultative Assembly (a kind of super-Parliament charged with determining the basic lines of state policy) truly representative of all the Indonesian people through the addition of functional and regional group delegations. Religious interests would thus continue to be recognized (although without the presence of Masjumi, the party of the majority of non-Javanese devout Muslims), as would regional interests (through special seats in the People's Consultative Assembly allotted to the various provinces). Ethnic divisions, however, were condemned as a harmful residue of the so-called divide-and-rule policy of Dutch imperialism, and were thus illegitimate as a basis for participation in political life. With regard to ethnic differences Sukarno called periodically for increased intermarriage.

What were the effects of Guided Democracy on progress toward the achievement of national integration in Indonesia? Before examining the specific implications of the Simalungun/Siantar data, some attention should be paid to the personal role of Sukarno. It is often claimed that, for all of the President's weaknesses, he did succeed in enhancing national unity. As a national leader with charismatic qualities he bridged the gaps among primordial groups and between elite and mass, personifying the nation in a critical period of nation-building.[9] His personal prestige helped to win mass

9. This is, of course, an adaptation of the familiar Weberian argument concerning charismatic authority as a transitional phase between traditional and rational-

support not only for the regime he created but also for the political community.

This view, if it can be maintained at all, needs considerable qualification. In the first place, it should be recalled that Sukarno is culturally a Javanese.[10] His appeal was greatest in the homeland of the ethnic Javanese (the provinces of East and Central Java), and only in these regions can it be argued that he was believed to possess charismatic, i.e. supernatural or mystical, qualities. The traditional component of Sukarno's ideological formulations, e.g. the emphasis on creating a political system in harmony with the "Indonesian personality" and on a return to democracy as practiced in the Indonesian village, was most attractive to the ethnic Javanese, who shared Sukarno's cultural background. Similarly, the increasingly sultanlike behavior of the President, his use of the traditional yellow in his personal flag, and so on, appealed primarily to the abangan Javanese. To these people, Sukarno may have been a sultan; to most Outer Islanders, particularly members of the "political public,"[11] he was a much more human figure, respected for his leadership during the Revolution, for his uncompromising stand on the West Irian issue, and to some extent for his attempts to win a place of respect for Indonesia in world politics. At the same time, he was suspected of partiality toward the Javanese and was criticized for the authoritarianism and centralization of the Djakarta regime and for the increasing honor, if not formal authority, given the Communist Party. Former members and supporters of Masjumi fervently, if for a long time passively, opposed Sukarno and his regime. The President stood, after all, squarely in the center of only one of the two major political cultures in Indonesia, the Javanese-aristocratic. Neither he nor any of his supporters could effectively bridge the gap between the Javanese-aristocratic culture and its chief antagonist, the Islamic-entrepreneurial culture, large sections of which had been alienated from the regime since 1958 or earlier.

---

legal authority. Max Weber, *The Theory of Social and Economic Organization* (New York, The Free Press of Glencoe, 1964), pp. 358–92.

10. Sukarno's father was Javanese and his mother Balinese, but he grew up in a Javanese environment. See Cindy Adams, *Sukarno, An Autobiography* (Indianapolis, Ind., Bobbs-Merrill, 1965).

11. Feith's term. See above, p. 6.

Despite these qualifications, it is nonetheless true that Sukarno was the preeminent political personality in postindependence Indonesia and personally symbolized the continuity of an Indonesian nation-state legitimized by the nationalist movement and the Revolution. To remove him from office required great political skill and finesse. In the aftermath of the events of October 1, 1965, the new government moved exceedingly slowly to strip the President of his office and power, despite considerable provocation and the urgings of anti-Sukarno student demonstrators. By treating him with consummate politeness and delicacy, by easing him gradually out of power, they hoped to assure the continuity of the regime and to avoid the alienation of the Javanese and all those who had come to consider the ideas (however interpreted) and person of Sukarno inseparable from the unity and goals of the nation. Like the Masjumi supporters during the Guided Democracy period, many of these individuals have in recent years become internal exiles. In building and maintaining regime support for the future they, together with the former supporters of the Communist Party, constitute the most pressing integrative problem facing the government of General Suharto.

If Sukarno's personal integrative role was something less than has been claimed for it, then what of the procedures and structures of government he was instrumental in establishing? On this point the Simalungun/Siantar data and more general considerations suggest that, far from promoting national integration, the structures and processes of Guided Democracy tended to undermine those national loyalties that had already emerged. Much of my argument here is implicit in the foregoing discussion. First, as of 1950 commitment to the concept of an Indonesian nation was already firmly rooted among most segments of the political-governmental elite in Simalungun/Siantar and had begun to filter down to the villages. There is no evidence to suggest that this commitment became any weaker in the succeeding years. All political parties, legal and banned, accepted the idea of common membership in the nation, and even the most disruptive conflicts of the postrevolutionary period—the agitation for an East Sumatran province and the provincial coup attempts of 1956–57—reflected opposition to the policies and personnel of the central government and to the regime, but not to the basis of the political community. This is, I believe, equally true of the up-heavals following the 1965 murder of the generals.

While neither the parliamentary nor the Guided Democracy regime seems to have had a measurable impact on loyalties toward the political community, at least in the short run, attitudes toward the regime became sharply polarized in the Sukarno period. From 1950 to 1955 local political leaders concentrated their energies on building local support which would enable their respective organizations to play an influential role in decision-making within the parliamentary regime. While not all of these leaders shared equally a commitment to that regime (Masjumi's demands for an Islamic state and PKI's espousal of a communist state represented the extreme poles) most were attempting, at least for the time being, to obtain their goals through the parliamentary process. The breakdown of parliamentary decision-making, or perhaps more accurately the continued failure of parliament to arrive at broadly acceptable solutions to policy differences, and the final assumption of power by President Sukarno led to a breakdown of the admittedly tenuous regime consensus that had existed among the local leadership. While much of the Simalungun/Siantar Javanese community and its PNI and PKI leadership supported Guided Democracy (although both parties opposed the weakening of the local legislatures which Guided Democracy entailed), the South Tapanuli Bataks and their Masjumi leadership firmly opposed it. North Tapanuli Bataks (who were in the paradoxical position of being grateful to President Sukarno for his religious tolerance but opposed to most of his other policies) and the local Parkindo leadership took a plague-on-both-your-houses position but continued to work to maximize their own influence within the new regime. The Simalungun Bataks similarly did not support either Guided Democracy or an Islamic state, although those Simalungun Bataks who were active in party and governmental circles did what they could to maintain an influential position for their ethnic group.

Beyond the fact that Guided Democracy had strong support from only a part of the local (or national) population, two of its features with regard to the maintenance of regime loyalties strike this observer as crucial. First, there was general recognition that Guided Democracy was a temporary phenomenon. Nearly all of the local political leaders in Simalungun/Siantar (with the exception of some of the more militant PNI youth) were aware of the fact that the regime was heavily dependent for its stability on Sukarno and would not long outlive him. No one could foresee with much clarity what events might precipitate the downfall of the regime, but all knew that it would happen, and in the comparatively near future. All political activity in the region was thus heavily future-oriented, with each group of leaders preparing itself for the eventual upheaval and giving little attention to making the formal structures and processes of the regime work. Politics in Simalungun/Siantar in 1963–64 was fraught with enormous tension, for the stakes were high and the rules and starting time of the game uncertain. The effect was to increase suspicion and hostility among the leaders and to intensify further party and ethnoreligious group polarization. The tension was especially high between the Communists on the one hand and the devout Muslims and Christians on the other, and this spilled over into some more generalized Javanese versus Batak hostility, but all groups and organizations eyed each other warily.

The second feature of Guided Democracy was its inability to command a sufficient monopoly over the instruments of authority or to control sufficient material resources to enable it to carry out its policies and programs effectively. Formally, the Sukarno regime was highly centralized. Much of the authority that had been given to local executives and legislatures in 1957 was withdrawn in 1959. It was also authoritarian, as formal decision-making power was concentrated in the executive branch, which exercised broad influence over both legislative and judicial matters. If the reconstituted national parliament and the People's Consultative Assembly approximated rubber stamps controlled by the President, the regency/municipality legislatures, despite valiant efforts by some of their members, were largely functionless and ignored by the Regional Heads.

The transfer of authority from the legislature to the executive was, of course, a conscious decision on the part of the President and his supporters. Its effects, however, in terms of increased control over the making and implementing of decisions, were not as hoped. One major difficulty was the low priority attached by the government to problems of economic stability and development.[12] Already at a low level of performance, the Indonesian economy was allowed to stagnate. Increasing expenditures, necessary particularly to maintain the modernized armed services and the swollen bureaucracy, and to pay for the building of huge monuments and a sports complex in Djakarta, were financed through the simple, but highly inflationary and thus ultimately self-defeating, mechanism of printing money.[13] Moreover, much potential government revenue was lost through extensive smuggling activities carried on by regional military commanders. The effects on governmental performance were (1) to reduce to a bare minimum funds available for domestic projects of all sorts, routine as well as developmental, and (2) to impair administrative efficiency at all levels, since salary increases did not even approach the rate at which prices rose. In Simalungun/Siantar, civil servants, schoolteachers, members of the regional legislatures, and others on fixed salaries were forced to take second and third jobs, work in the rice fields, or accept bribes in order to maintain a minimum standard of living.[14] Governmental revenues could not cover even routine administrative expenditures, forcing repeated requests (only sometimes met) to Medan and Djakarta for subsidies.

Another major difficulty with regard to effective policy implementation lay in the fact that, despite formal centralization and concentration of authority in the hands of the President, it was the regional military officials who exercised predominant influence in their areas. This was especially true during the period of martial law (1957–63) but military power did not seem to have been much diminished in the North Sumatra of 1964. While most decisions at the regency/municipality level were left to the locally responsible officials (there were, in any event, few decisions of any importance that could be made at this level), the provincial military officials had an

12. An excellent discussion of Indonesia's economy may be found in Douglas S. Paauw, "From Colonial to Guided Economy," in Ruth McVey, *Indonesia.*

13. Between December 1964 and March 1965, for example, money in circulation rose from 263 billion to 818 billion rupiahs.

14. For a rather optimistic assessment of the economic effects of moonlighting, see Everett D. Hawkins, "Job Inflation in Indonesia," *Asian Survey,* 6 (May 1966), 264–75.

informal veto and, if they wished to use it (as in the selection of the Regional Head of Siantar in 1964), dominant influence in appointments to key offices. In many instances in various parts of the country provincial officials implemented or did not implement central policies as they saw fit.[15]

In the final analysis, neither the personal qualities and ideological formulations of President Sukarno nor the structures and processes he was instrumental in shaping (and an acknowledged master at manipulating) were conducive to national integration. Sukarno's charisma and his ideology had profound meaning for only a segment of the Indonesian population (and were explicitly rejected by many others), and the inculcation of the ideology was hampered by limited control over material resources and the instruments of authority. In Simalungun/Siantar ideological indoctrination was not taken very seriously, either by the government officials who were required to take a brief course in Medan and to listen to the speeches of "indoctrination teams" who periodically visited the region, or by university students who were required to hear a weekly ideological lecture by the municipality regional head.[16]

Structurally, formal authoritarianism and centralization without the informal means to acquire and maintain control meant that the regional military hierarchies were to a large extent worlds unto themselves. While they certainly did not reject the formal structures of the regime or the concept of an Indonesian political community, their relative independence from central authority and popular pressure served to undermine loyalties at both levels. Political parties and subsidiary organizations in Simalungun/Siantar, in North Sumatra, and at the national level whose leaders were at least in some measure representative of and responsive to the demands of the public were shunted aside in favor of structures that had few ties with significant local and supralocal groups and to which popular access was

15. Herbert Feith, "Indonesia," in George McT. Kahin, ed., *Governments and Politics of Southeast Asia*, pp. 240–41, 256–57, and passim.

16. Nowhere was the generational cleavage more apparent than in these lectures. The Regional Head (an old revolutionary active in the prewar PNI in Karo) alternated reading of Sukarno's speeches with attempts at interpretation; the student response was boredom or barely muffled laughter. The text used in this course (and also in the high schools, where it was taught by teachers for the most part indifferent or opposed to the regime) was Mr. Soepardo et al. *Manusia dan Masjarakat Baru Indonesia (Civics)* [A New Indonesian Man and Society] (Djakarta, 1962).

severely limited. The effect was to deny popular participation in the political process at all levels and to increase the psychological distance between the villager, who came more and more to feel that there was little he could do to influence even local decisions, and the regency/municipality, provincial, and central governments. The levers of power were no longer open, close at hand, and accessible through organizations he could understand and support, but rather hidden from view, far removed from the local scene, and at best only vaguely related to the attitudes and values he brought to the political arena. In Simalungun/Siantar in 1963–64 the prevailing attitudes toward the regime were alienation, heightened concern for personal or local affairs per se, wait-and-see attitudes, and preparation for an eventual power struggle among the various competing groups. None of these postures contributed to integration either at the regime level or, because of the primordial antagonisms and feelings of alienation and withdrawal they intensified, at the community level.

In essence, the transition from parliamentary to Guided Democracy in Simalungun/Siantar was a shift away from a political system that encouraged, and was getting, popular participation in government toward a political process dominated by individuals without an organizational base in the society, who neither communicated with nor could speak for the majority of the local population. Indonesian politics during the Guided Democracy period was awash on a flood of rhetoric and sloganeering designed to obscure sociopolitical diversity rather than to provide it with a meaningful ideological and institutional framework. Beneath the rhetoric, conflict among members of the elite was intense but for the most part removed from the masses of the population. In this pattern of elite dominance and mass isolation, Geertz has argued, can be seen a revival of an ancient tradition in Indonesian politics, the

> theory of the exemplary center, the notion that the capital city (or more accurately the king's palace) was at once a microcosm of the supernatural order . . . and the material embodiment of political order. The capital was not merely the nucleus, the engine, or the pivot of the state; it *was* the state.[17]

17. Clifford Geertz, "Ideology as a Cultural System," in David E. Apter, ed., *Ideology and Discontent* (New York, The Free Press of Glencoe, 1964), p. 66. Robert Heine-

[Under Guided Democracy] the supra-local polity, the national state, shrinks more and more to the limits of its traditional domain, the capital city—Djakarta—plus a number of semi-independent tributary cities and towns held to a minimal loyalty by the threat of centrally-applied force.[18]

It is difficult, and perhaps presumptuous, to go beyond discussion of the effects of Guided Democracy to propose solutions to Indonesia's integrative problems. At the same time, it is necessary that the attempt be made, not only because Indonesia's present "New Order" must try to solve these problems but also because of their relevance to many other new states. The basic integrative problem in Indonesia, I have argued, has to do with regime rather than community loyalties, particularly with regard to the elite (including the provincial and regency/municipality-level elites) and the political public, among whom the sense of national identity is strong. The problem has been to establish a regime broadly inclusive of the major political cultures, at the national and local levels, which can at the same time deal reasonably effectively and in a mutually acceptable fashion with major social, economic, and foreign policy issues. To accomplish this, both vertical and horizontal divisions must be closed or at least appreciably narrowed.

In the Indonesian case I believe the cure to be, at least in part, implicit in the disease. The major failing of Guided Democracy was that it contributed to instead of mitigating integrative problems by creating a "participation gap" resulting in the alienation or withdrawal of many individuals and groups from the political system. Popular commitment to the regime declined principally because so few people had access, directly or indirectly, to its decision-making centers. Moreover, the regime did not possess the capacity effectively to impose a unifying ideology and one-party system on its people in the manner of totalitarian states.

In the absence of such a capacity the solution to the participation gap,

Geldern, "Conceptions of State and Kingship in Southeast Asia," *Far Eastern Quarterly,* 2 (November 1942), 15–30, provides a more detailed discussion of the "theory of the exemplary center" with regard to all of the Hindu-Buddhist kingdoms of ancient Southeast Asia.

18. C. Geertz, "Ideology as a Cultural System," p. 69.

which seems undiminished in post-Sukarno Indonesian politics, is to restore a reasonable balance between executive and legislative authority, to expand the authority of local government (particularly at the regency/municipality level, where legislatures already exist and can easily be reactivated), and to permit political parties (especially those that have established themselves as nationally significant) to organize freely and to campaign for local and national legislative seats. While it need not be unlimited (as in the 1950s), some freedom to organize is crucial, for any conceivable imposed alternative in the Indonesian setting—a one-party system (inevitably dominated by an internally divided military), no parties, an attempt to encourage an Anglo-American or Philippine-style two-party system—will significantly reduce the sense of popular participation in organizations that are meaningful to the villager and nonelite urbanite. It was this admittedly still embryonic sense of participation that was the most hopeful sign of progress toward national integration in Simalungun/Siantar in the early 1950s.

From the viewpoint of the current national leadership, advocacy of popular participation through a return to some form of multiparty system and parliamentary government immediately raises two problems to which I have already referred: fear of the disintegrative consequences for the national community of parties heavily dependent on primordially related support, and fear of governmental immobilism. The first of these problems does not seem to be critical. Despite intense ethnic and ethnic-related loyalties, the people of Simalungun/Siantar participated in party politics and generally in their social lives within the framework of national loyalties already molded by the colonial and revolutionary experiences. Their very participation, moreover, meant an involvement in supralocal, and fundamentally national, affairs which if permitted to continue as in the early 1950s would have contributed on balance to an intensification of national loyalties.

The second problem is more difficult, and only with considerable temerity can the broad outlines of a solution be suggested. If governmental immobilism is to be avoided, Indonesia must develop a national ideology that (1) is broad enough to appeal to all of the major strata of Indonesian society and explicitly recognizes the legitimacy of demands rooted in diverse cultural backgrounds, and (2) provides a set of formal and informal rules of a political game whose outcomes are accepted as legitimate and binding. This ideology cannot be made up from whole cloth but must have its roots in what is common in Indonesian culture, historical experience, and contemporary aspirations. It is, of course, much easier to propose such an ideology than to formulate one, particularly for a society with as many divergent values as the Indonesian.

The ideology of Guided Democracy, which was heavily dependent on the Javanese-aristocratic political culture, attempted to submerge cultural diversity in notions of a single Indonesian ethnic group and an Indonesian personality, severely limited popular participation in any meaningful sense, and was widely recognized as a temporary arrangement, clearly does not meet the requirements. The original formulation of Pantja Sila as an incorporative, pluralistic ideology came much closer. Its fate at the hands of various groups contending for power indicates, however, the enormity of the problem of achieving even a minimal consensus on the nature of the regime.

While it is difficult to propose an acceptable ideological framework for the Indonesian political system, the task should not be an impossible one for several reasons. First, there is considerable consensus on the definition of the political community, which serves to orient political leaders toward resolving their differences within that community. This is true not only at the national level but in Simalungun/Siantar as well, where local politicians (especially from 1957 to 1959, but also later) were motivated to cooperate with each other because of their common desire for strong local government in which the legislature would be predominant. Second, the two major political cultures in contemporary Indonesia are not mutually exclusive. In Java, which contains over half the national population, the diverse strands of religious belief—santri, abangan, and prijaji—are in fact all aspects of a syncretic religious tradition. Except perhaps at the furthest extremes, each group shares some of the practices, beliefs, and traditions of the others. Outer Island Muslims, moreover, are linked to the Javanese religious tradition through its santri component. Third, the problem of incorporation of the extremes is made somewhat easier by the removal of the Communist Party from the political arena, although the interests of the millions of people who supported PKI or one of its mass organizations must still somehow be brought into the system. The weakness of PNI, and most especially its dependence on the traditional aristocracy and modern bureaucracy for its local leadership on Java, make it a probably unsuitable alternative, and there is at present no other party that might fill the vacuum.[19] Finally, there is the fact of common aspirations for a more modern society and economy. Between elite and mass and among the various cultural groups there seems to be, in the post-1965 period, a measure of agreement that economic problems come first and that every effort must be made to restore stability and to begin the arduous process of development. While economic issues can be extremely divisive (and in fact tended to deepen the Java-Outer Islands cleavage in the 1950s) there is also the possibility that agreement to place primary emphasis on the economy may have a beneficial effect on consensus in other policy areas and on the rules by which decisions are made.

It is important to stress that I do not mean to minimize the gravity of the obstacles to national integration created by a political order based on popular participation through open partisan competition. Among the various lessons of the Simalungun/Siantar case, none is clearer than the potentially disruptive quality of a party system dependent on primordial loyalties for its local support. Within the locality, one of the principal effects of the organization of the party system was the intensification of the already powerful hostilities between Christian North Tapanuli Bataks (who supported Parkindo) and Muslim South Tapanuli Bataks (who supported Masjumi). If purely local, specifically ethnic parties are allowed to form, as in the case of KRSST, the result is a perpetuation and strengthening of the sense of ethnic community instead of, rather than in combination with, developing regime and national community loyalties. Even the most pan-primordial party in the region, PNI, has been dominated by members of particular ethnic groups at the village and subdistrict levels and has been rent by ethnic-based hostilities at the level of regency/municipality leadership.

Moreover, the continued importance of the elite–mass gap (albeit in less stark a form than originally presented) suggests that it is by no means cer-

19. The PNI on Java has been discussed recently by Donald Hindley, "Political Power and the October 1965 Coup in Indonesia," *Journal of Asian Studies*, 26 (February 1967), 237–49; W. F. Wertheim, "Indonesia Before and After the Untung Coup," *Pacific Affairs*, 39 (Spring-Summer 1966), 115–27; and Daniel S. Lev, "Political Parties in Indonesia," *Journal of Southeast Asian History*, 8 (1967), 52–67.

tain that national party leadership will in fact articulate the interests of the local membership. Elite–mass ideological differences related to modernization and the difficulties involved in the control of leaders by members are serious problems in new states' politics and were apparent in our discussion of organizational linkage in Simalungun/Siantar. In the cases of Masjumi and Parkindo membership involvement in party decision-making and factional conflict was minimal, particularly during the Guided Democracy period but also earlier. It was also true, however, that local partisans understood and supported the objectives of their regency/municipality, provincial, and national leaders, which were directed toward the protection and advancement of the religious community. In the cases of PNI and PKI, firmer bonds between leaders and members were necessitated by weak primordial support and the atmosphere of intense competition. At the same time, as we have indicated, the national leaders of these parties were primarily interested in maximizing their own positions and those of their party organizations in the national political process. To the extent that they articulated local interests, they did so in terms of ideologies of Marhaenism and Marxism which had little meaning for the people whose support they sought.[20]

Despite the enormity of these problems, the Simalungun/Siantar experience also demonstrates the importance for ultimate national integration of dealing with local social groups on their own terms. The impact of PKI strategy is most relevant here, for it was PKI that most explicitly set itself against the recognition of primordial interests in the political process. The result, of course, was that PKI was successful only in those areas where primordial loyalties were, at least in part, submerged in the economic interests of plantation workers and squatters. Elsewhere the party found few supporters: in Upper Simalungun because of the particularly strong sense of communal loyalty, the continued importance of the traditional aristocracy,

20. It should be added that predominantly Javanese parties such as PNI and PKI have tended, at the national level, to ignore the interests of their Outer Island branches. Of a total of 23 branches attending the PNI Party Congress in 1963, representatives from East and Central Java represented 33 percent of the total voting delegation. Computed from Dewan Pimpinan PNI, *Laporan Umum kepada Kongres ke-X Partai Nasional Indonesia* [PNI Leadership Council, *General Report to the Tenth PNI Congress*] (Purwokerto, 1963). "In a situation like that," as a North Tapanuli Batak PNI-Siantar official said, "how much of a role can we hope to play?"

the atheism of PKI, the fact that PNI drained off the most revolutionary and detraditionalized segment of the ethnic group, and most fundamentally because the nature of the Communist appeal seemed irrelevant to the Simalungun Bataks; in Pematangsiantar because the most critical principle of differentiation among individuals is ethnic or ethnoreligious affiliation and PKI refused to relate itself to these differences.[21]

It seems evident that an imposed one-party system, at least of the mobilizational, national-elite-dominated type, would generate at best only slightly more support than PKI was able to achieve.[22] In such a situation, the

21. The attachment of the people of Siantar to primordial group loyalties, as expressed in their 1955 vote and in interviews in 1963–64, suggests the complexities of generalizing about urbanization and its effects in the new states. While my findings confirm those of Edward Bruner with regard to the North Tapanuli Batak community in Medan and are consistent with the general argument of Hildred Geertz, they seem to be at odds with studies of urbanization and tribalism in Africa. See Edward Bruner, "Urbanization and Ethnic Identity in North Sumatra," *American Anthropologist, 63* (1961); Hildred Geertz, "Indonesian Cultures and Communities," in Ruth McVey, ed., *Indonesia,* pp. 37–41; and various publications of the Rhodes-Livingstone Institute, e.g. A. L. Epstein, *Politics in an Urban African Community* (Manchester, Manchester University Press, 1958). The differences are perhaps in degree rather than in kind, for in both Luanshya, Northern Rhodesia, and Pematangsiantar ethnic loyalties are clearly present in local political life, in conjunction with other attitudes related to the particular characteristics of urbanization and the wider political environments of the two towns. Parenthetically, it may be added that cultural assimilation is a solution for integrative problems in Simalungun/Siantar only in the very long run. The present strength of ethnic loyalties indicates that they will be with us for a long time to come and provides an additional reason for dealing with them on their own terms instead of denying their existence or calling for intermarriage.

22. Although I do not believe it to be a suitable solution in the Indonesian case, one-partyism may, in some countries and under specified conditions, provide a nation-wide structure within which the interests of various groups may be represented. For opposing views on the nature, role, and relevance of one-party systems for national integration, see Chief H. O. Davies, "The New African Profile," *Foreign Affairs* (January 1962); David E. Apter, "Some Reflections on the Role of a Political Opposition in New Nations," *Comparative Studies in Society and History, 4* (1962); and Julius Nyerere, "Democracy and the Party System," in Paul E. Sigmund, ed., *The Ideologies of the Developing Nations* (New York, 1967). On one-party mobilization systems, see David Apter, *The Politics of Modernization* (Chicago, University of Chicago Press, 1965).

position of all groups in the region vis-à-vis the structures of authority
would be comparable to the position of the Simalungun Bataks during the
Guided Democracy period: no organized channels of communication and a
heavy reliance on intermittent and unstable personal relationships between
the villager and the government official or military officer (with or without
intermediaries), with responsiveness to village demands beyond local control
and dependent upon the exigencies of intrabureaucracy and intramilitary
power struggles. It is this pattern that the Indonesian political leadership
must avoid if it is to bring about an effective integration of the political
system.

As of mid-1969 it is still difficult to evaluate the potential effects of
General Suharto's "New Order" regime on national integration. In its first
months, the government moved to destroy PKI, consolidate its own position, and by a series of gradual steps remove President Sukarno from office.
The result was a new power structure, dominated by the army (which has
long had integrative problems of its own), but containing important civilian
elements, most of whom are technical experts and nonpartisan bureaucrats
rather than party politicians. The stated program of the regime is to reverse
the economic decline experienced during the past decade and in general to
concentrate on domestic development rather than foreign policy problems.
Political prisoners, leaders of the banned parties and of the regional rebellions, have been released (although the jails are now full of communists
and others implicated in the murder of the generals). Pantja Sila has been
restored to its former prominence in state ideology (although it is now used
for both anti-communist and anti-Islamic purposes), and is currently fea-
tured along with the Constitution of 1945 (in which the executive branch is
predominant) as the central symbol of the regime. Elections have been
promised for 1971, but on what basis is not yet clear. Despite considerable
agitation for political party reform, the government has shown no inclina-
tion to alter a situation in which the old parties (minus PKI and plus a new
Muslim party) continue to exist in a kind of twilight zone, not totally insig-
nificant but not very important either.

It is thus by no means certain that the "New Order" will be better able
than the old to provide a solid basis for national unity. The critical problem
lies in the relationship between participation and effectiveness, and so far,

at least, no adequate formula for solving this problem has been devised. Even if elections are held it seems unlikely that the government will permit a redistribution of authority either away from the center or toward a re-vitalized legislature and party system. Like its immediate predecessor, the Suharto government believes in the efficacy of centralized decision-making and a firm grip, in as few hands as possible, on the instruments of political power. Unlike Sukarno's Guided Democracy system, however, the New Order claims legitimacy not through the charismatic role of a single dom-inant personality but rather through a commitment to pragmatic policy planning and implementation within the framework of the secular nation-state. Whether under such a regime Indonesia can move in the direction of more effective national integration remains to be seen.

Let us turn, finally and very briefly, to the broader question. How can multiethnic nations with elite–mass gaps of serious proportions such as the contemporary new states of Asia and Africa achieve national integration? My analysis, while limited to a single case in a single country and therefore far from definitive, suggests that authoritarianism, centralization, and mo-bilization are not the answers.[23] Beyond the specifics of the Indonesian case, it seems clear that in most new states the resources required to operate effec-tively an authoritarian, highly centralized regime are not readily available to the national elites.[24] To be sure, it is possible that such regimes (e.g. of the communist variety) may emerge and successfully integrate their societies through the exaction of enormous costs in human freedom, although recent events in China and Yugoslavia indicate that communist parties, too, may be imperfect integrative instruments.

Fortunately for the new states and for humanity in general, there are

23. The case for authoritarian regimes in the new states has been most recently made in Claude Ake, *A Theory of Political Integration* (Homewood, Ill., The Dorsey Press, 1967).

24. This point has been forcefully argued for the Ivory Coast, Mali, Ghana, Senegal, and Guinea in A. R. Zolberg, *Creating Political Order, The Party-States of West Africa* (Chicago, Rand McNally, 1966), esp. ch. 5. Zolberg makes a distinction between a "modern" sector of the polity, in which the authority of the single-party regime is great, and a large "residual" sector in which it is very weak. For Indonesia, see the perceptive article by Soedjatmoko, "Indonesia: Problems and Opportunities," *Australian Outlook* (December 1967), 263–86.

alternatives to massive, intensive, and prolonged compulsion as a means of bringing about integration. The keys, I believe, are participation through nation-wide but locally meaningful organizations and a national ideology that (1) defines and limits participation in such a way that people develop commitments to the regime and nation while still acting through traditional or semitraditional political organizations, and (2) provides enough of a consensus on the rules of the game to enable government to deal effectively with problems of economic and social development.

What I have argued, in effect, is that the very forces generally thought inimical to the development of national unity are in fact inseparable from it. This is so because in the absence of severe compulsion (and perhaps even with compulsion) primordial loyalties will retain, and may even intensify, their strength in most new states and because most people identify with the nation not only in terms of an abstract conception of direct loyalty (although this is important) but also in terms of primordial (and other) group identifications *within the context of* the nation. There is no reason why primordialism, understood in this way, should be destructive of national integration. In fact, it is the opposition to properly limited and channeled primordialism that is most likely to disrupt and weaken national sentiments developed when the foreign enemy was present.

In many old states, it is generally recognized that democratic stability depends upon the existence of a variety of associations intermediary between the individual and the state. This is no less true for the new states where the principal associations are traditional or at least semitraditional in content rather than modern voluntary associations as commonly found in the West. Although the intensity of primordial group loyalties is generally greater than that of loyalties to voluntary associations, and although overlapping memberships are generally fewer, it is still possible that groups of the former type may be brought into a working relationship with each other. Indeed, if these societies are to achieve both democracy and effective government within the framework of a multiethnic nation-state, it is imperative that such a relationship be established. For any new state this is a tall order, but the results—compared to those of any conceivable alternative—are worth the effort.

INDEX

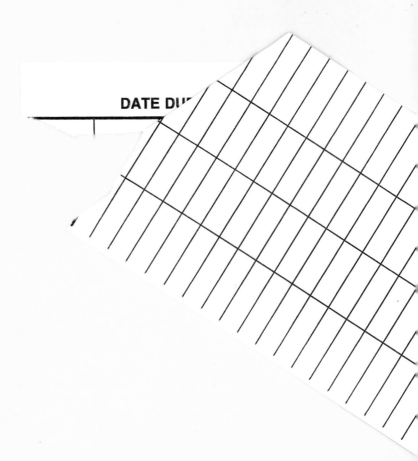

DATE DUE